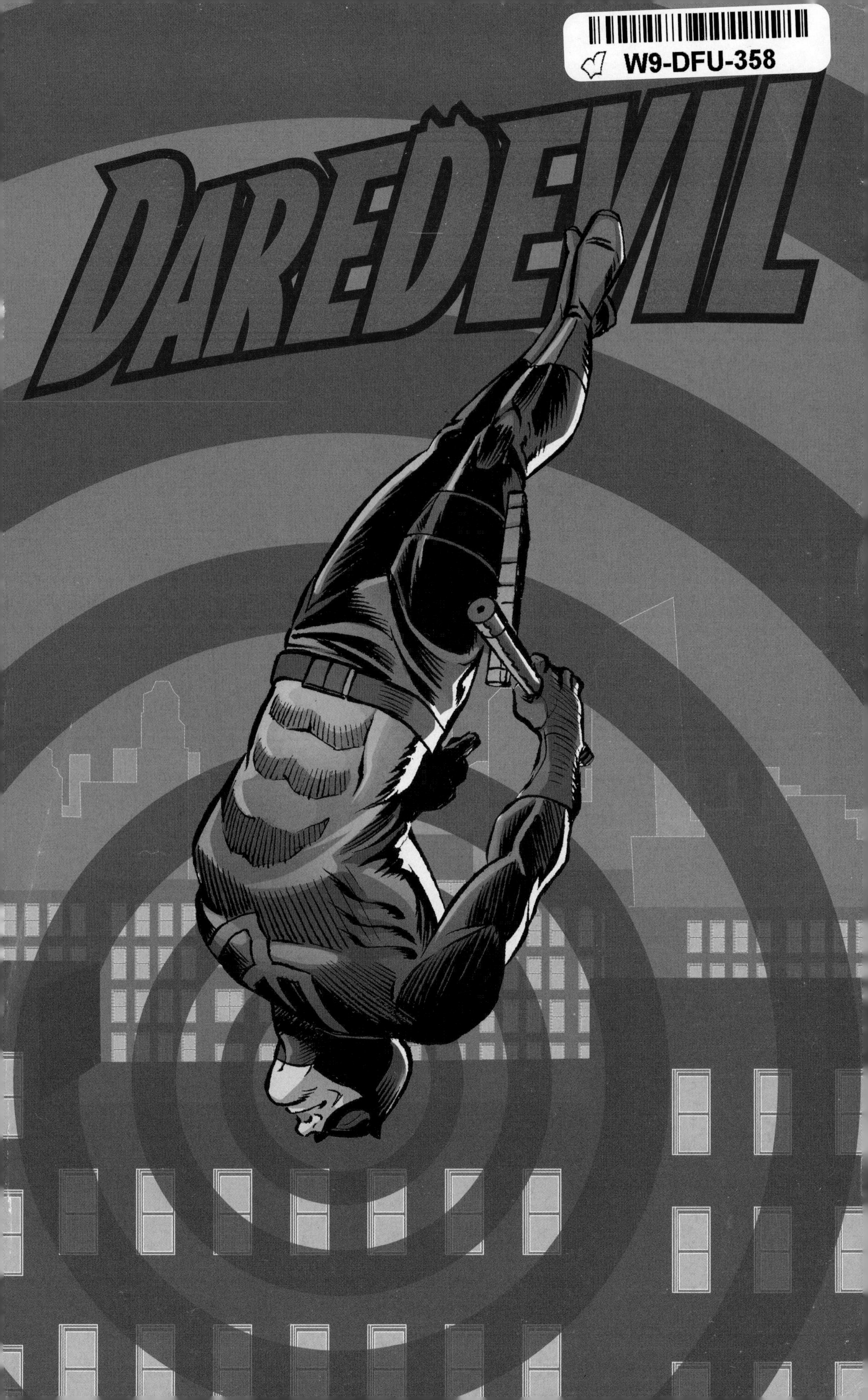
DAREDEVIL

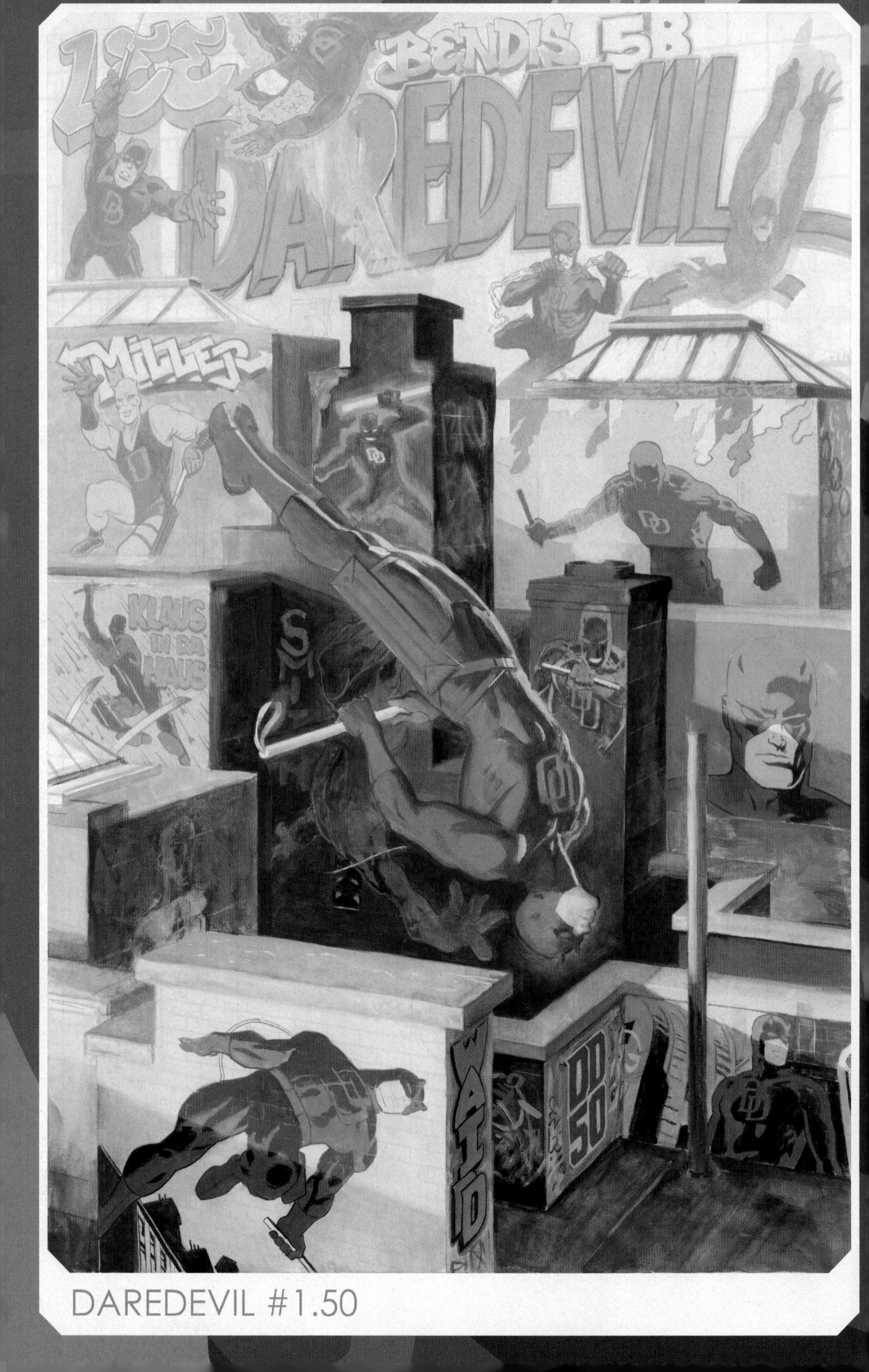
DAREDEVIL
MILLER
KLAUS IN DA HAUS
WAID
DD 50

DAREDEVIL #1.50

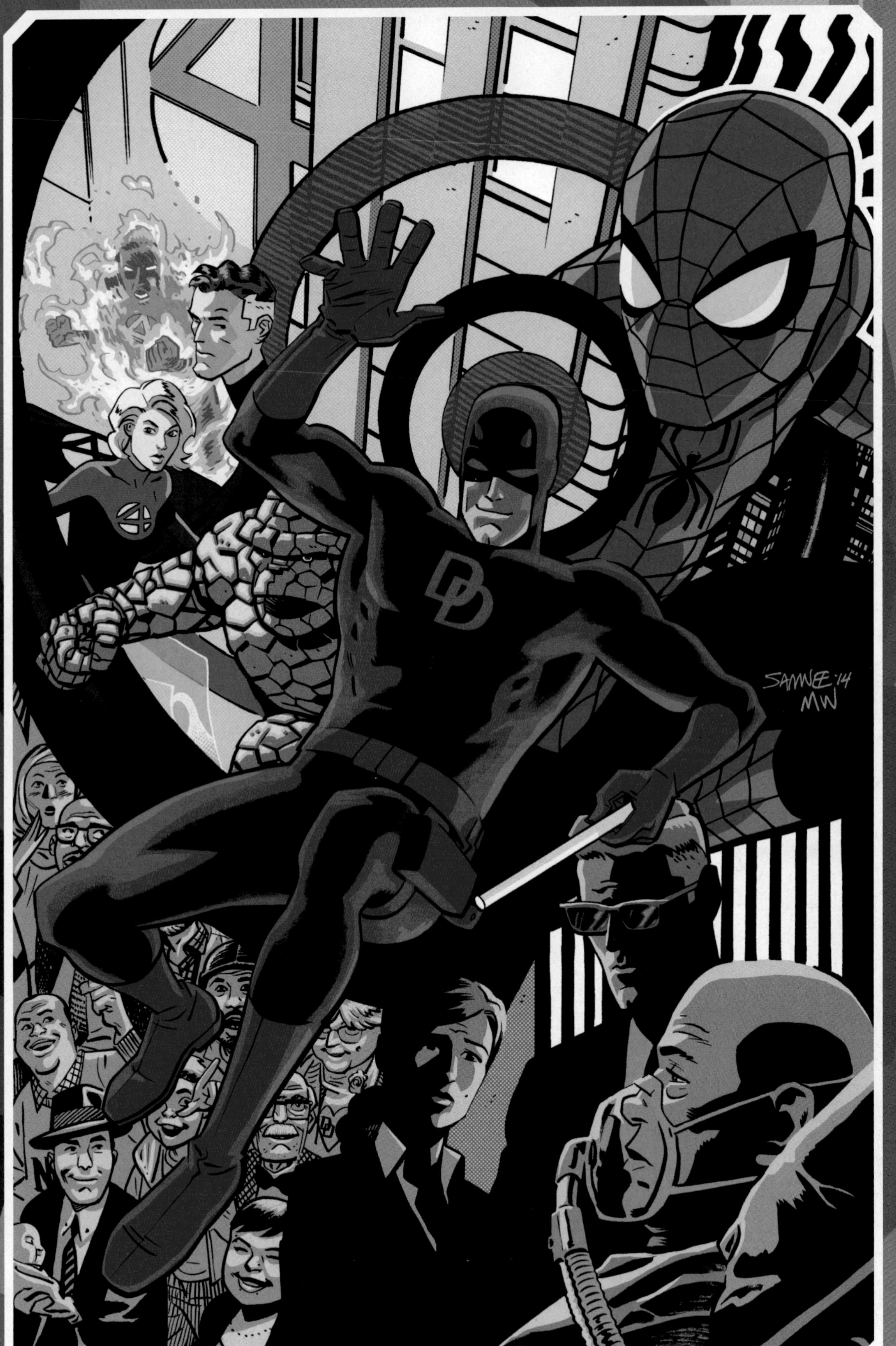
SAMNEE '14
MW

DAREDEVIL #1.50 VARIANT BY CHRIS SAMNEE & JAVIER RODRIGUEZ

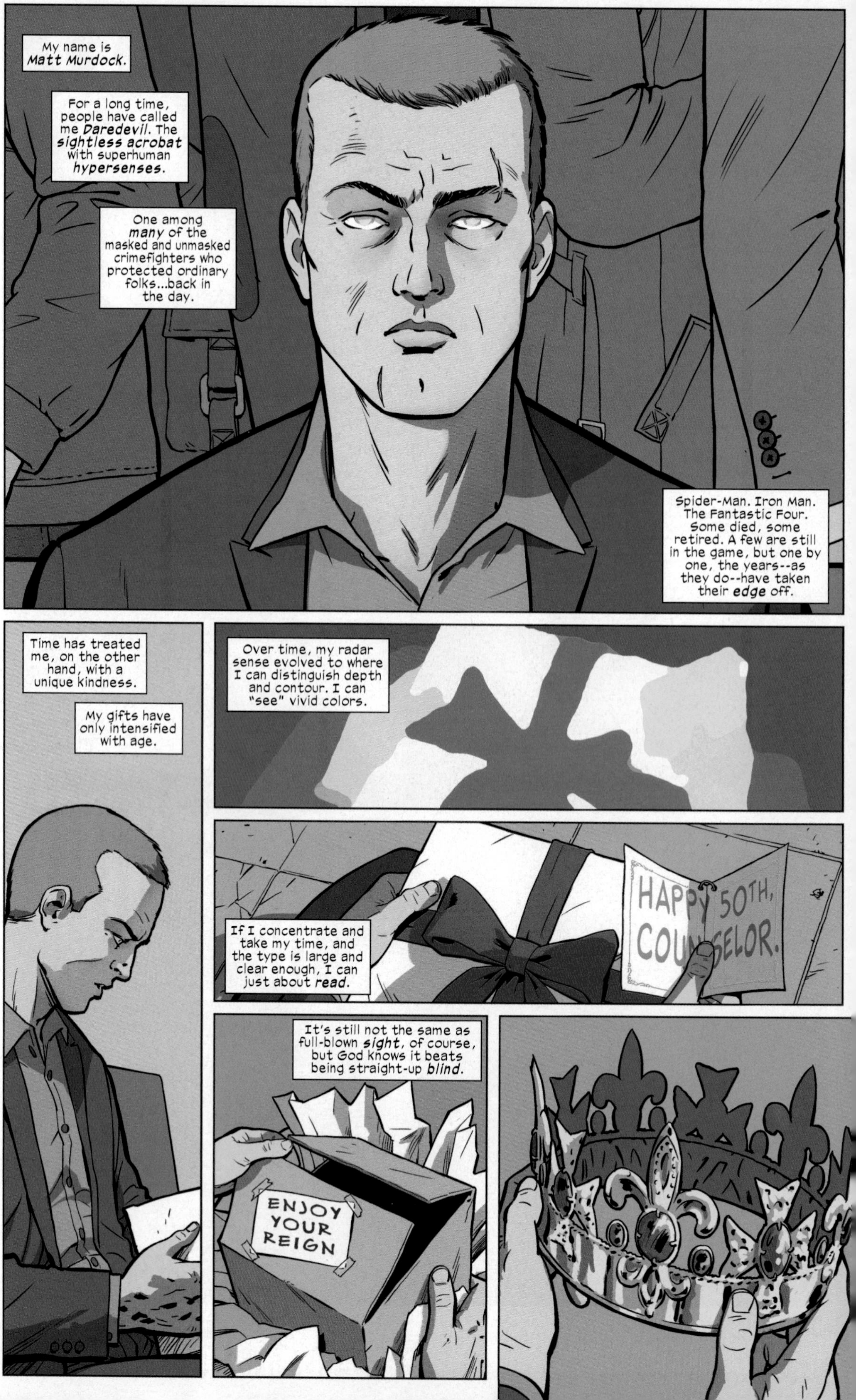
My name is Matt Murdock.
For a long time, people have called me Daredevil. The sightless acrobat with superhuman hypersenses.
One among many of the masked and unmasked crimefighters who protected ordinary folks...back in the day.
Spider-Man. Iron Man. The Fantastic Four. Some died, some retired. A few are still in the game, but one by one, the years--as they do--have taken their edge off.
Time has treated me, on the other hand, with a unique kindness.
My gifts have only intensified with age.
Over time, my radar sense evolved to where I can distinguish depth and contour. I can "see" vivid colors.
If I concentrate and take my time, and the type is large and clear enough, I can just about read.
HAPPY 50TH, COUNSELOR.
It's still not the same as full-blown sight, of course, but God knows it beats being straight-up blind.
ENJOY YOUR REIGN

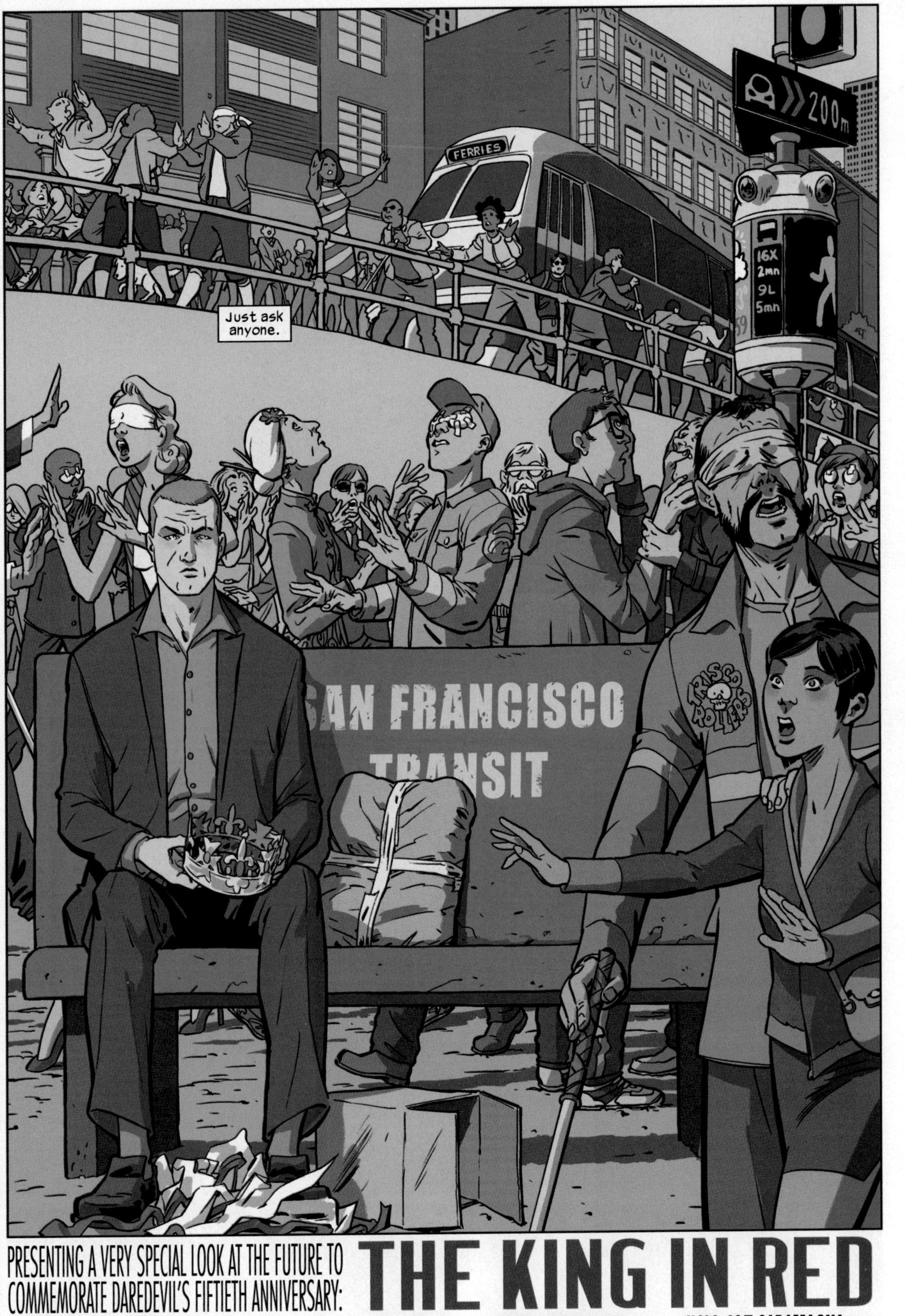
FERRIES
200m
16X
2mn
9L
5mn
Just ask anyone.
SAN FRANCISCO TRANSIT

PRESENTING A VERY SPECIAL LOOK AT THE FUTURE TO COMMEMORATE DAREDEVIL'S FIFTIETH ANNIVERSARY:

THE KING IN RED

MARK WAID & JAVIER RODRIGUEZ STORYTELLERS **ALVARO LOPEZ** INKS **JAVIER RODRIGUEZ** COLORS **VC'S JOE CARAMAGNA** LETTERER

PAOLO RIVERA COVER **MARCOS MARTIN and SAMNEE & RODRIGUEZ** VARIANT COVER **ELLIE PYLE** EDITOR **AXEL ALONSO** EDITOR IN CHIEF **JOE QUESADA** CHIEF CREATIVE OFFICER

DAN BUCKLEY PUBLISHER **ALAN FINE** EXEC. PRODUCER WITH GRATITUDE TO **STAN LEE & BILL EVERETT, KARL KESEL, TOM PEYER,** AND **STEPHEN WACKER**

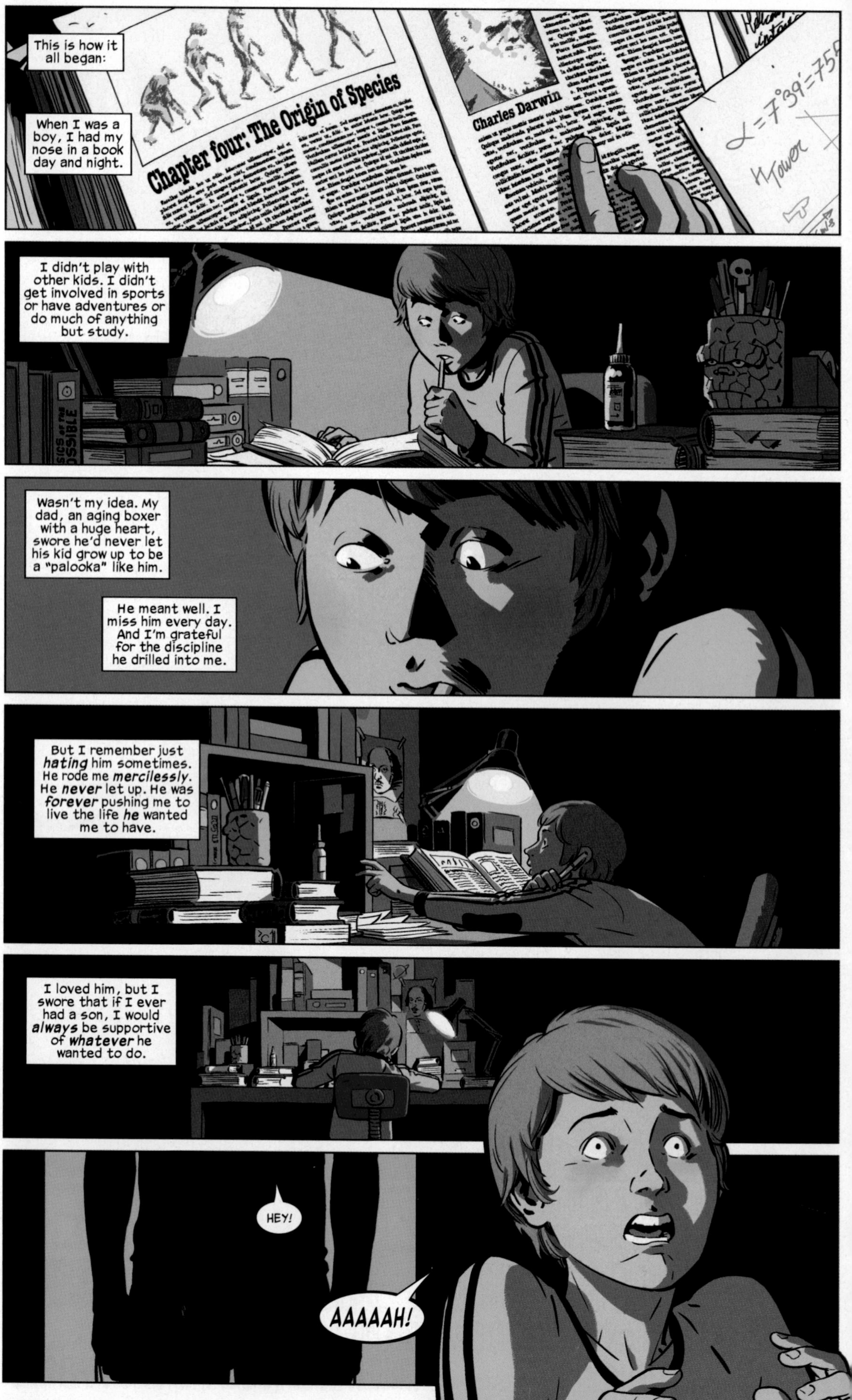
This is how it all began:
Chapter four: The Origin of Species
Charles Darwin
When I was a boy, I had my nose in a book day and night.
I didn't play with other kids. I didn't get involved in sports or have adventures or do much of anything but study.
Wasn't my idea. My dad, an aging boxer with a huge heart, swore he'd never let his kid grow up to be a "palooka" like him.
He meant well. I miss him every day. And I'm grateful for the discipline he drilled into me.
But I remember just *hating* him sometimes. He rode me *mercilessly*. He *never* let up. He was *forever* pushing me to live the life *he* wanted me to have.
I loved him, but I swore that if I ever had a son, I would *always* be supportive of *whatever* he wanted to do.
HEY!
AAAAAH!

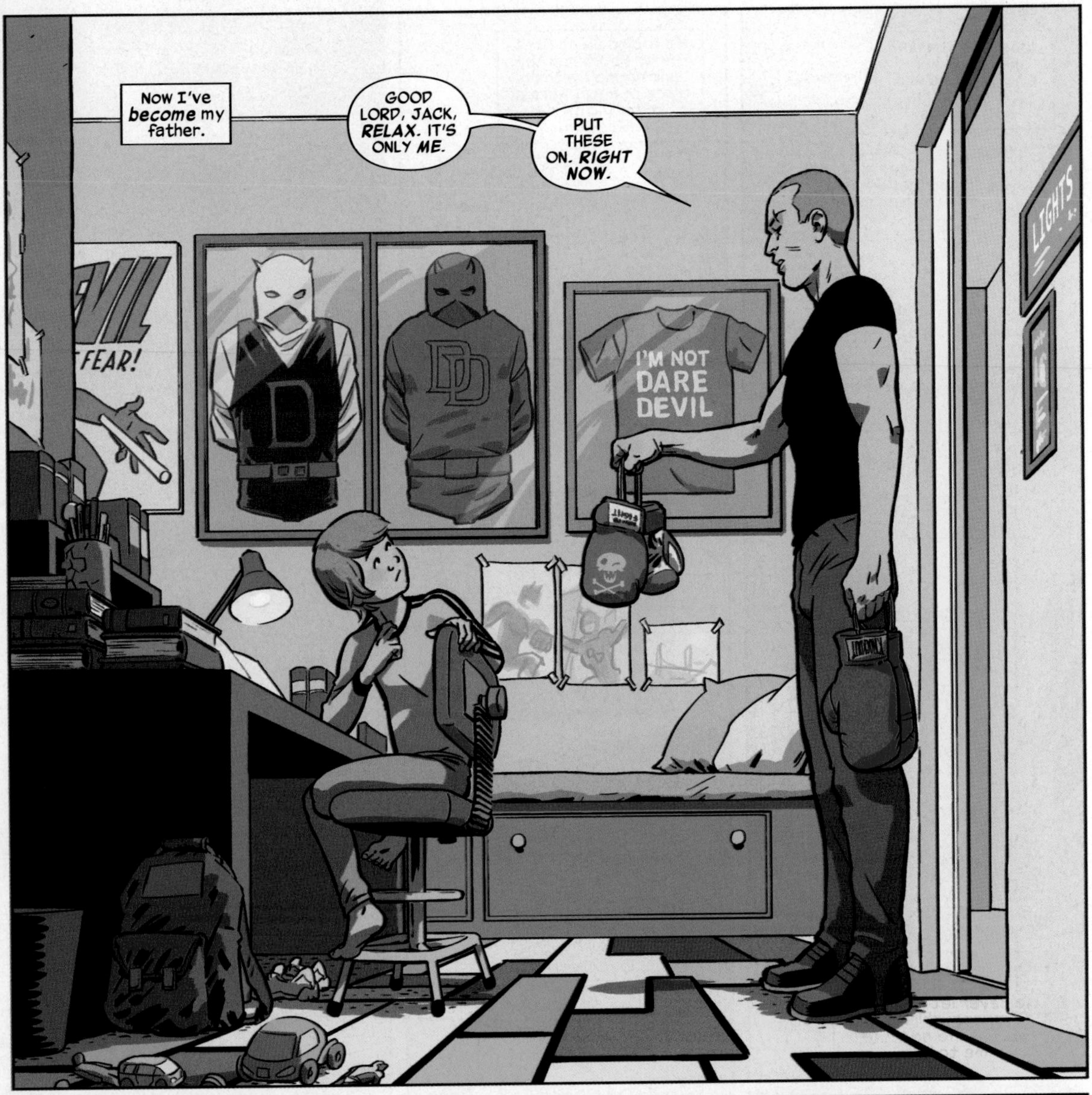
Now I've *become* my father.
GOOD LORD, JACK, *RELAX*. IT'S ONLY *ME*.
PUT THESE ON. *RIGHT NOW*.
I'M NOT DARE DEVIL
FEAR!

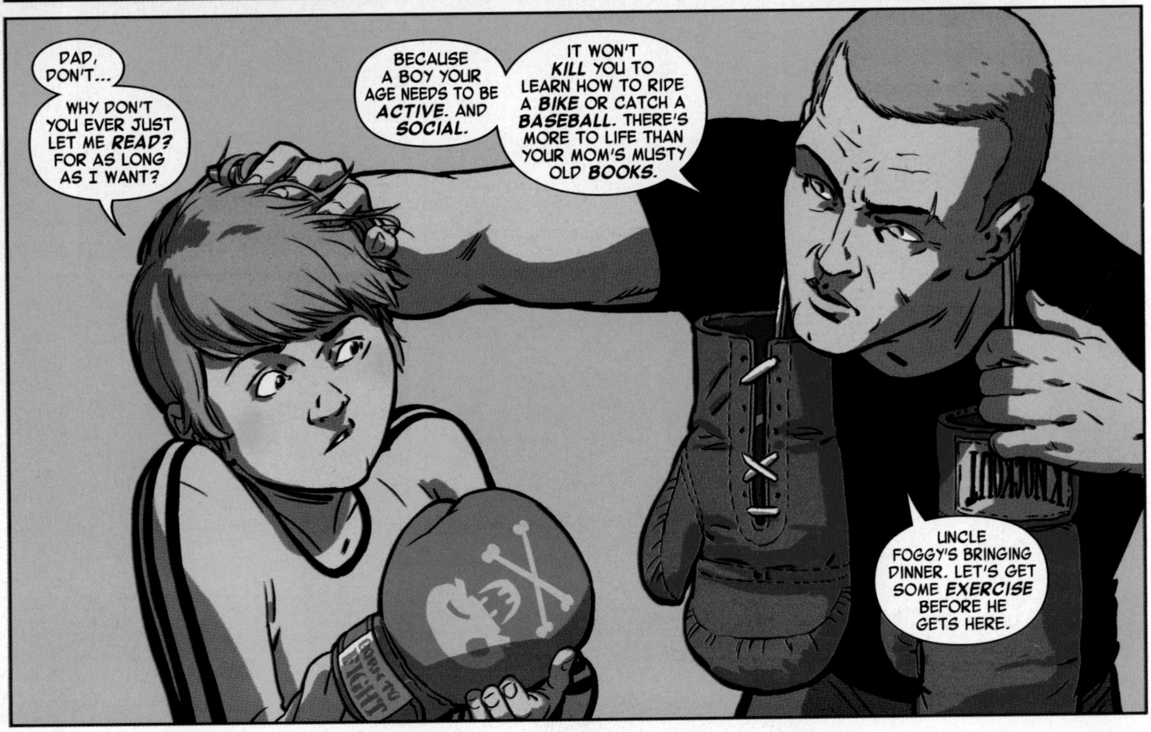
DAD, DON'T...
WHY DON'T YOU EVER JUST LET ME *READ?* FOR AS LONG AS I WANT?
BECAUSE A BOY YOUR AGE NEEDS TO BE *ACTIVE*. AND *SOCIAL*.
IT WON'T *KILL* YOU TO LEARN HOW TO RIDE A *BIKE* OR CATCH A *BASEBALL*. THERE'S MORE TO LIFE THAN YOUR MOM'S MUSTY OLD *BOOKS*.
UNCLE FOGGY'S BRINGING DINNER. LET'S GET SOME *EXERCISE* BEFORE HE GETS HERE.

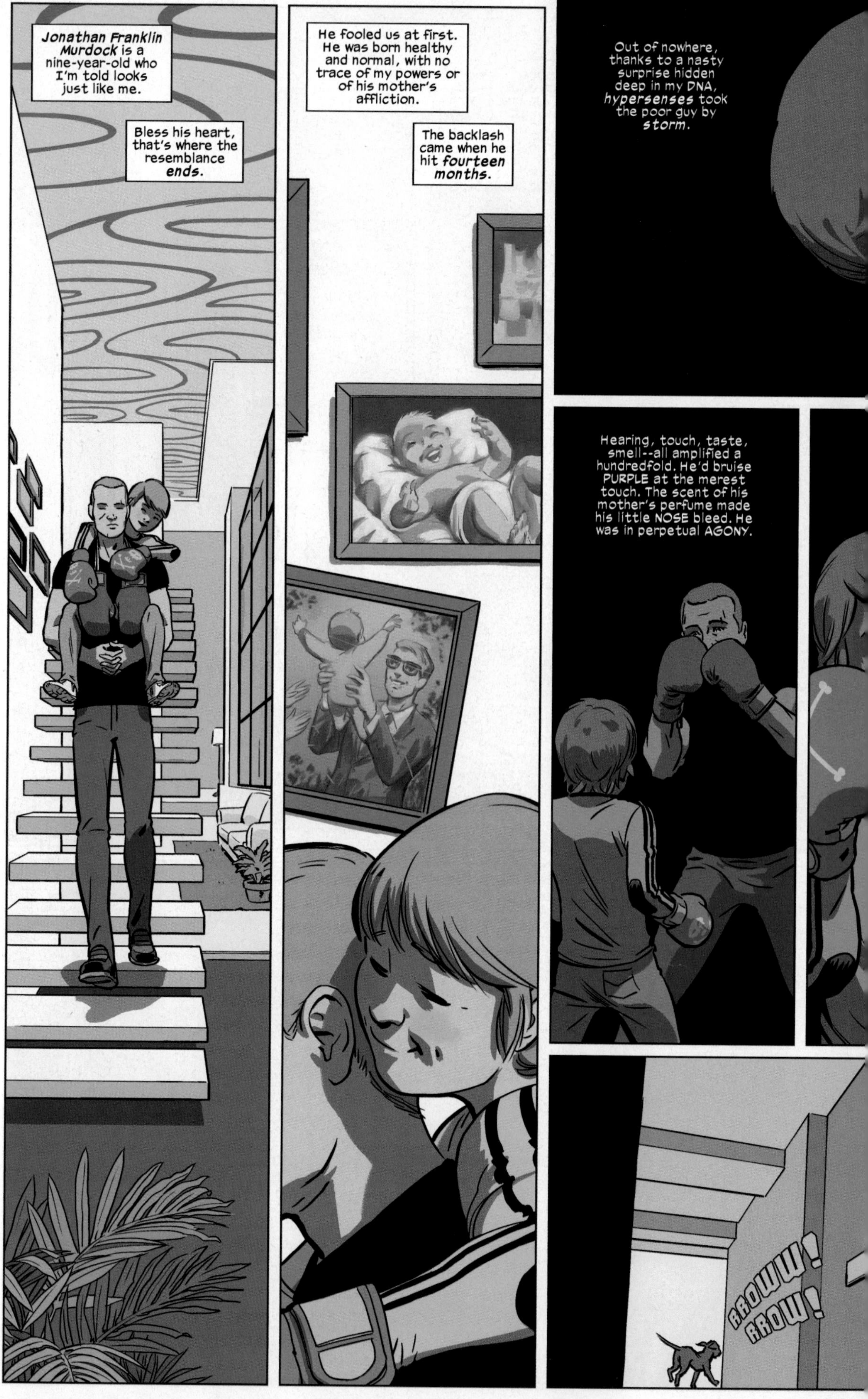

Jonathan Franklin Murdock is a nine-year-old who I'm told looks just like me.
Bless his heart, that's where the resemblance *ends*.
He fooled us at first. He was born healthy and normal, with no trace of my powers or of his mother's affliction.
The backlash came when he hit *fourteen months*.
Out of nowhere, thanks to a nasty surprise hidden deep in my DNA, *hypersenses* took the poor guy by *storm*.
Hearing, touch, taste, smell--all amplified a hundredfold. He'd bruise PURPLE at the merest touch. The scent of his mother's perfume made his little NOSE bleed. He was in perpetual AGONY.
ARROWW! ARROW!

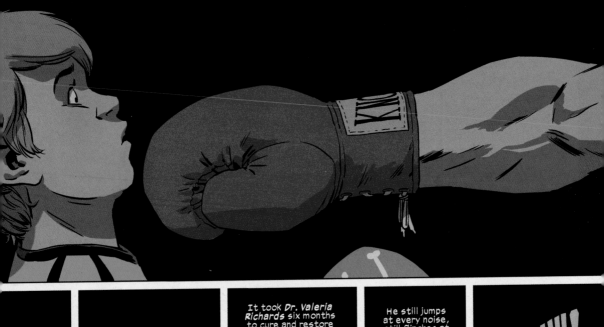

It took *Dr. Valeria Richards* six months to cure and restore him, but even so, the *psychological* scars were permanent.

— POF

He still jumps at every noise, still flinches at every contact. Every second of every moment, he's like a jack-in-the-box with one note left to go.

RROWW!
RRUFF
RRUFF
RROW!

AAAH!

He flinches at absolutely *everything.*

JACK, IT'S *ALL RIGHT!* IT'S JUST THE *DOG,* OKAY? IT'S JUST THE DOG...!

That's my boy.

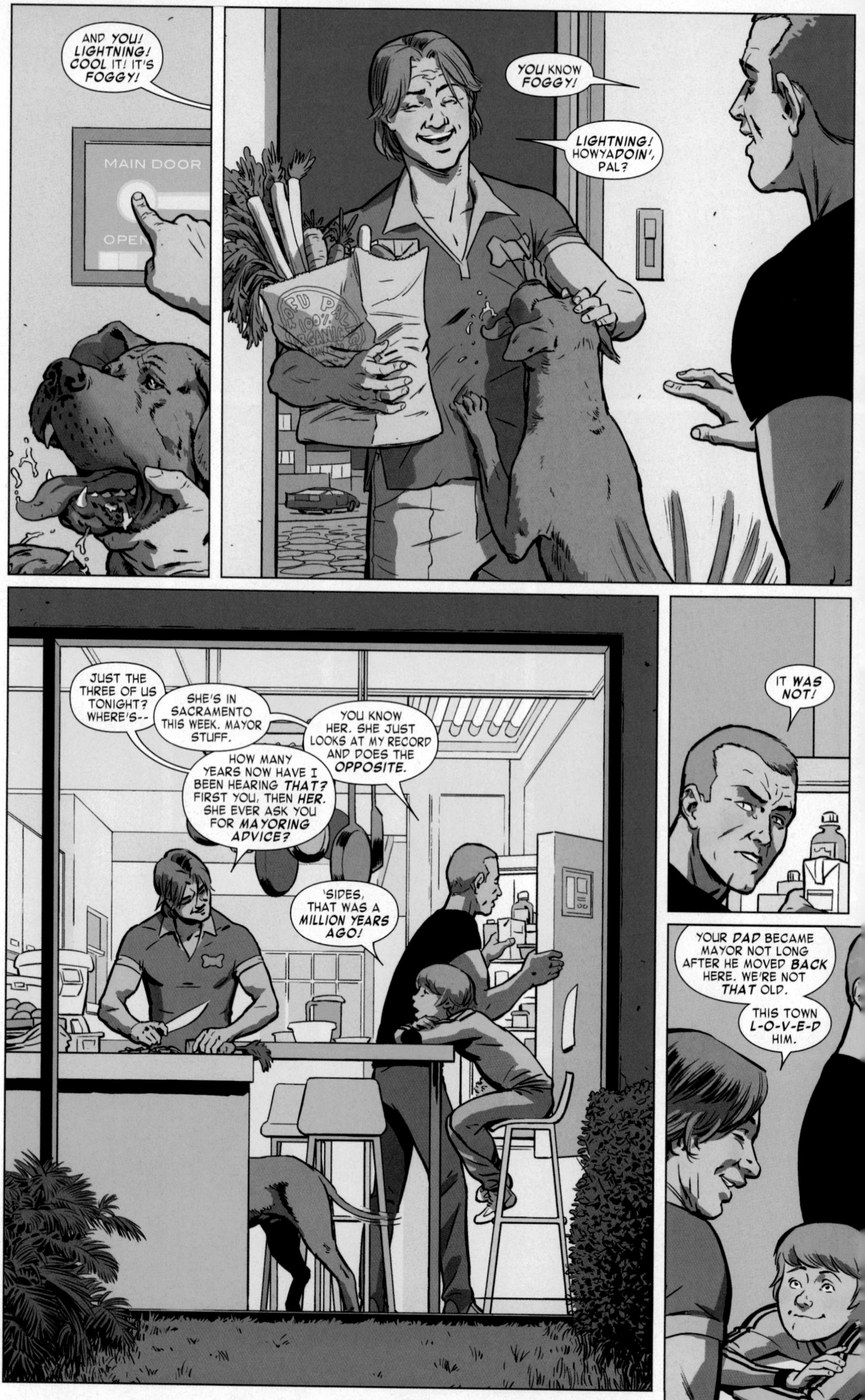
AND YOU! LIGHTNING! COOL IT! IT'S FOGGY!
MAIN DOOR
OPEN
YOU KNOW FOGGY!
LIGHTNING! HOWYADOIN', PAL?
JUST THE THREE OF US TONIGHT? WHERE'S--
SHE'S IN SACRAMENTO THIS WEEK. MAYOR STUFF.
YOU KNOW HER. SHE JUST LOOKS AT MY RECORD AND DOES THE OPPOSITE.
HOW MANY YEARS NOW HAVE I BEEN HEARING THAT? FIRST YOU, THEN HER. SHE EVER ASK YOU FOR MAYORING ADVICE?
'SIDES, THAT WAS A MILLION YEARS AGO!
IT WAS NOT!
YOUR DAD BECAME MAYOR NOT LONG AFTER HE MOVED BACK HERE. WE'RE NOT THAT OLD.
THIS TOWN L-O-V-E-D HIM.

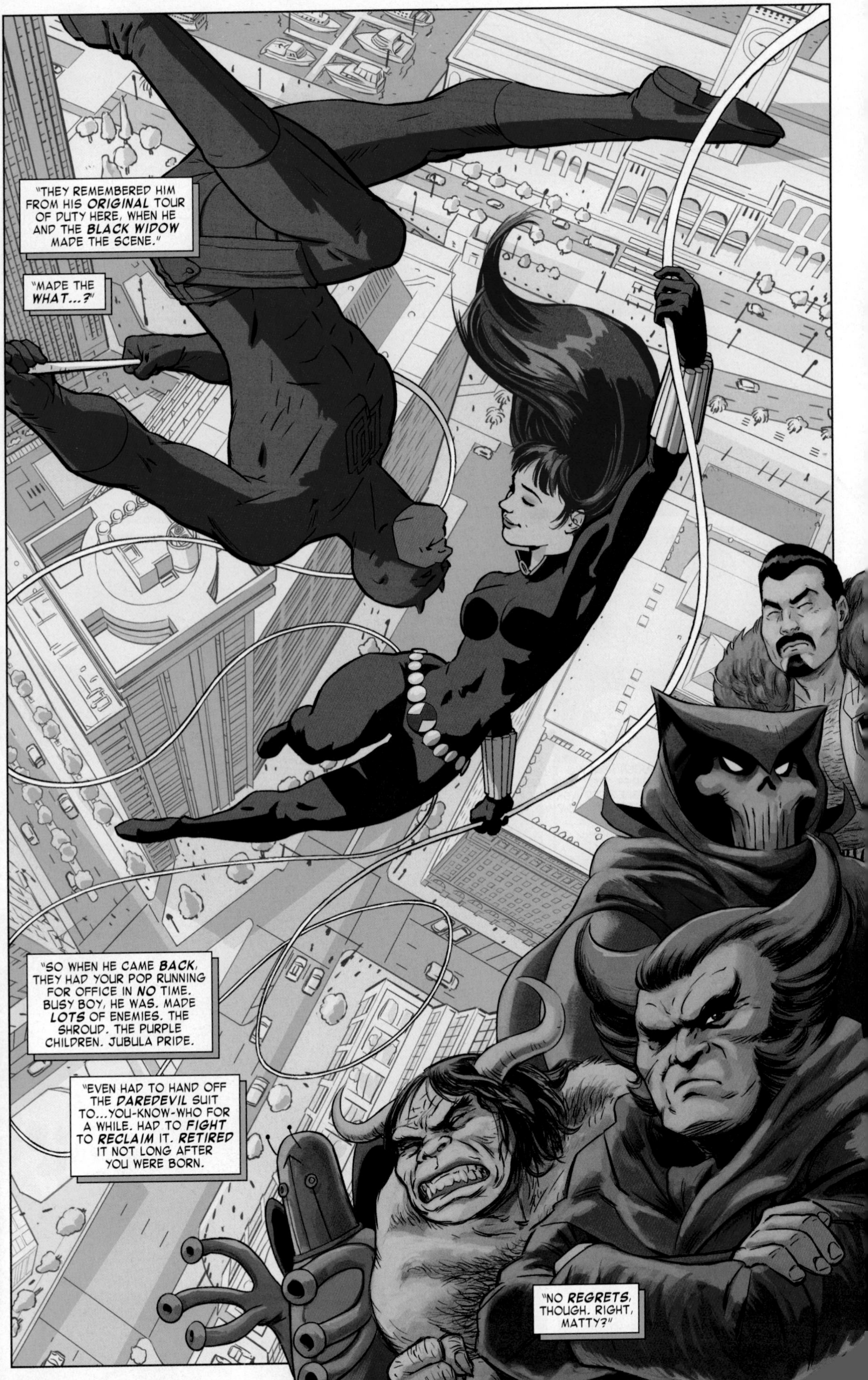
"THEY REMEMBERED HIM FROM HIS ORIGINAL TOUR OF DUTY HERE, WHEN HE AND THE BLACK WIDOW MADE THE SCENE."
"MADE THE WHAT...?"
"SO WHEN HE CAME BACK, THEY HAD YOUR POP RUNNING FOR OFFICE IN NO TIME. BUSY BOY, HE WAS. MADE LOTS OF ENEMIES. THE SHROUD. THE PURPLE CHILDREN. JUBULA PRIDE.
"EVEN HAD TO HAND OFF THE DAREDEVIL SUIT TO...YOU-KNOW-WHO FOR A WHILE. HAD TO FIGHT TO RECLAIM IT. RETIRED IT NOT LONG AFTER YOU WERE BORN.
"NO REGRETS, THOUGH. RIGHT, MATTY?"

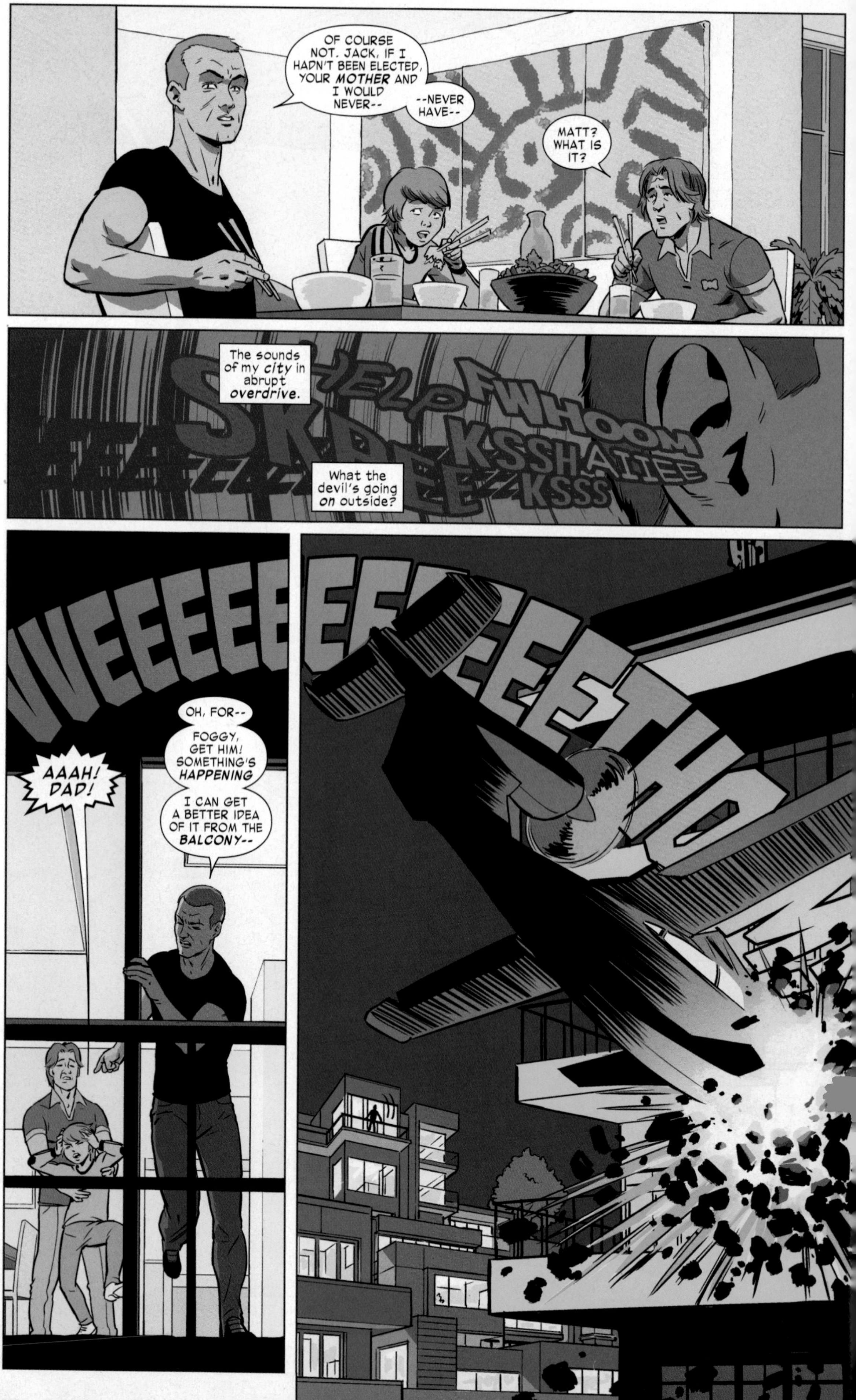
OF COURSE NOT. JACK, IF I HADN'T BEEN ELECTED, YOUR MOTHER AND I WOULD NEVER--
--NEVER HAVE--
MATT? WHAT IS IT?
The sounds of my city in abrupt overdrive.
HELP
SKREE
FWHOOM
KSSHAIEE
KSSS
What the devil's going on outside?
VEEEEEEEEEEEEEETHO
OH, FOR--
FOGGY, GET HIM! SOMETHING'S HAPPENING
I CAN GET A BETTER IDEA OF IT FROM THE BALCONY--
AAAH! DAD!

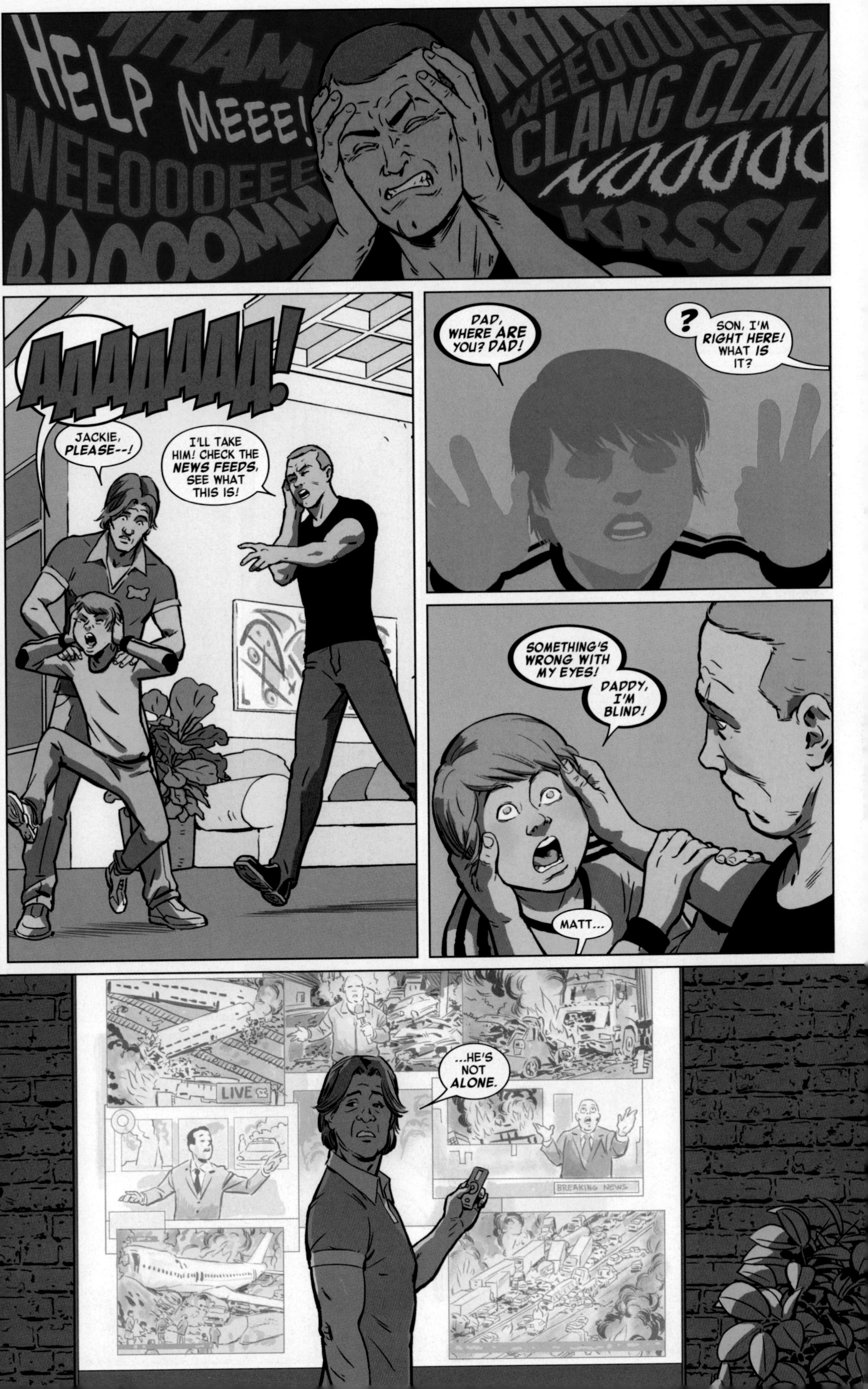
HELP MEEE!
WEEOOOEEE
CLANG CLANG
NOOOOO
KRSSH
AAAAAAA!
JACKIE, PLEASE--!
I'LL TAKE HIM! CHECK THE NEWS FEEDS, SEE WHAT THIS IS!
DAD, WHERE ARE YOU? DAD!
?
SON, I'M RIGHT HERE! WHAT IS IT?
SOMETHING'S WRONG WITH MY EYES!
DADDY, I'M BLIND!
MATT...
LIVE
BREAKING NEWS
...HE'S NOT ALONE.

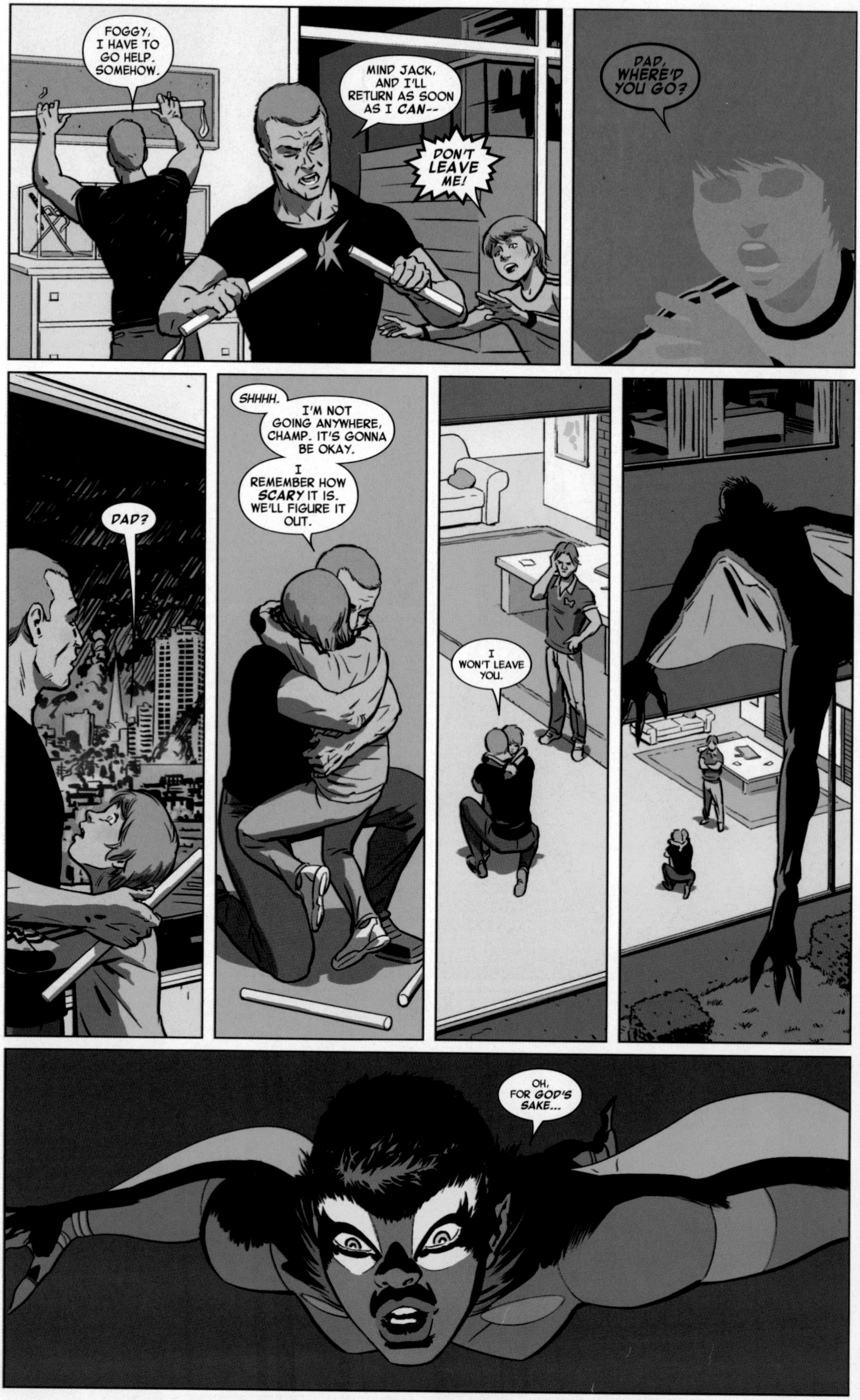
FOGGY, I HAVE TO GO HELP. SOMEHOW.
MIND JACK, AND I'LL RETURN AS SOON AS I CAN--
DON'T LEAVE ME!
DAD, WHERE'D YOU GO?
DAD?
SHHHH.
I'M NOT GOING ANYWHERE, CHAMP. IT'S GONNA BE OKAY.
I REMEMBER HOW SCARY IT IS. WE'LL FIGURE IT OUT.
I WON'T LEAVE YOU.
OH, FOR GOD'S SAKE...

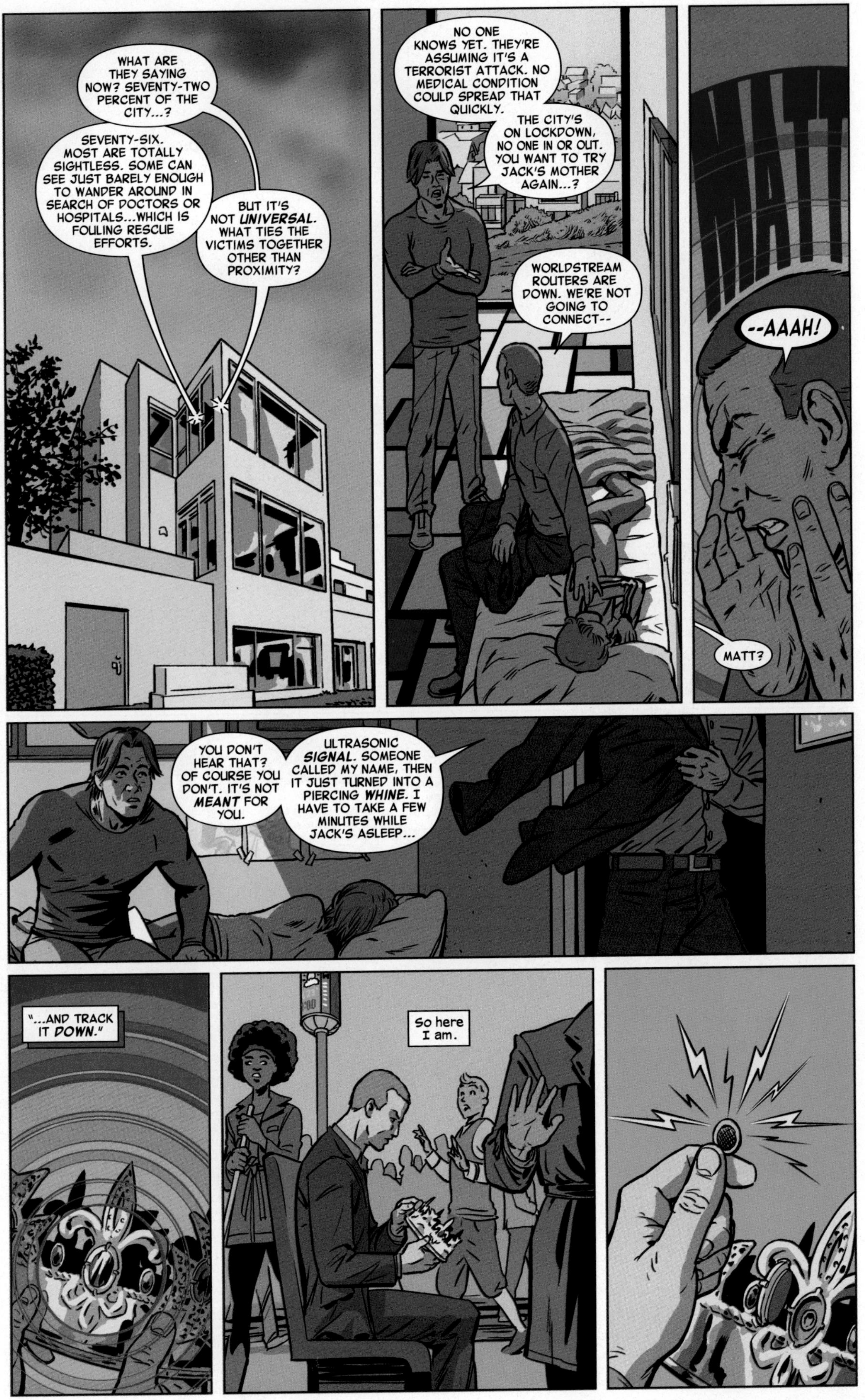
WHAT ARE THEY SAYING NOW? SEVENTY-TWO PERCENT OF THE CITY...?
SEVENTY-SIX. MOST ARE TOTALLY SIGHTLESS. SOME CAN SEE JUST BARELY ENOUGH TO WANDER AROUND IN SEARCH OF DOCTORS OR HOSPITALS...WHICH IS FOULING RESCUE EFFORTS.
BUT IT'S NOT UNIVERSAL. WHAT TIES THE VICTIMS TOGETHER OTHER THAN PROXIMITY?
NO ONE KNOWS YET. THEY'RE ASSUMING IT'S A TERRORIST ATTACK. NO MEDICAL CONDITION COULD SPREAD THAT QUICKLY.
THE CITY'S ON LOCKDOWN, NO ONE IN OR OUT. YOU WANT TO TRY JACK'S MOTHER AGAIN...?
WORLDSTREAM ROUTERS ARE DOWN. WE'RE NOT GOING TO CONNECT--
MATT
--AAAH!
MATT?
YOU DON'T HEAR THAT? OF COURSE YOU DON'T. IT'S NOT MEANT FOR YOU.
ULTRASONIC SIGNAL. SOMEONE CALLED MY NAME, THEN IT JUST TURNED INTO A PIERCING WHINE. I HAVE TO TAKE A FEW MINUTES WHILE JACK'S ASLEEP...
"...AND TRACK IT DOWN."
So here I am.

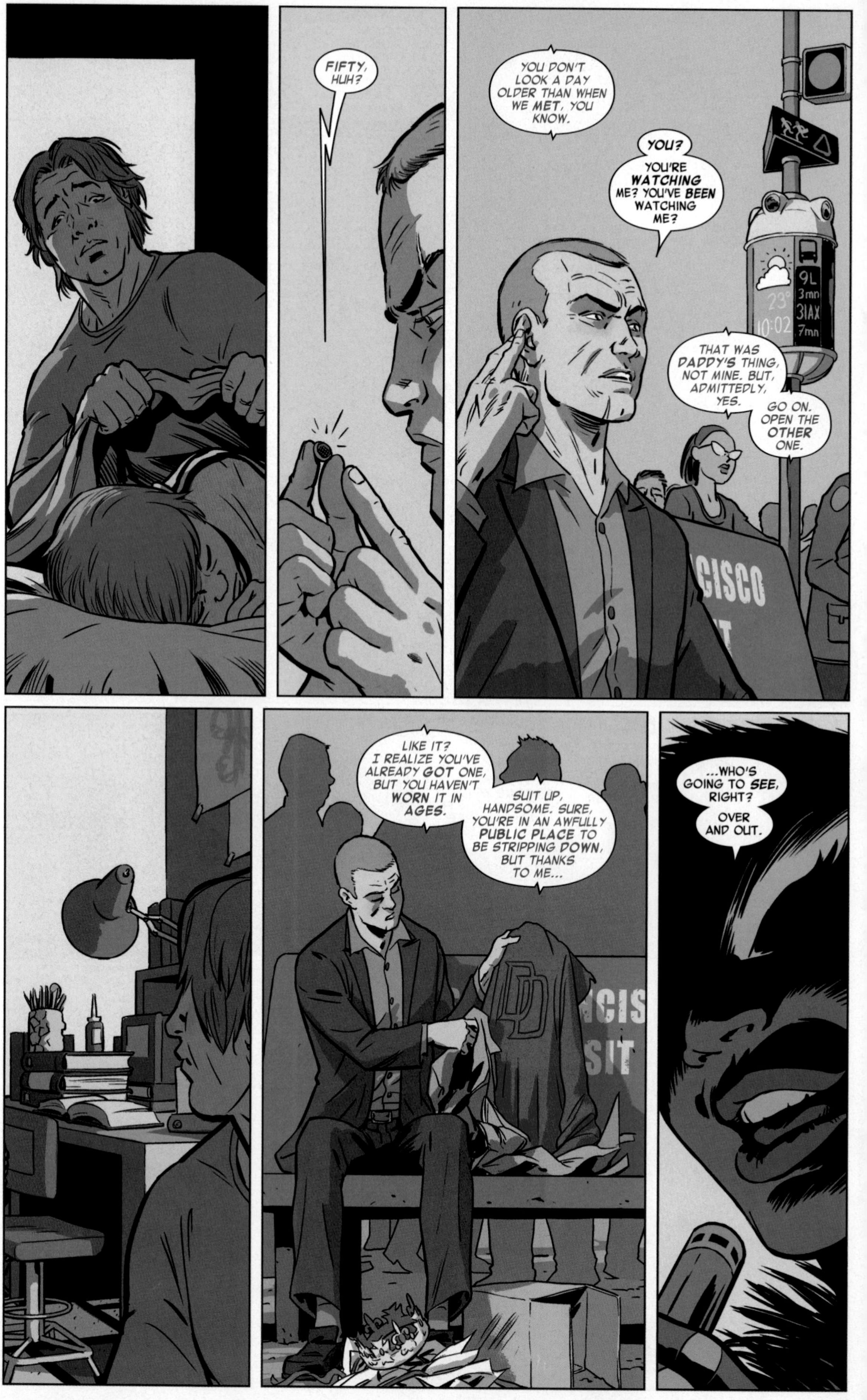
FIFTY, HUH?
YOU DON'T LOOK A DAY OLDER THAN WHEN WE MET, YOU KNOW.
YOU?
YOU'RE WATCHING ME? YOU'VE BEEN WATCHING ME?
9L 3mn
31AX 7mn
23°
10:02
THAT WAS DADDY'S THING, NOT MINE. BUT, ADMITTEDLY, YES.
GO ON. OPEN THE OTHER ONE.
LIKE IT? I REALIZE YOU'VE ALREADY GOT ONE, BUT YOU HAVEN'T WORN IT IN AGES.
SUIT UP, HANDSOME. SURE, YOU'RE IN AN AWFULLY PUBLIC PLACE TO BE STRIPPING DOWN, BUT THANKS TO ME...
...WHO'S GOING TO SEE, RIGHT?
OVER AND OUT.

She *is* behind this, then. But how--?

MATTY?

HOLY GOOGLE GLASS, MATTY, I THINK I'VE GOT A LEAD ON THE EPIDEMIC.

EYES FRONT CYBER-OPTIC FLUID

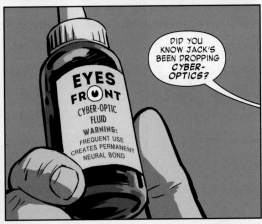

EYES FRONT

CYBER-OPTIC FLUID

WARNING: FREQUENT USE CREATES PERMANENT NEURAL BOND

DID YOU KNOW JACK'S BEEN DROPPING CYBER-OPTICS?

"GUESS WHAT PERCENTAGE OF BAY AREA RESIDENTS USE THIS STUFF TO STAY CONNECTED TO THE WORLDSTREAM 24/7?

"SEVENTY-SIX."

120 Sea Street San Francisco CA

Cecilia Shiro Management Consultants Richmond CA Online.....

In a relationship Cinema - Dance - Music

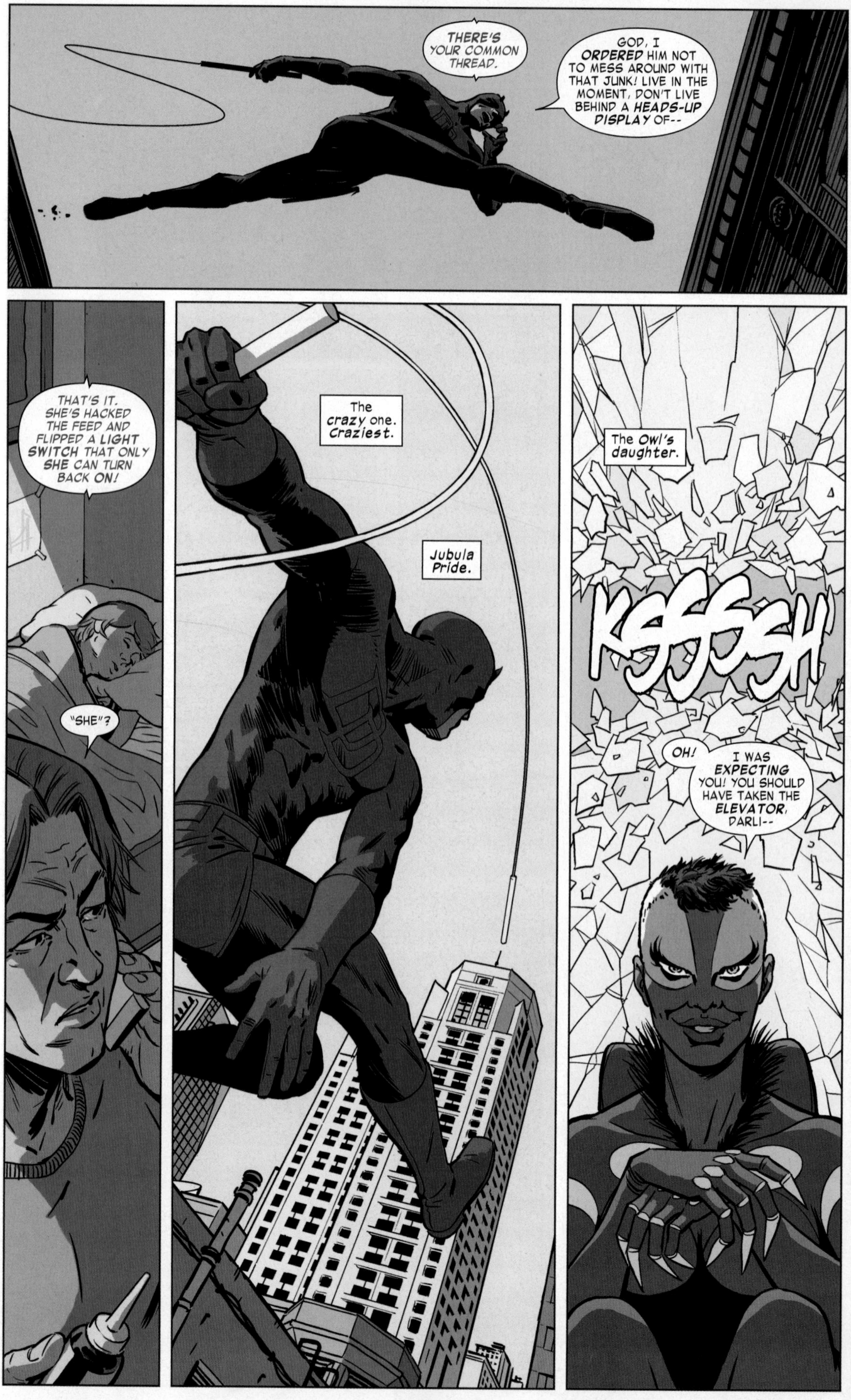

THERE'S YOUR COMMON THREAD.
GOD, I ORDERED HIM NOT TO MESS AROUND WITH THAT JUNK! LIVE IN THE MOMENT, DON'T LIVE BEHIND A HEADS-UP DISPLAY OF--
THAT'S IT. SHE'S HACKED THE FEED AND FLIPPED A LIGHT SWITCH THAT ONLY SHE CAN TURN BACK ON!
"SHE"?
The crazy one. Craziest.
Jubula Pride.
The Owl's daughter.
KSSSSH
OH!
I WAS EXPECTING YOU! YOU SHOULD HAVE TAKEN THE ELEVATOR, DARLI--

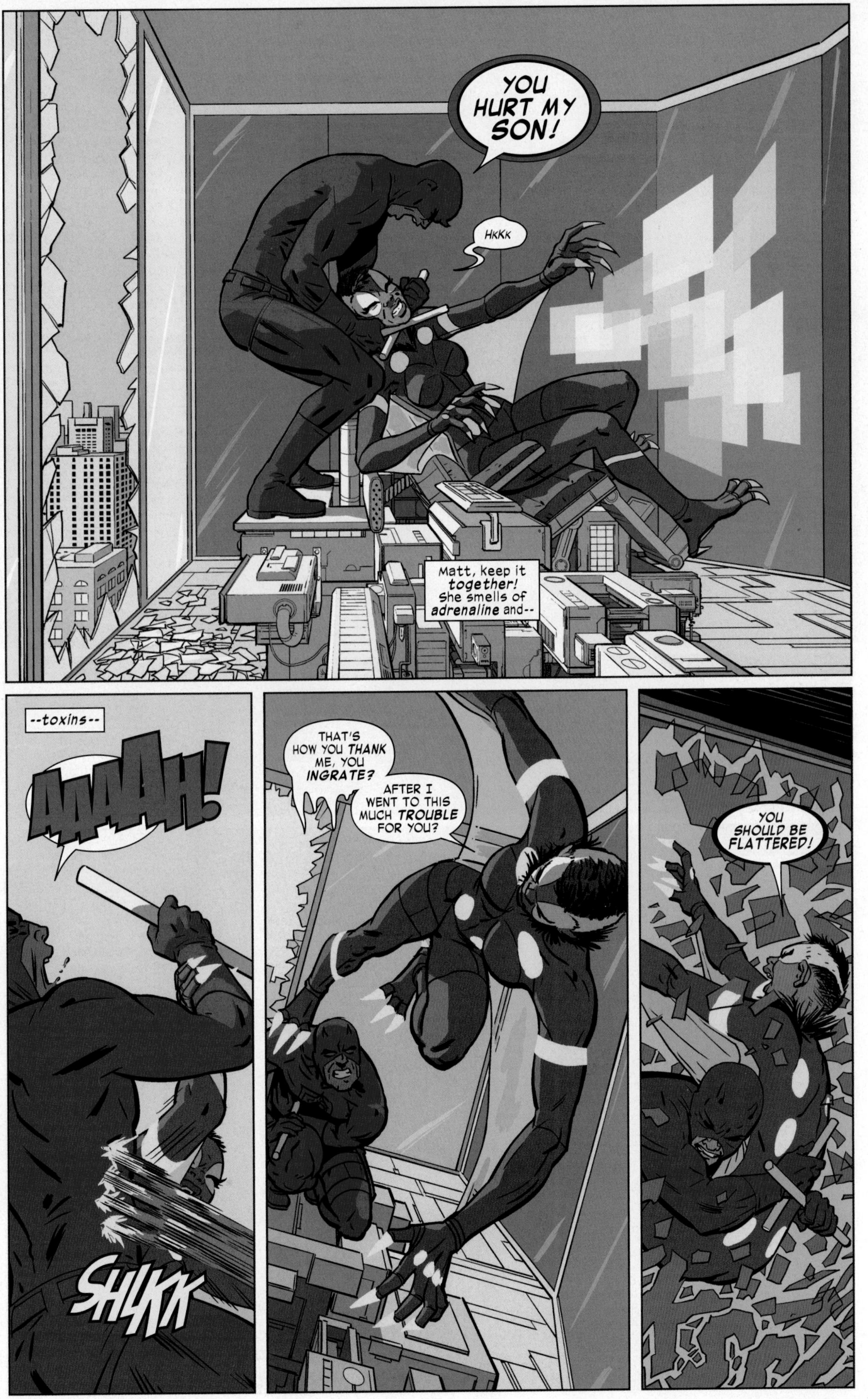
YOU HURT MY SON!
HKKK
Matt, keep it together! She smells of adrenaline and--
--toxins--
AAAAAH!
SHKK
THAT'S HOW YOU THANK ME, YOU INGRATE?
AFTER I WENT TO THIS MUCH TROUBLE FOR YOU?
YOU SHOULD BE FLATTERED!

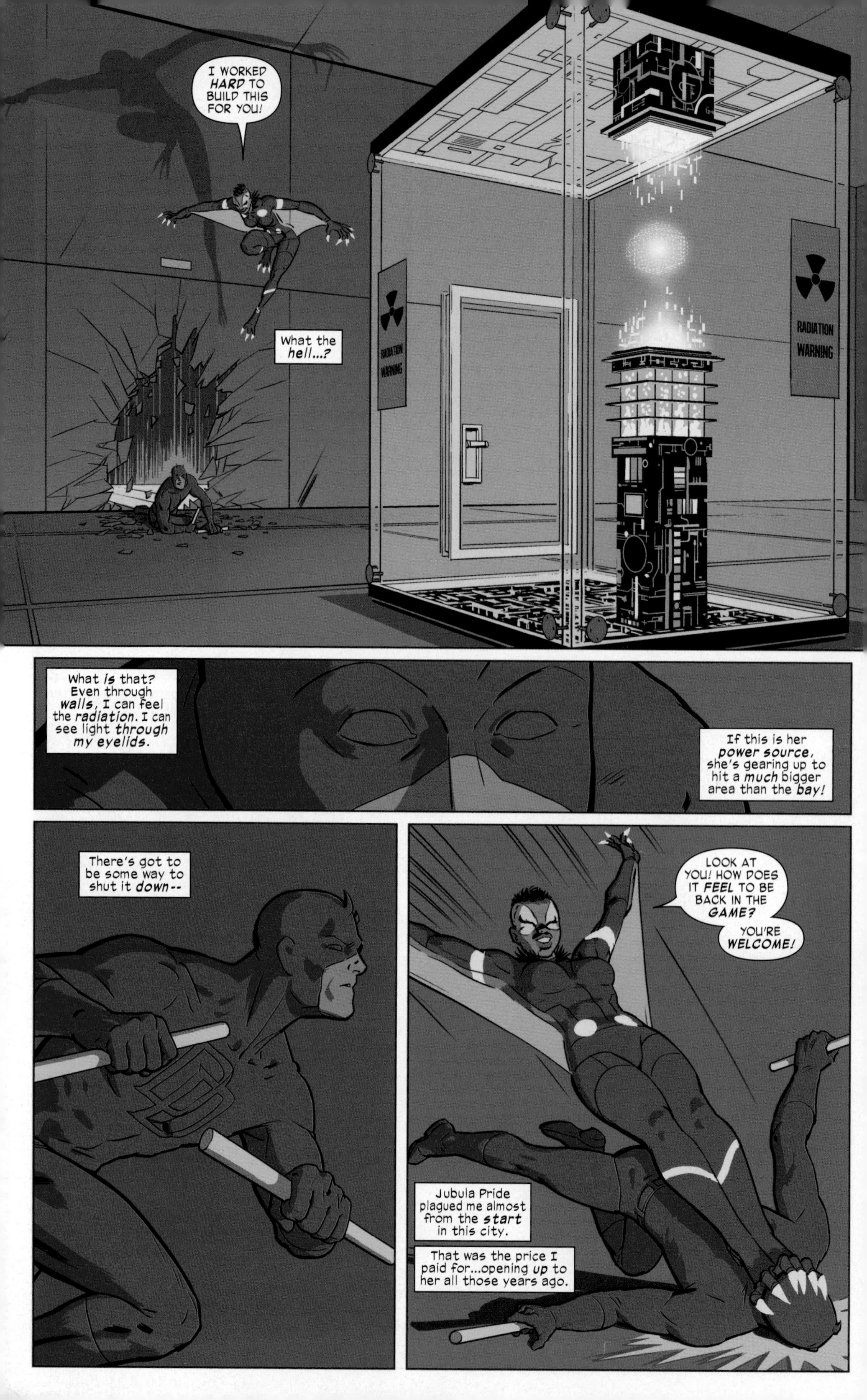

I WORKED HARD TO BUILD THIS FOR YOU!
What the hell...?
RADIATION WARNING
RADIATION WARNING
What is that? Even through walls, I can feel the radiation. I can see light through my eyelids.
If this is her power source, she's gearing up to hit a much bigger area than the bay!
There's got to be some way to shut it down--
LOOK AT YOU! HOW DOES IT FEEL TO BE BACK IN THE GAME?
YOU'RE WELCOME!
Jubula Pride plagued me almost from the start in this city.
That was the price I paid for...opening up to her all those years ago.

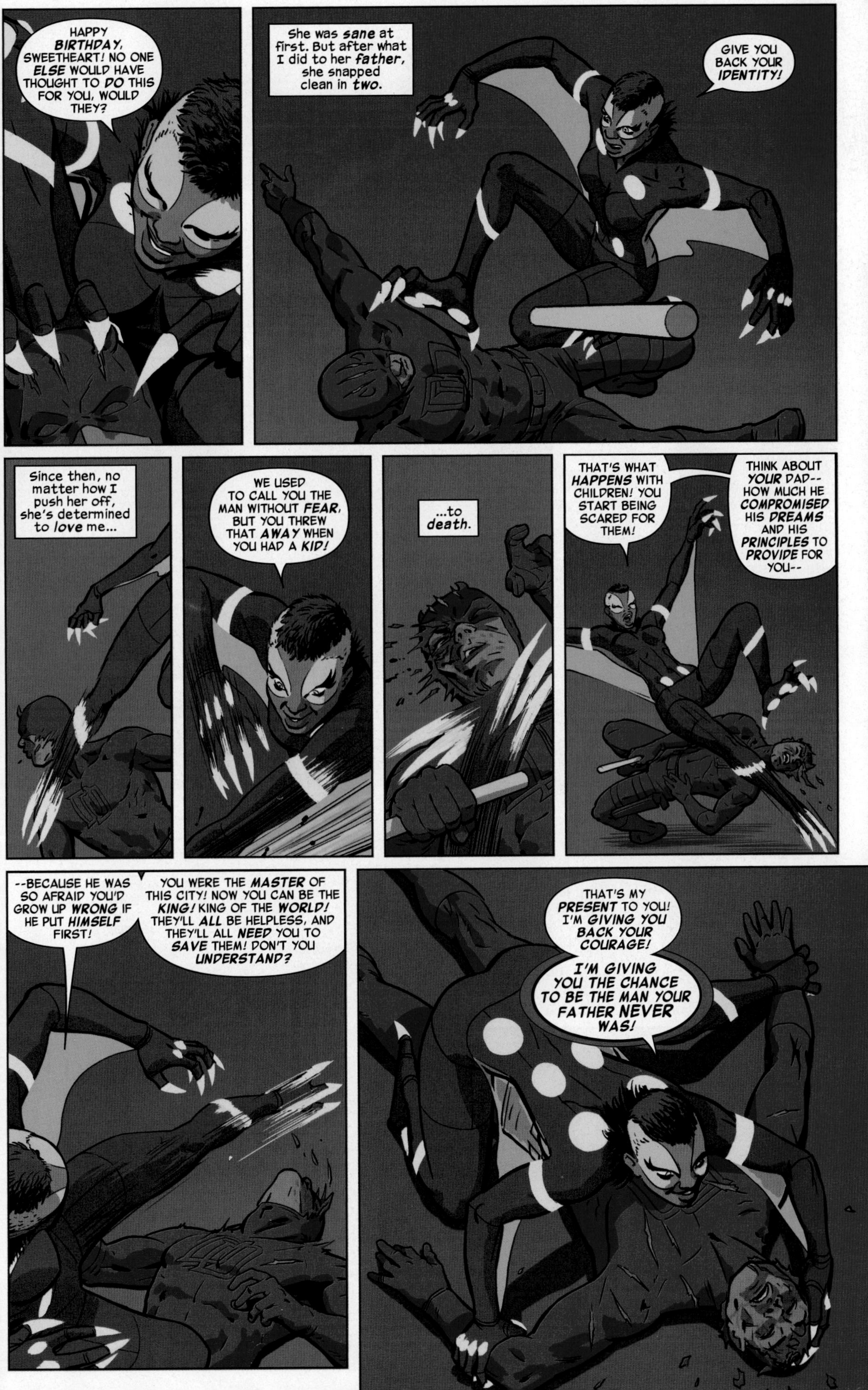
HAPPY BIRTHDAY, SWEETHEART! NO ONE ELSE WOULD HAVE THOUGHT TO DO THIS FOR YOU, WOULD THEY?
She was sane at first. But after what I did to her father, she snapped clean in two.
GIVE YOU BACK YOUR IDENTITY!
Since then, no matter how I push her off, she's determined to love me...
WE USED TO CALL YOU THE MAN WITHOUT FEAR, BUT YOU THREW THAT AWAY WHEN YOU HAD A KID!
...to death.
THAT'S WHAT HAPPENS WITH CHILDREN! YOU START BEING SCARED FOR THEM!
THINK ABOUT YOUR DAD-- HOW MUCH HE COMPROMISED HIS DREAMS AND HIS PRINCIPLES TO PROVIDE FOR YOU--
--BECAUSE HE WAS SO AFRAID YOU'D GROW UP WRONG IF HE PUT HIMSELF FIRST!
YOU WERE THE MASTER OF THIS CITY! NOW YOU CAN BE THE KING! KING OF THE WORLD! THEY'LL ALL BE HELPLESS, AND THEY'LL ALL NEED YOU TO SAVE THEM! DON'T YOU UNDERSTAND?
THAT'S MY PRESENT TO YOU! I'M GIVING YOU BACK YOUR COURAGE!
I'M GIVING YOU THE CHANCE TO BE THE MAN YOUR FATHER NEVER WAS!

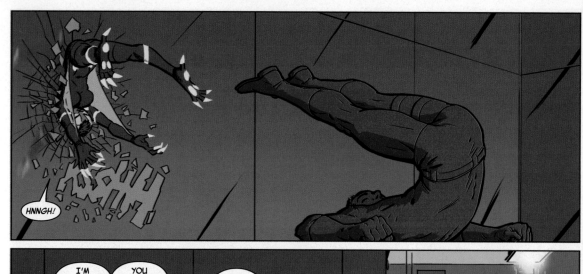

HNNNGH!

I'M *LUCKY* TO BE ANYTHING LIKE MY DAD.

YOU WANT TO KNOW HOW *ELSE* WE'RE ALIKE?

NO-- *DON'T--!*

WE BOTH DIED *YOUNG.*

Within seconds, I can smell the skin on my face burning.

The air blisters my lungs.

And my *radar sense* is screaming like a *Geiger counter* in a *uranium mine.*

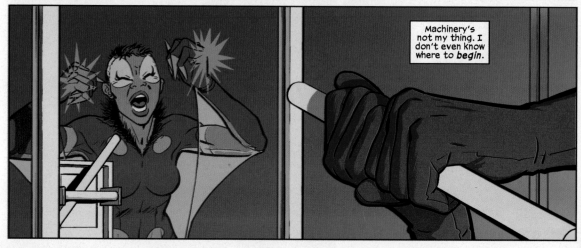

Machinery's not my thing. I don't even know where to *begin.*

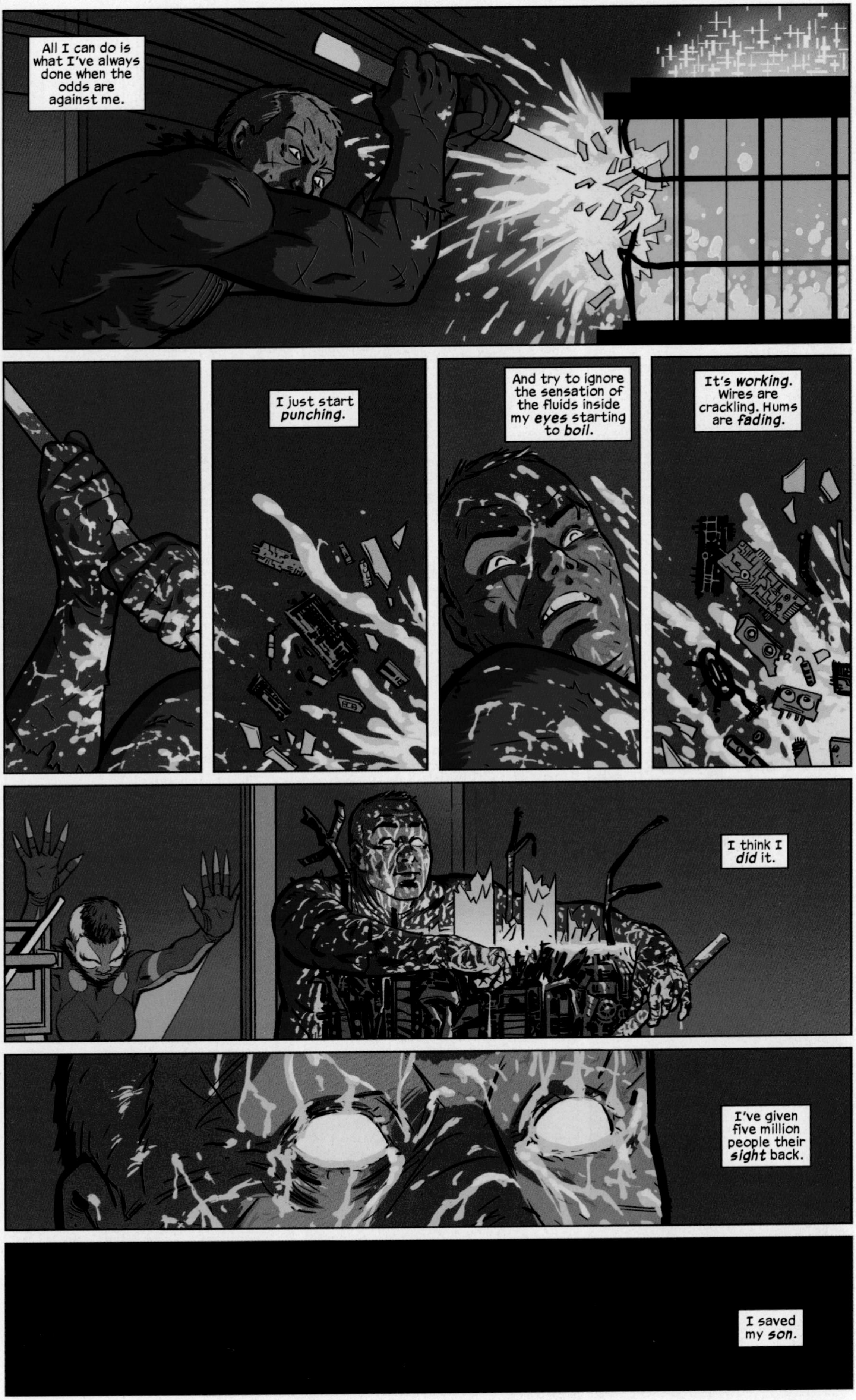
All I can do is what I've always done when the odds are against me.
I just start punching.
And try to ignore the sensation of the fluids inside my eyes starting to boil.
It's working. Wires are crackling. Hums are fading.
I think I did it.
I've given five million people their sight back.
I saved my son.

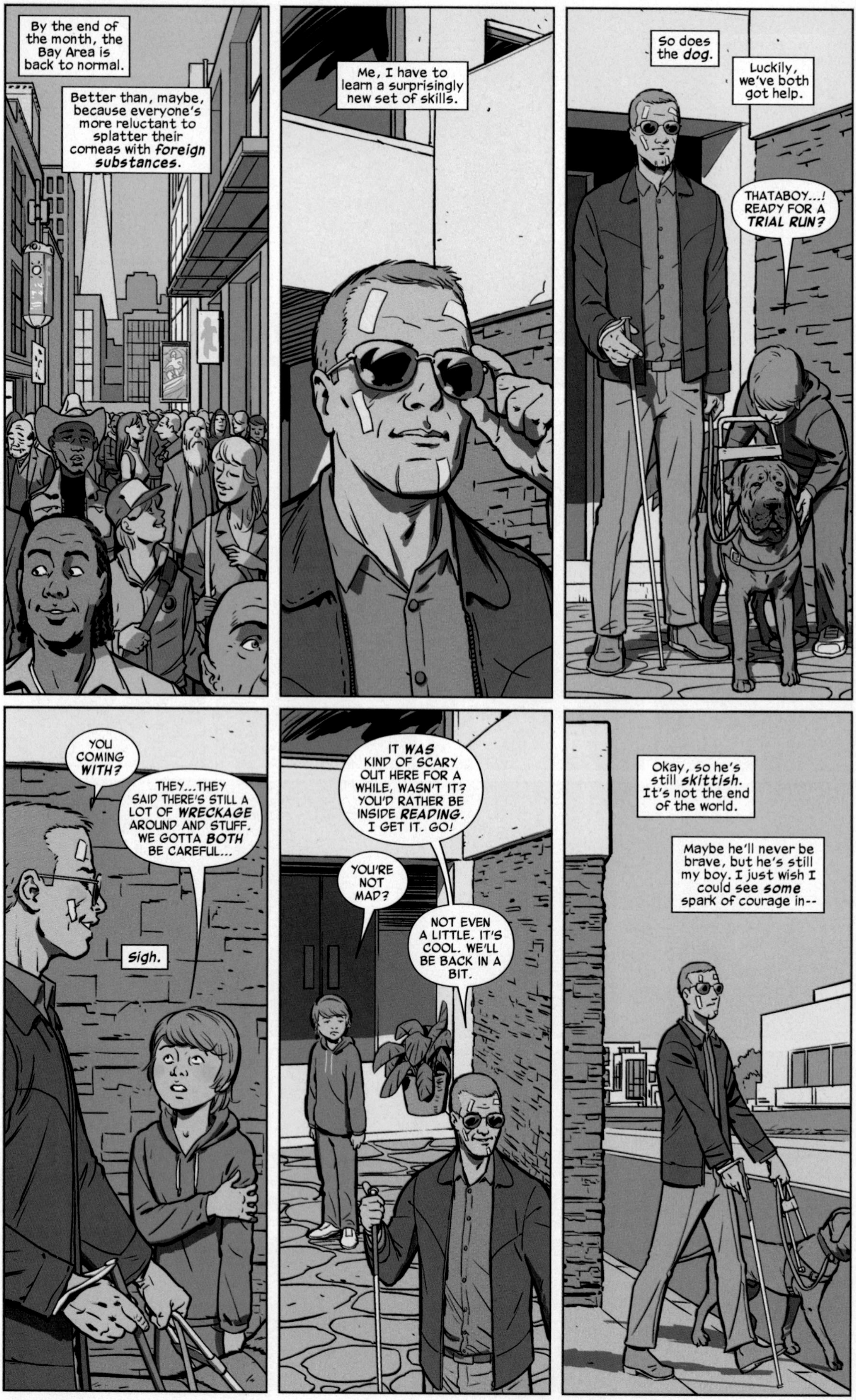
By the end of the month, the Bay Area is back to normal.
Better than, maybe, because everyone's more reluctant to splatter their corneas with foreign substances.
Me, I have to learn a surprisingly new set of skills.
So does the dog.
Luckily, we've both got help.
THATABOY...! READY FOR A TRIAL RUN?
YOU COMING WITH?
THEY...THEY SAID THERE'S STILL A LOT OF WRECKAGE AROUND AND STUFF. WE GOTTA BOTH BE CAREFUL...
Sigh.
IT WAS KIND OF SCARY OUT HERE FOR A WHILE, WASN'T IT? YOU'D RATHER BE INSIDE READING. I GET IT. GO!
YOU'RE NOT MAD?
NOT EVEN A LITTLE. IT'S COOL. WE'LL BE BACK IN A BIT.
Okay, so he's still skittish. It's not the end of the world.
Maybe he'll never be brave, but he's still my boy. I just wish I could see some spark of courage in--

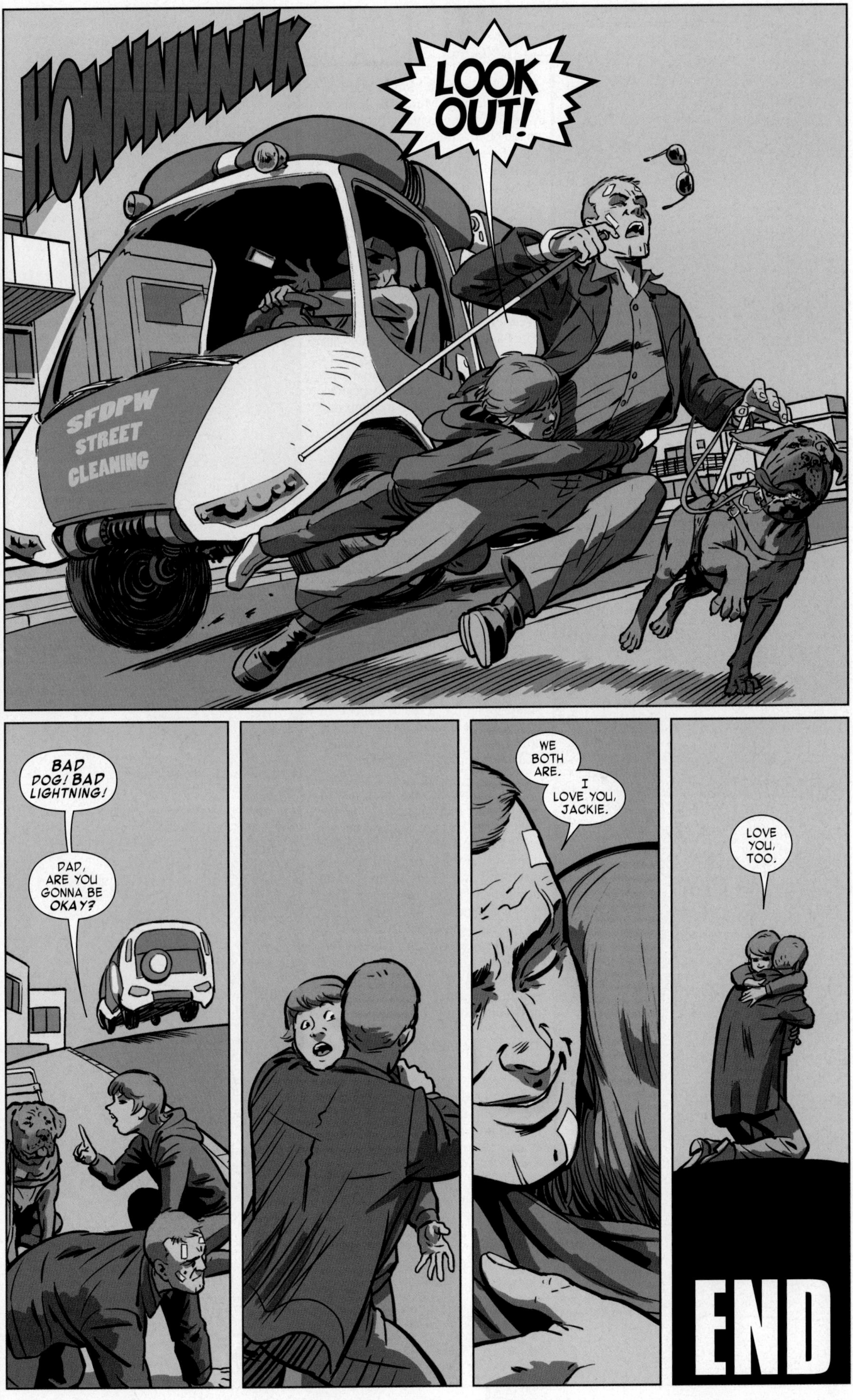
HONNNNNNK
LOOK OUT!
SFDPW
STREET
CLEANING
BAD DOG! BAD LIGHTNING!
DAD, ARE YOU GONNA BE OKAY?
WE BOTH ARE.
I LOVE YOU, JACKIE.
LOVE YOU, TOO.
END

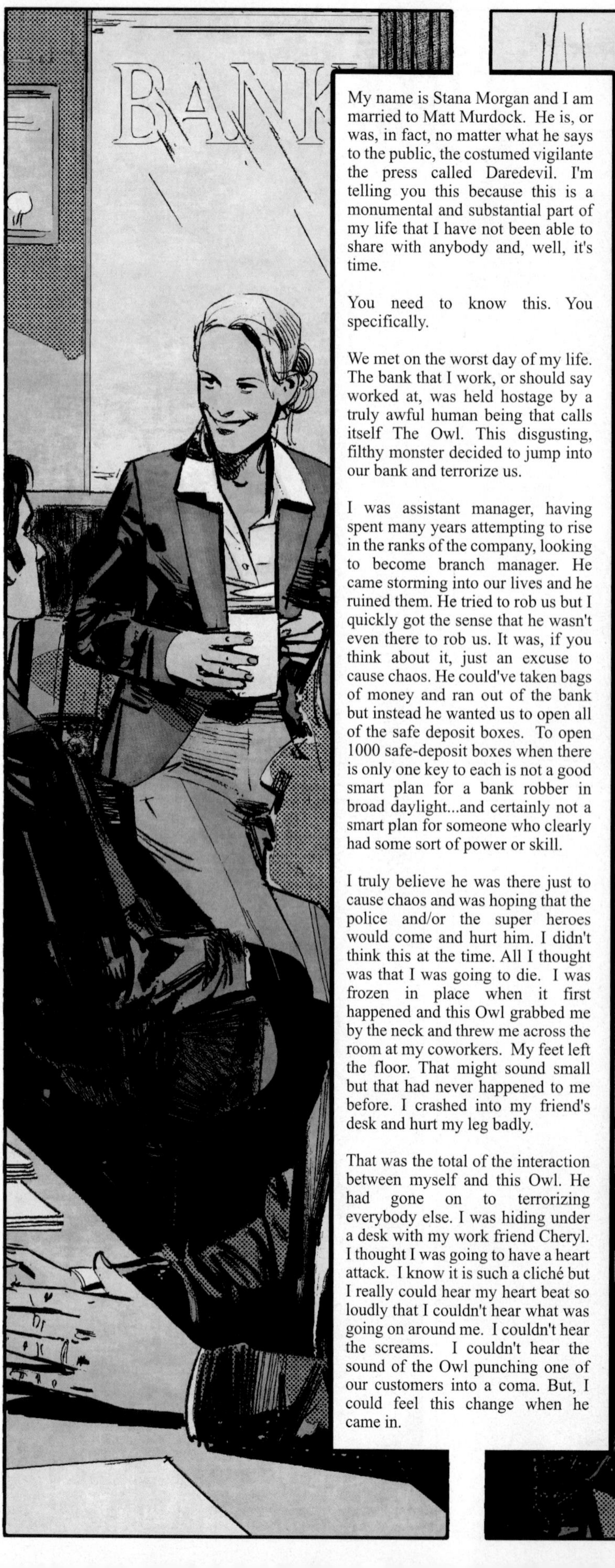
BANK

My name is Stana Morgan and I am married to Matt Murdock. He is, or was, in fact, no matter what he says to the public, the costumed vigilante the press called Daredevil. I'm telling you this because this is a monumental and substantial part of my life that I have not been able to share with anybody and, well, it's time.

You need to know this. You specifically.

We met on the worst day of my life. The bank that I work, or should say worked at, was held hostage by a truly awful human being that calls itself The Owl. This disgusting, filthy monster decided to jump into our bank and terrorize us.

I was assistant manager, having spent many years attempting to rise in the ranks of the company, looking to become branch manager. He came storming into our lives and he ruined them. He tried to rob us but I quickly got the sense that he wasn't even there to rob us. It was, if you think about it, just an excuse to cause chaos. He could've taken bags of money and ran out of the bank but instead he wanted us to open all of the safe deposit boxes. To open 1000 safe-deposit boxes when there is only one key to each is not a good smart plan for a bank robber in broad daylight...and certainly not a smart plan for someone who clearly had some sort of power or skill.

I truly believe he was there just to cause chaos and was hoping that the police and/or the super heroes would come and hurt him. I didn't think this at the time. All I thought was that I was going to die. I was frozen in place when it first happened and this Owl grabbed me by the neck and threw me across the room at my coworkers. My feet left the floor. That might sound small but that had never happened to me before. I crashed into my friend's desk and hurt my leg badly.

That was the total of the interaction between myself and this Owl. He had gone on to terrorizing everybody else. I was hiding under a desk with my work friend Cheryl. I thought I was going to have a heart attack. I know it is such a cliché but I really could hear my heart beat so loudly that I couldn't hear what was going on around me. I couldn't hear the screams. I couldn't hear the sound of the Owl punching one of our customers into a coma. But, I could feel this change when he came in.

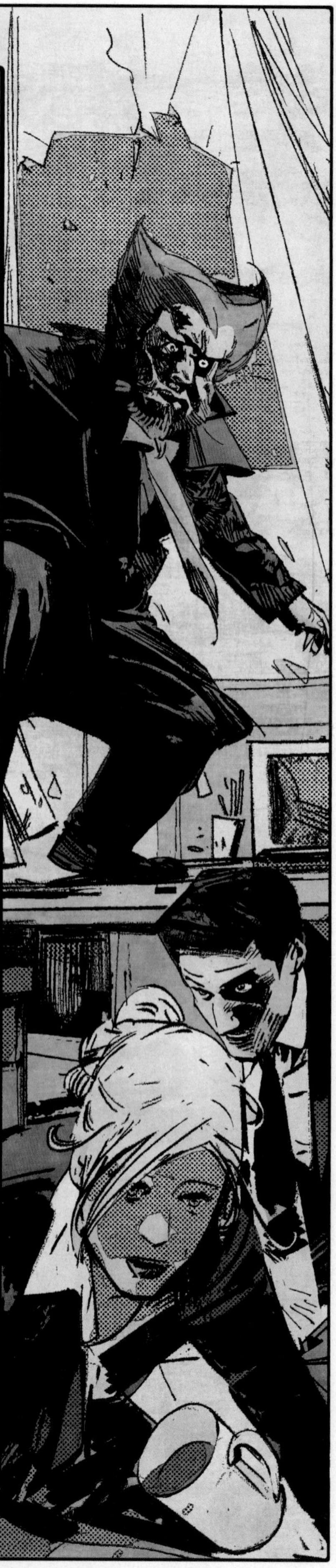

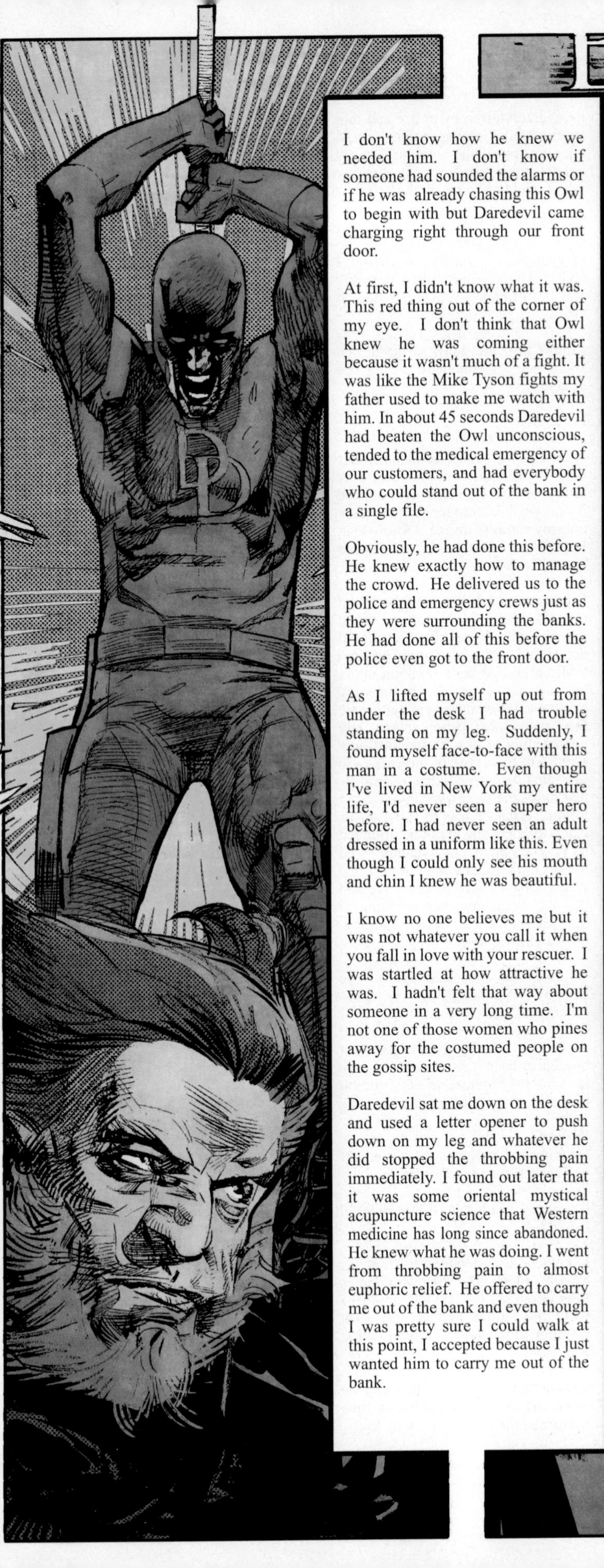

I don't know how he knew we needed him. I don't know if someone had sounded the alarms or if he was already chasing this Owl to begin with but Daredevil came charging right through our front door.

At first, I didn't know what it was. This red thing out of the corner of my eye. I don't think that Owl knew he was coming either because it wasn't much of a fight. It was like the Mike Tyson fights my father used to make me watch with him. In about 45 seconds Daredevil had beaten the Owl unconscious, tended to the medical emergency of our customers, and had everybody who could stand out of the bank in a single file.

Obviously, he had done this before. He knew exactly how to manage the crowd. He delivered us to the police and emergency crews just as they were surrounding the banks. He had done all of this before the police even got to the front door.

As I lifted myself up out from under the desk I had trouble standing on my leg. Suddenly, I found myself face-to-face with this man in a costume. Even though I've lived in New York my entire life, I'd never seen a super hero before. I had never seen an adult dressed in a uniform like this. Even though I could only see his mouth and chin I knew he was beautiful.

I know no one believes me but it was not whatever you call it when you fall in love with your rescuer. I was startled at how attractive he was. I hadn't felt that way about someone in a very long time. I'm not one of those women who pines away for the costumed people on the gossip sites.

Daredevil sat me down on the desk and used a letter opener to push down on my leg and whatever he did stopped the throbbing pain immediately. I found out later that it was some oriental mystical acupuncture science that Western medicine has long since abandoned. He knew what he was doing. I went from throbbing pain to almost euphoric relief. He offered to carry me out of the bank and even though I was pretty sure I could walk at this point, I accepted because I just wanted him to carry me out of the bank.

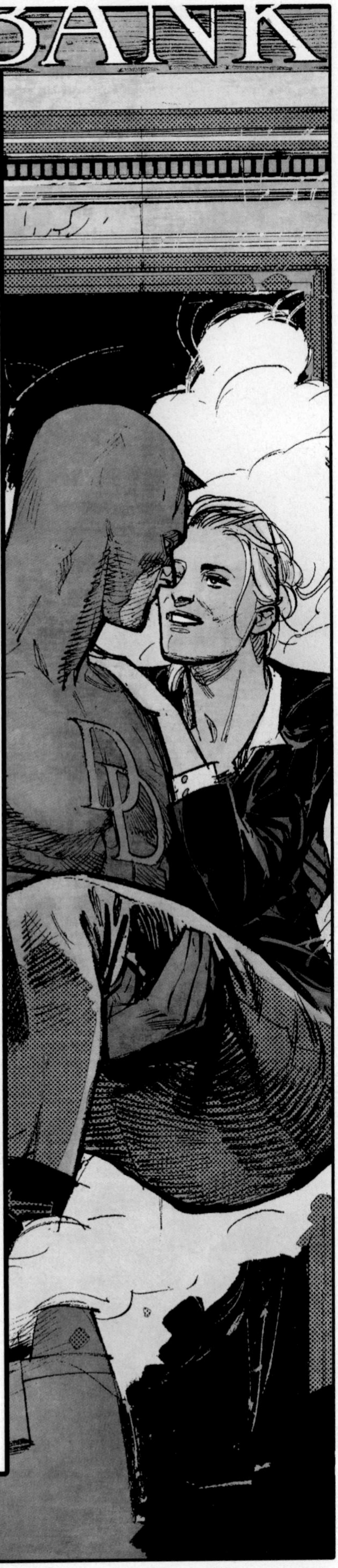
BANK

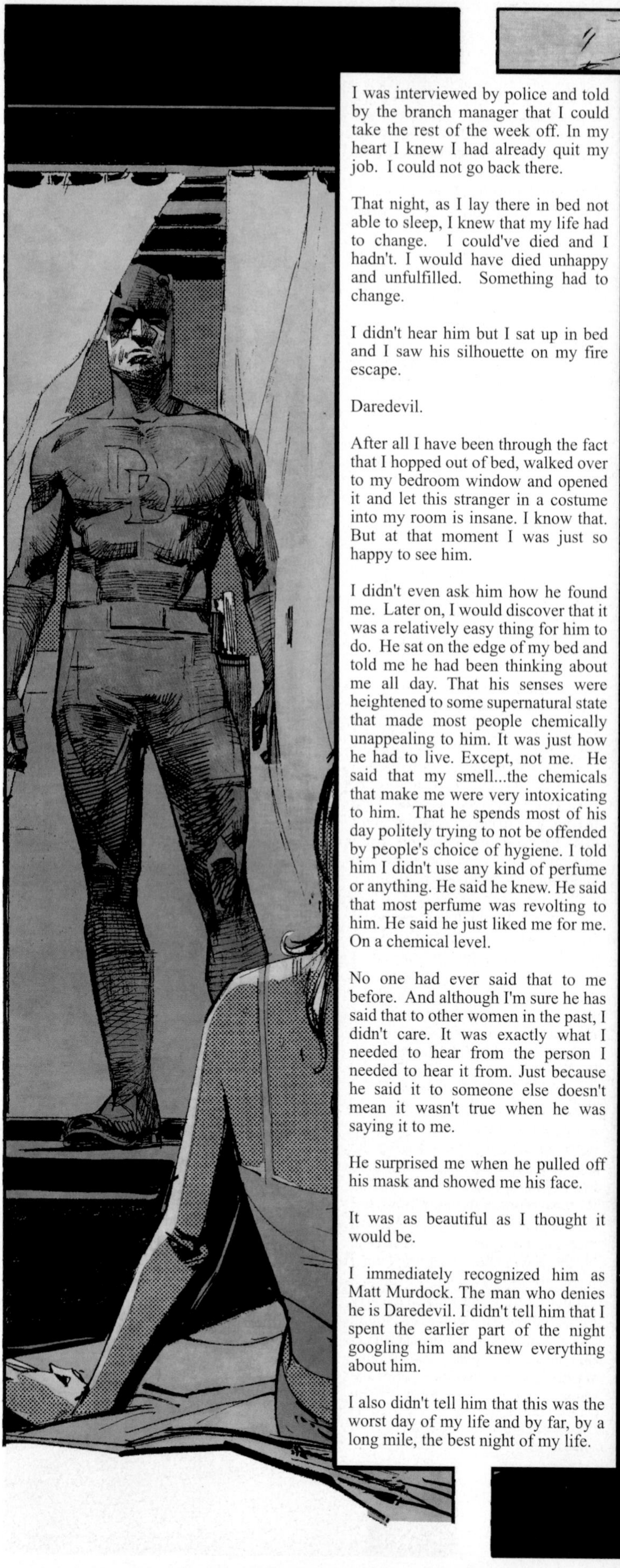

I was interviewed by police and told by the branch manager that I could take the rest of the week off. In my heart I knew I had already quit my job. I could not go back there.

That night, as I lay there in bed not able to sleep, I knew that my life had to change. I could've died and I hadn't. I would have died unhappy and unfulfilled. Something had to change.

I didn't hear him but I sat up in bed and I saw his silhouette on my fire escape.

Daredevil.

After all I have been through the fact that I hopped out of bed, walked over to my bedroom window and opened it and let this stranger in a costume into my room is insane. I know that. But at that moment I was just so happy to see him.

I didn't even ask him how he found me. Later on, I would discover that it was a relatively easy thing for him to do. He sat on the edge of my bed and told me he had been thinking about me all day. That his senses were heightened to some supernatural state that made most people chemically unappealing to him. It was just how he had to live. Except, not me. He said that my smell...the chemicals that make me were very intoxicating to him. That he spends most of his day politely trying to not be offended by people's choice of hygiene. I told him I didn't use any kind of perfume or anything. He said he knew. He said that most perfume was revolting to him. He said he just liked me for me. On a chemical level.

No one had ever said that to me before. And although I'm sure he has said that to other women in the past, I didn't care. It was exactly what I needed to hear from the person I needed to hear it from. Just because he said it to someone else doesn't mean it wasn't true when he was saying it to me.

He surprised me when he pulled off his mask and showed me his face.

It was as beautiful as I thought it would be.

I immediately recognized him as Matt Murdock. The man who denies he is Daredevil. I didn't tell him that I spent the earlier part of the night googling him and knew everything about him.

I also didn't tell him that this was the worst day of my life and by far, by a long mile, the best night of my life.

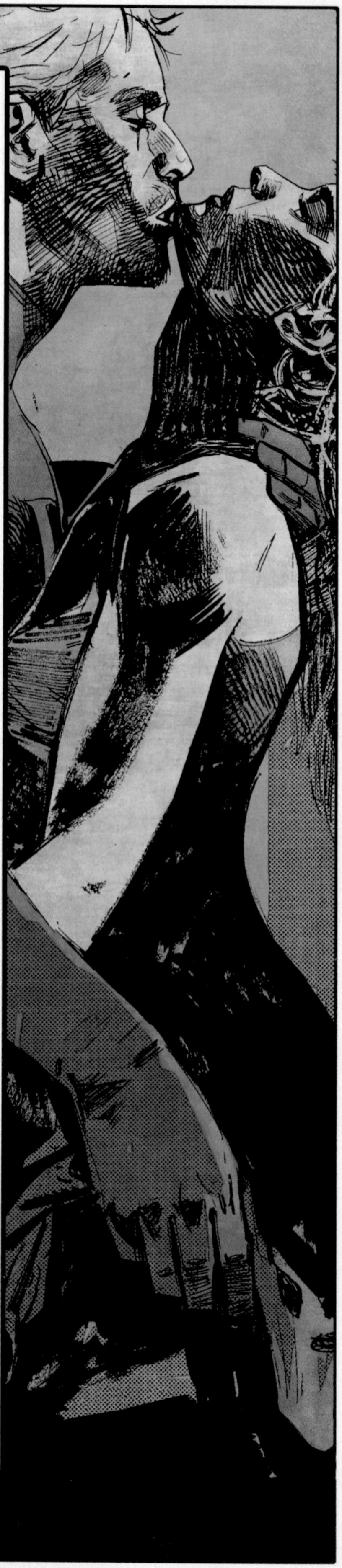

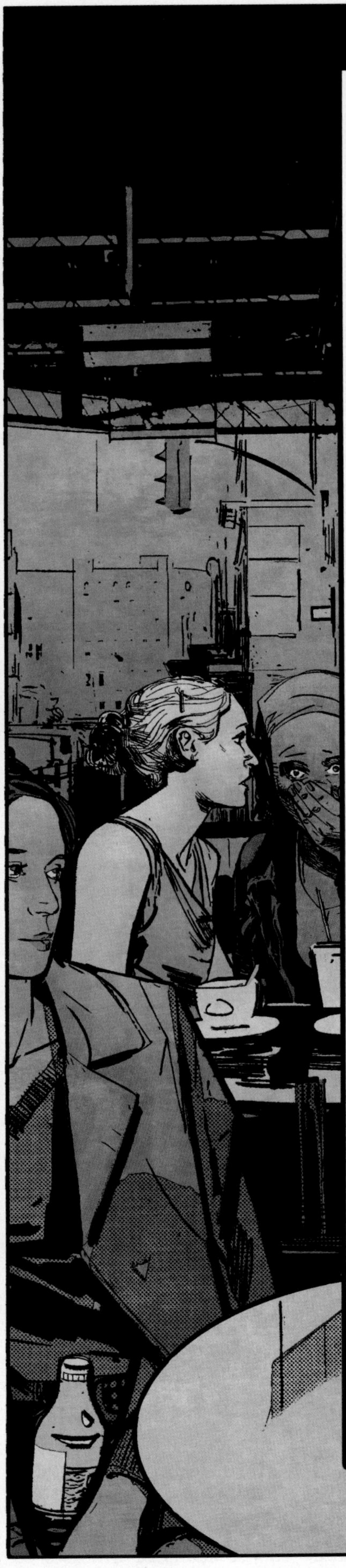

The next day he made it very clear that for numerous reasons we had to keep what was happening between us a secret. He said that he lives a dangerous life and the people around him are in danger as well.

If he could keep me a secret we could enjoy each other just as people.

He kept saying he didn't want to rush things but we both knew that we were going to. Once you get to a certain age, there are a lot of things you know about yourself and the world. You know how some relationships are going to end before they even begin. You know how certain new people in your life will be life-defining. And once you find these people, there is no reason to dance around it.

I was very in love and I was almost certain that he was, too. He kept putting my hand on his heart as if he wanted me to hear and feel it the way he could hear and feel mine without even touching it.

As the days and late nights progressed, we fully expressed our love to each other. I have a best friend, or should I say had, a best friend named Jeannie. Not telling her about this was almost a betrayal to our friendship. Though I was, in a way, betraying Matthew by telling Jeannie about my life now...I had to.

Obviously, I thought she was going to be happy for me. I truly did. No person on the planet Earth had to sit through more whining from me about the parade of disappointments I have had in my life. I thought my happiness would relieve her.

Instead, she stared at me as if I told her I had murdered her cat. I waited for her to speak her mind. She looked me right in the eye and told me that I was going to be murdered. That I had just signed my life away for a "midnight booty call." She said that super heroes bring death to everyone around them. She said that Oprah had done a show about it years ago. I told her I disagreed--that I was in love and that she should be happy for me. The days that followed were the longest we have ever gone without speaking. When I finally decided to corner her at work and asked her if she was mad at me she said that she was certain that I was going to die and that she didn't want to be there to see it.

She kissed me, hugged me, told me she loved me and told me never to speak to her again. I have never been so angry at someone in my entire life. I confessed to Matthew what had transpired. He asked me to marry him.

At his law office, his partner Frank Nelson officiated the ceremony. In attendance were some of Matt's friends. I had to look them up later: Luke Cage, Danny Rand, this very funny woman named Jessica Jones. They could not have been happier for us and more welcoming of me into their circle. I was angry that I had gone my whole life surrounded by people who judged me while Matt had found a circle like this. I didn't know what I was missing.

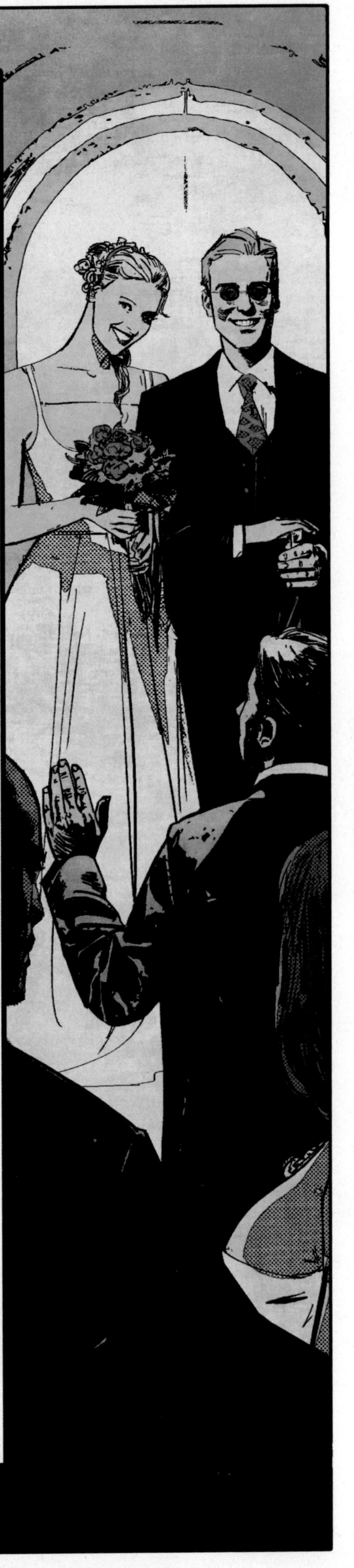

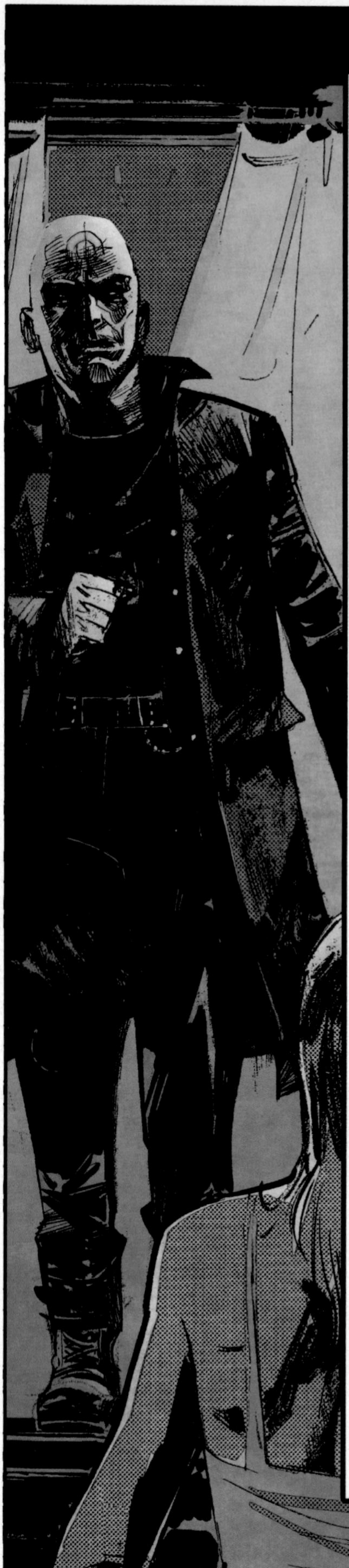

The months that followed were everything I had always hoped my life would be, I was happy, I was happy on a level that I did not know I needed to be. Sometimes days would go by without Matt and I seeing each other, but I understood. Sometimes he was away. Sometimes what he was doing was actually in the newspaper or online so I knew where he was and I knew who he was with. I wasn't jealous.

Matt was a good man. A man who I could trust wholeheartedly. I just hoped that he was safe and that he would come back. And he always did. I have a cousin who was married to a police officer. She told me that the trick was that you just have to learn to share them.

I don't know why I bought the pregnancy test. I didn't get crazy, or nauseous, or constipated, or any of those other things my girlfriends have felt when they thought they were pregnant. I had never bought one before.

But I did. And I was.

Maybe I wanted to be and I willed it. I was married and happy and I wanted to bring a baby into this miraculously happy life I had finally put together.

If you are reading this, you know that this is my last will and testament, my last rites and confession, and you know that my friend Jeannie was right.

To my darling baby, I am writing this for you.

One day you'll be old enough to understand it and I just wanted you to know from me, to you, that I love you. That you were born out of love. That your mother and father love you entirely and each other, as well. As you get older, you'll see what a gift that is. I would've given anything to be by your side at every minute of your life, but know that your mother died a happy woman who knew the risks. It was worth it.

But I hope you never see this. I hope I am crazy for writing it.

I can't wait for your father to find out about you.

I know he will cry.

I know he'd been wanting this forever.

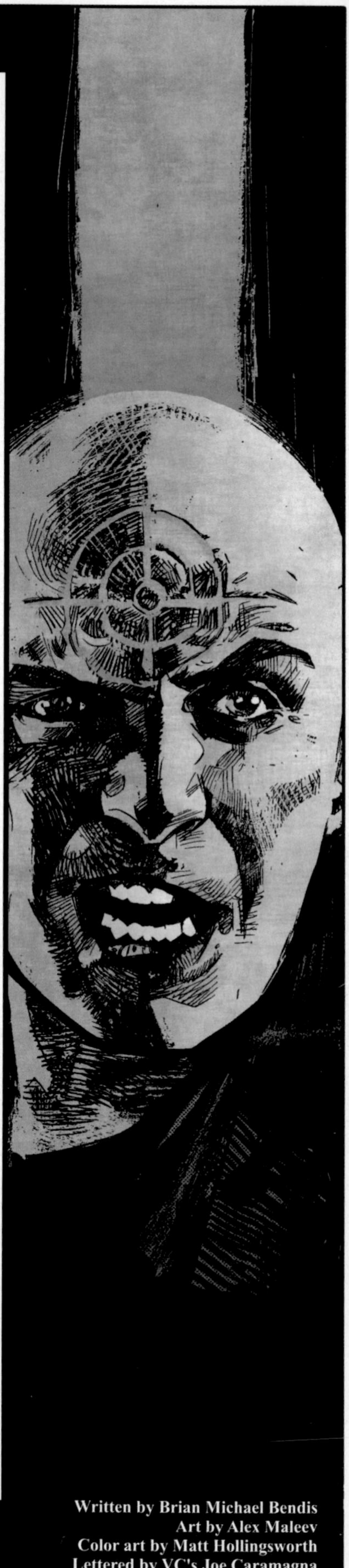

Written by Brian Michael Bendis
Art by Alex Maleev
Color art by Matt Hollingsworth
Lettered by VC's Joe Caramagna

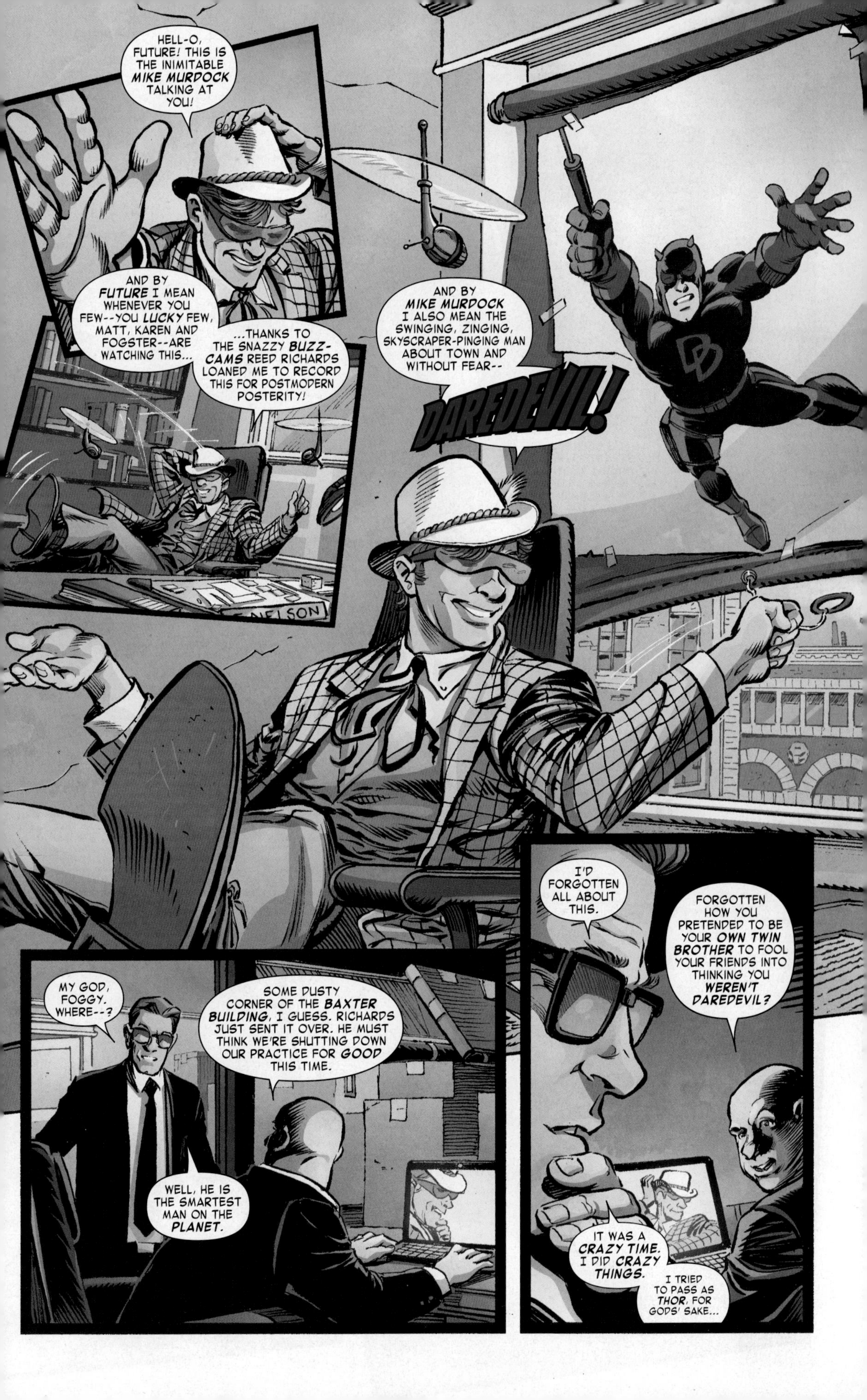

HELL-O, FUTURE! THIS IS THE INIMITABLE MIKE MURDOCK TALKING AT YOU!
AND BY FUTURE I MEAN WHENEVER YOU FEW--YOU LUCKY FEW, MATT, KAREN AND FOGSTER--ARE WATCHING THIS...
...THANKS TO THE SNAZZY BUZZ-CAMS REED RICHARDS LOANED ME TO RECORD THIS FOR POSTMODERN POSTERITY!
NELSON
AND BY MIKE MURDOCK I ALSO MEAN THE SWINGING, ZINGING, SKYSCRAPER-PINGING MAN ABOUT TOWN AND WITHOUT FEAR--
DAREDEVIL!
MY GOD, FOGGY. WHERE--?
SOME DUSTY CORNER OF THE BAXTER BUILDING, I GUESS. RICHARDS JUST SENT IT OVER. HE MUST THINK WE'RE SHUTTING DOWN OUR PRACTICE FOR GOOD THIS TIME.
WELL, HE IS THE SMARTEST MAN ON THE PLANET.
I'D FORGOTTEN ALL ABOUT THIS.
FORGOTTEN HOW YOU PRETENDED TO BE YOUR OWN TWIN BROTHER TO FOOL YOUR FRIENDS INTO THINKING YOU WEREN'T DAREDEVIL?
IT WAS A CRAZY TIME. I DID CRAZY THINGS.
I TRIED TO PASS AS THOR, FOR GODS' SAKE...

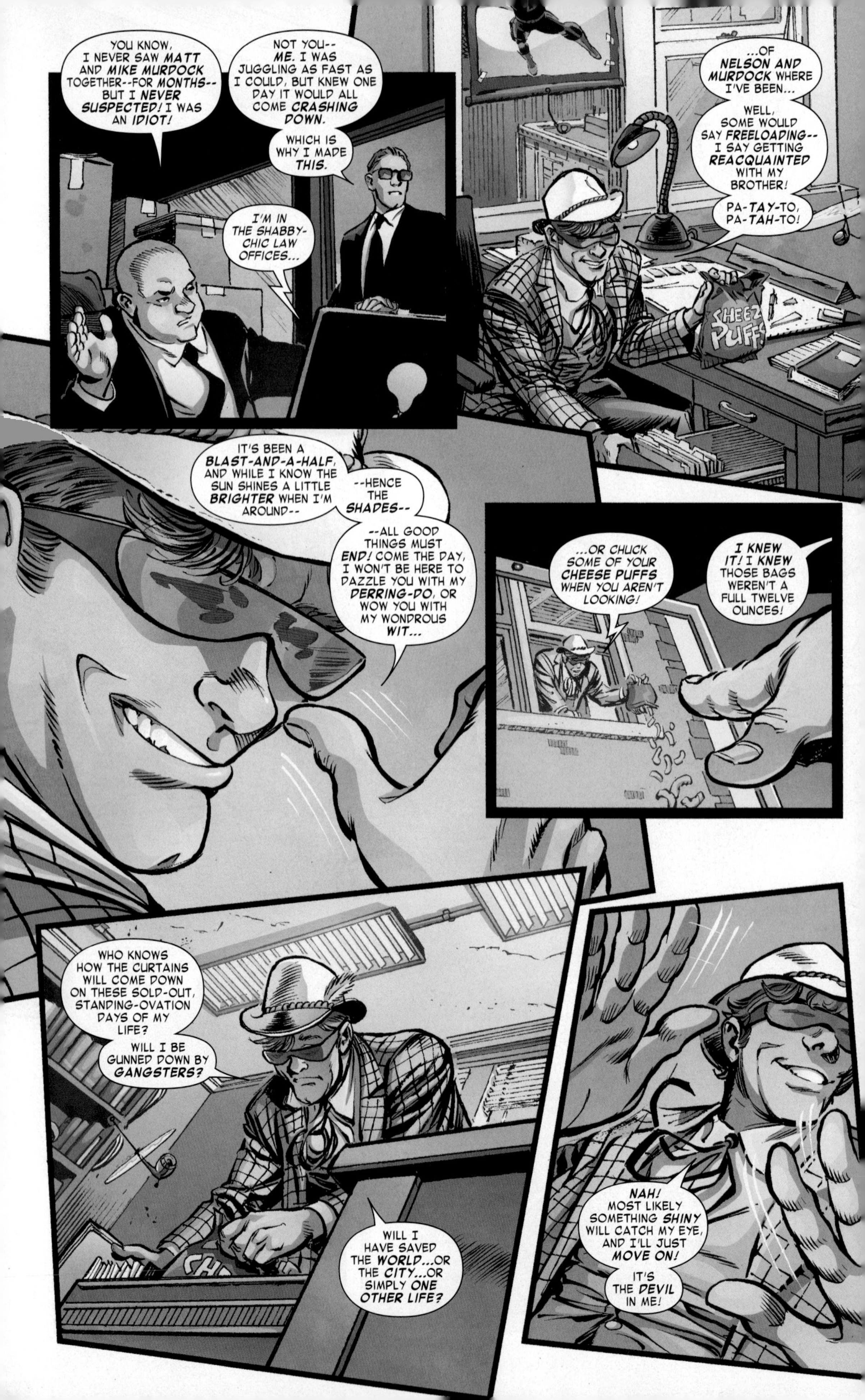
YOU KNOW, I NEVER SAW MATT AND MIKE MURDOCK TOGETHER--FOR MONTHS--BUT I NEVER SUSPECTED! I WAS AN IDIOT!
NOT YOU--ME. I WAS JUGGLING AS FAST AS I COULD, BUT KNEW ONE DAY IT WOULD ALL COME CRASHING DOWN.
WHICH IS WHY I MADE THIS.
I'M IN THE SHABBY-CHIC LAW OFFICES...
...OF NELSON AND MURDOCK WHERE I'VE BEEN...
WELL, SOME WOULD SAY FREELOADING--I SAY GETTING REACQUAINTED WITH MY BROTHER!
PA-TAY-TO, PA-TAH-TO!
CHEEZ PUFFS
IT'S BEEN A BLAST-AND-A-HALF, AND WHILE I KNOW THE SUN SHINES A LITTLE BRIGHTER WHEN I'M AROUND--
--HENCE THE SHADES--
--ALL GOOD THINGS MUST END! COME THE DAY, I WON'T BE HERE TO DAZZLE YOU WITH MY DERRING-DO, OR WOW YOU WITH MY WONDROUS WIT...
...OR CHUCK SOME OF YOUR CHEESE PUFFS WHEN YOU AREN'T LOOKING!
I KNEW IT! I KNEW THOSE BAGS WEREN'T A FULL TWELVE OUNCES!
WHO KNOWS HOW THE CURTAINS WILL COME DOWN ON THESE SOLD-OUT, STANDING-OVATION DAYS OF MY LIFE?
WILL I BE GUNNED DOWN BY GANGSTERS?
WILL I HAVE SAVED THE WORLD...OR THE CITY...OR SIMPLY ONE OTHER LIFE?
NAH! MOST LIKELY SOMETHING SHINY WILL CATCH MY EYE, AND I'LL JUST MOVE ON!
IT'S THE DEVIL IN ME!

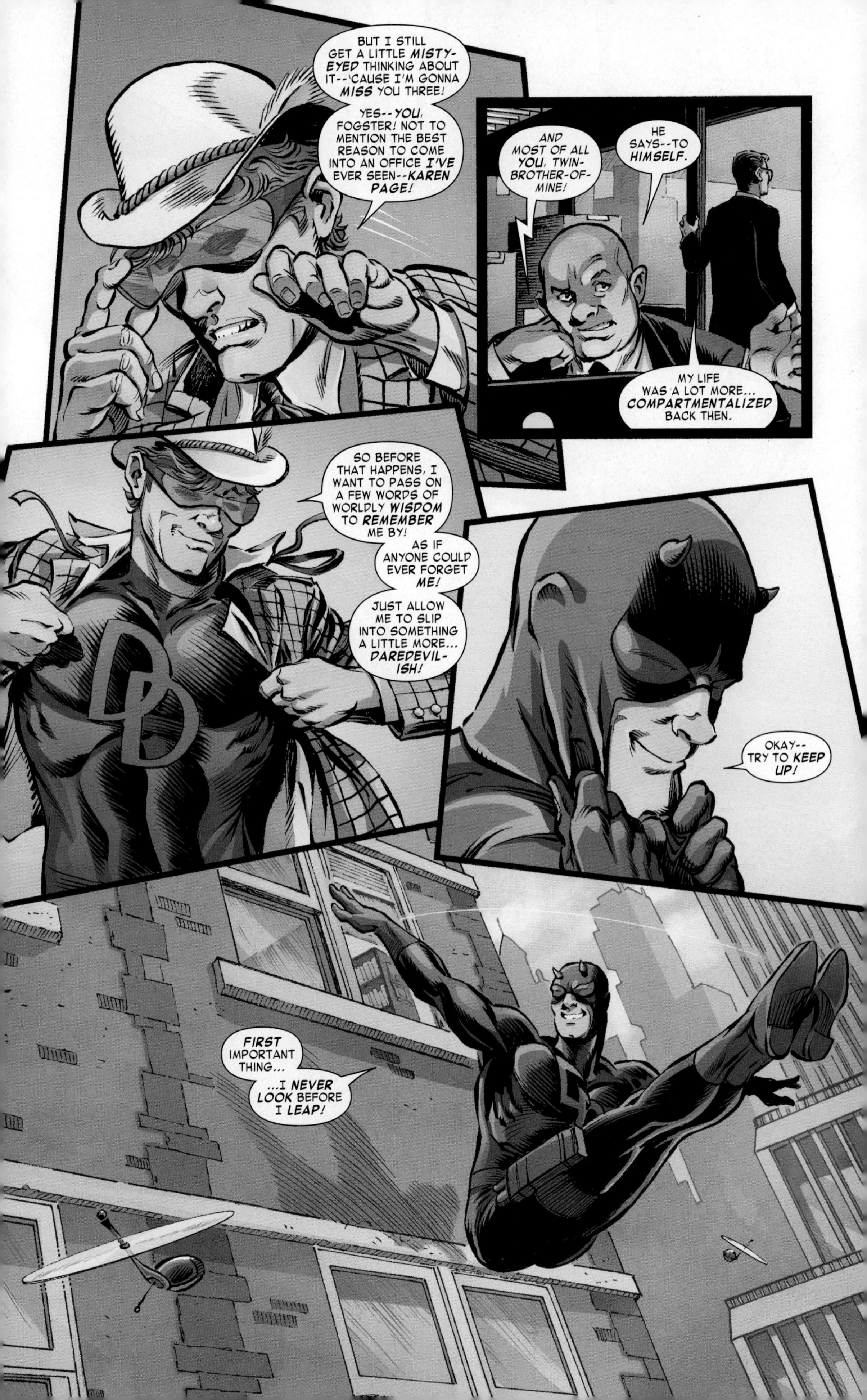
BUT I STILL GET A LITTLE MISTY-EYED THINKING ABOUT IT--'CAUSE I'M GONNA MISS YOU THREE!
YES--YOU, FOGSTER! NOT TO MENTION THE BEST REASON TO COME INTO AN OFFICE I'VE EVER SEEN--KAREN PAGE!
AND MOST OF ALL YOU, TWIN-BROTHER-OF-MINE!
HE SAYS--TO HIMSELF.
MY LIFE WAS A LOT MORE... COMPARTMENTALIZED BACK THEN.
SO BEFORE THAT HAPPENS, I WANT TO PASS ON A FEW WORDS OF WORLDLY WISDOM TO REMEMBER ME BY!
AS IF ANYONE COULD EVER FORGET ME!
JUST ALLOW ME TO SLIP INTO SOMETHING A LITTLE MORE... DAREDEVIL-ISH!
OKAY--TRY TO KEEP UP!
FIRST IMPORTANT THING...
...I NEVER LOOK BEFORE I LEAP!

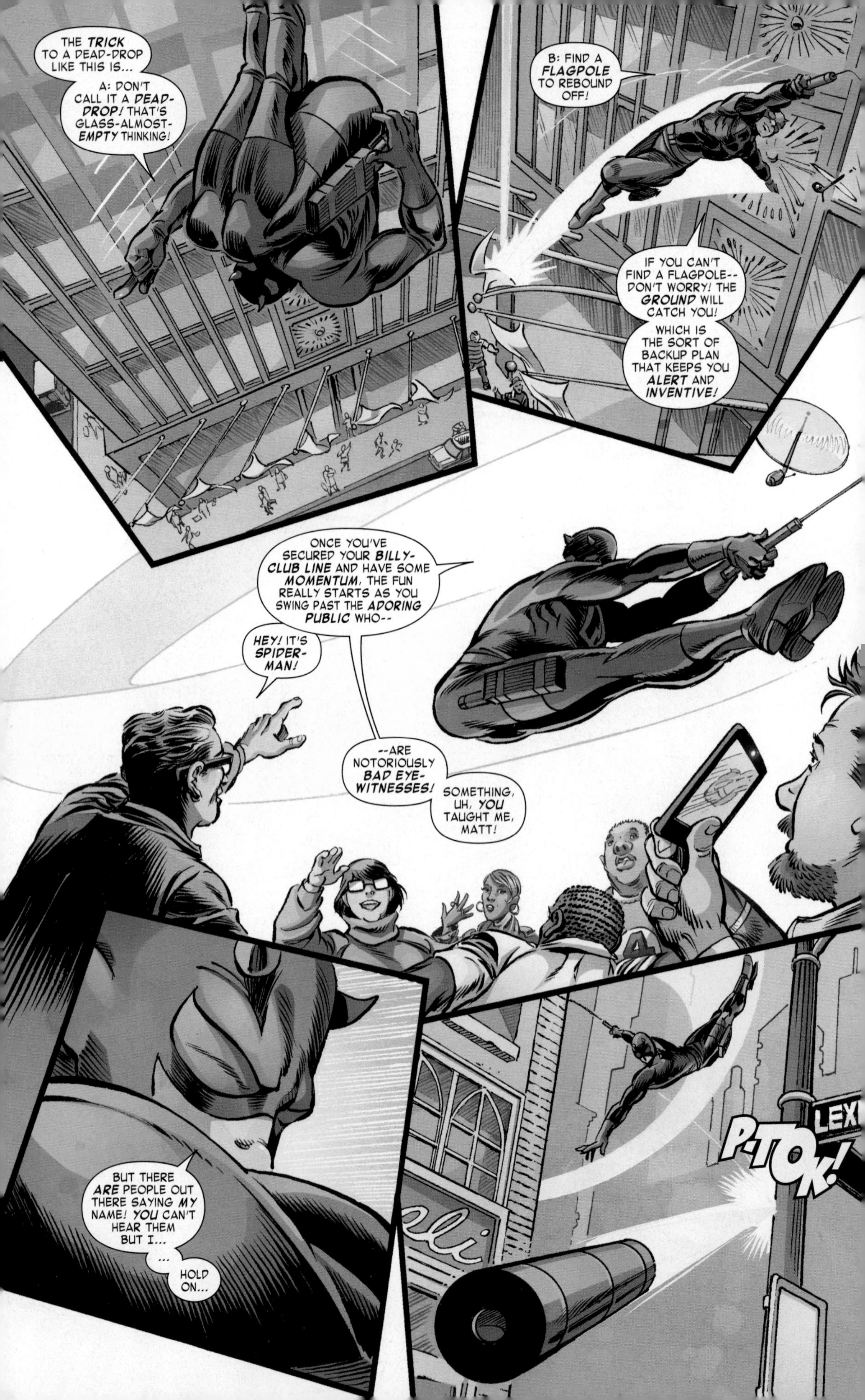
THE TRICK TO A DEAD-DROP LIKE THIS IS...
A: DON'T CALL IT A DEAD-DROP! THAT'S GLASS-ALMOST-EMPTY THINKING!
B: FIND A FLAGPOLE TO REBOUND OFF!
IF YOU CAN'T FIND A FLAGPOLE--DON'T WORRY! THE GROUND WILL CATCH YOU!
WHICH IS THE SORT OF BACKUP PLAN THAT KEEPS YOU ALERT AND INVENTIVE!
ONCE YOU'VE SECURED YOUR BILLY-CLUB LINE AND HAVE SOME MOMENTUM, THE FUN REALLY STARTS AS YOU SWING PAST THE ADORING PUBLIC WHO--
HEY! IT'S SPIDER-MAN!
--ARE NOTORIOUSLY BAD EYE-WITNESSES!
SOMETHING, UH, YOU TAUGHT ME, MATT!
BUT THERE ARE PEOPLE OUT THERE SAYING MY NAME! YOU CAN'T HEAR THEM BUT I...
...
HOLD ON...
LEX
P-TOK!

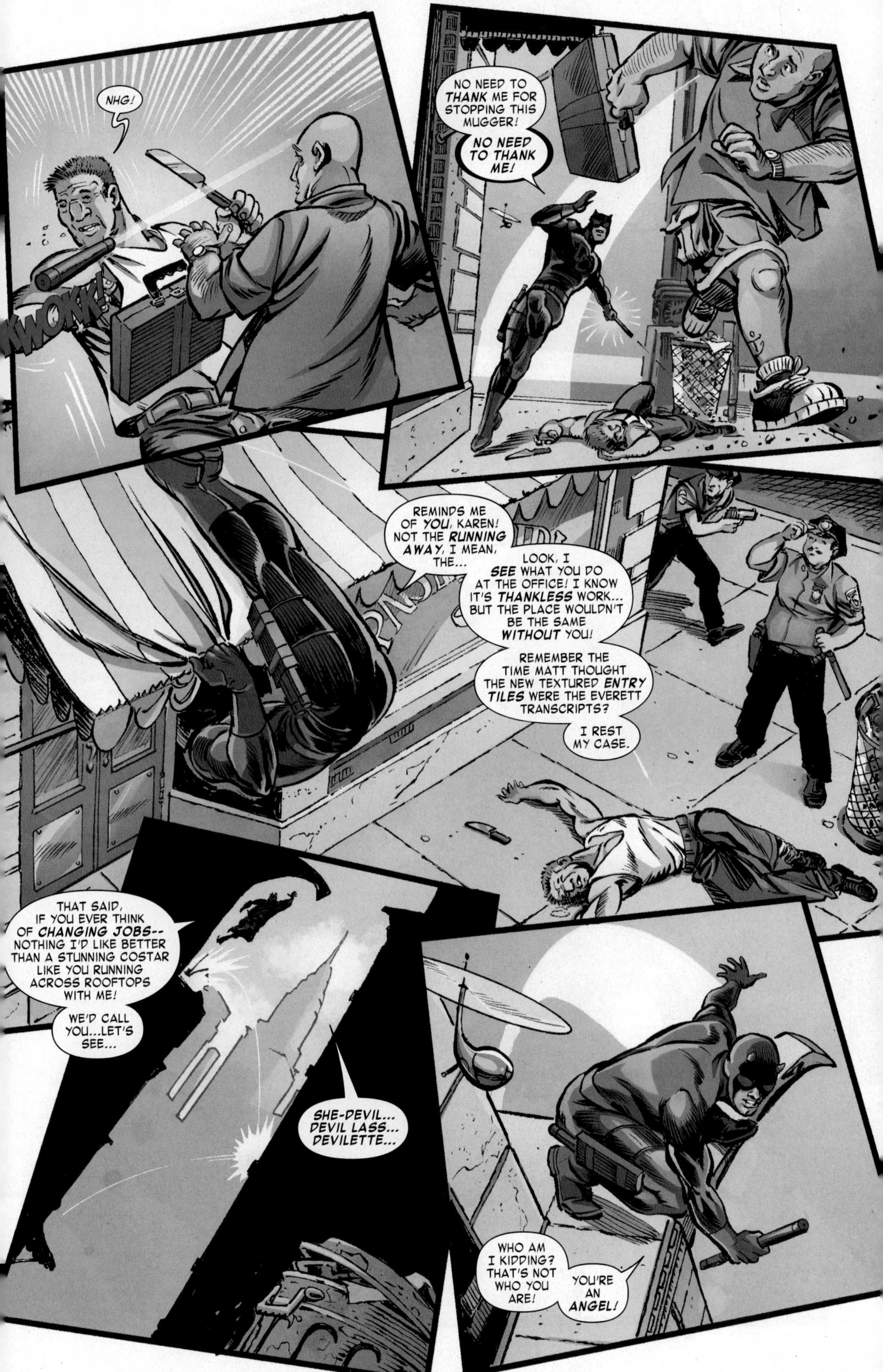
NHG!
KWOKK!
NO NEED TO THANK ME FOR STOPPING THIS MUGGER!
NO NEED TO THANK ME!
REMINDS ME OF YOU, KAREN! NOT THE RUNNING AWAY, I MEAN, THE...
LOOK, I SEE WHAT YOU DO AT THE OFFICE! I KNOW IT'S THANKLESS WORK... BUT THE PLACE WOULDN'T BE THE SAME WITHOUT YOU!
REMEMBER THE TIME MATT THOUGHT THE NEW TEXTURED ENTRY TILES WERE THE EVERETT TRANSCRIPTS?
I REST MY CASE.
THAT SAID, IF YOU EVER THINK OF CHANGING JOBS-- NOTHING I'D LIKE BETTER THAN A STUNNING COSTAR LIKE YOU RUNNING ACROSS ROOFTOPS WITH ME!
WE'D CALL YOU...LET'S SEE...
SHE-DEVIL... DEVIL LASS... DEVILETTE...
WHO AM I KIDDING? THAT'S NOT WHO YOU ARE!
YOU'RE AN ANGEL!

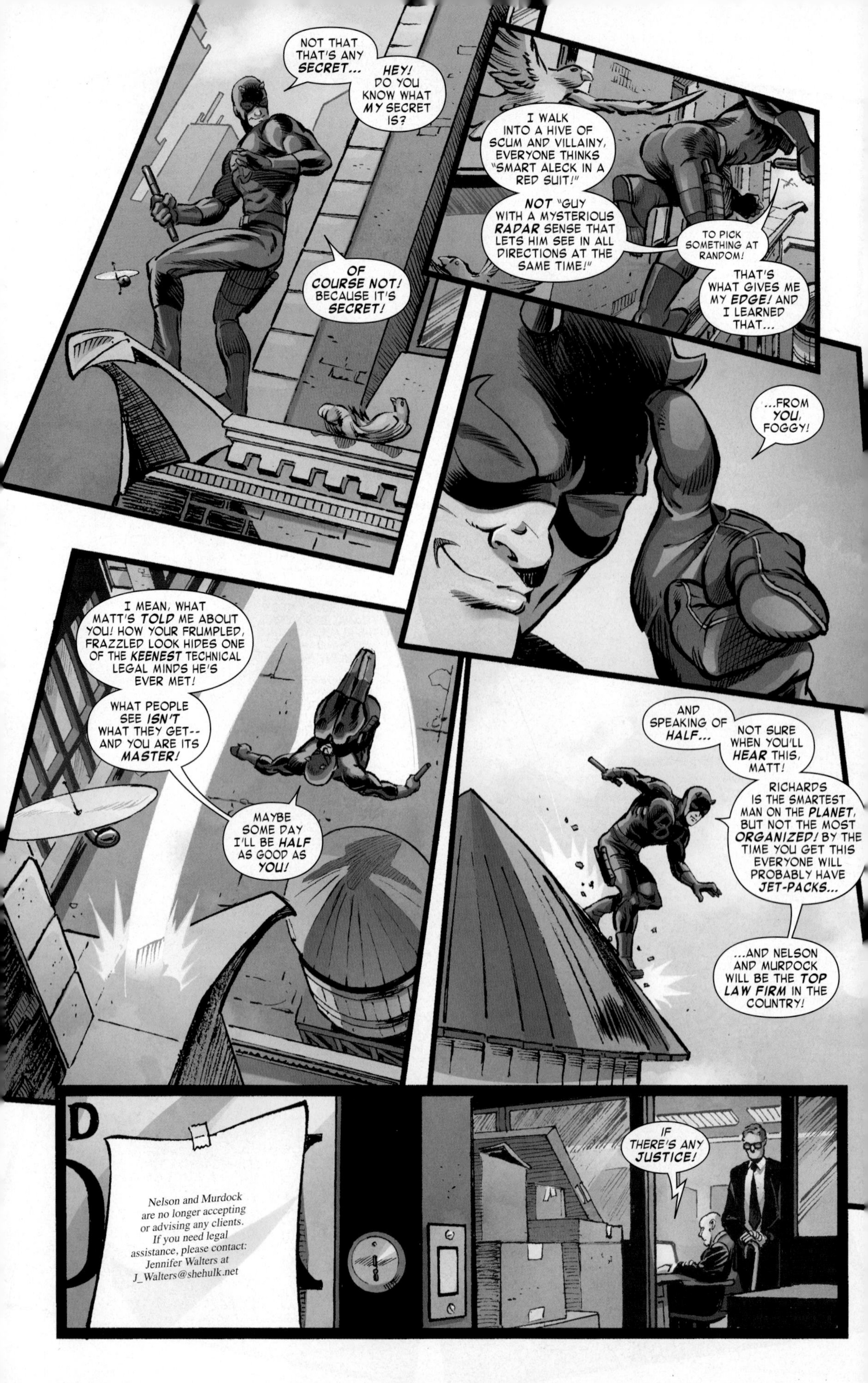
NOT THAT THAT'S ANY SECRET...
HEY! DO YOU KNOW WHAT MY SECRET IS?
OF COURSE NOT! BECAUSE IT'S SECRET!
I WALK INTO A HIVE OF SCUM AND VILLAINY, EVERYONE THINKS "SMART ALECK IN A RED SUIT!"
NOT "GUY WITH A MYSTERIOUS RADAR SENSE THAT LETS HIM SEE IN ALL DIRECTIONS AT THE SAME TIME!"
TO PICK SOMETHING AT RANDOM!
THAT'S WHAT GIVES ME MY EDGE! AND I LEARNED THAT...
...FROM YOU, FOGGY!
I MEAN, WHAT MATT'S TOLD ME ABOUT YOU! HOW YOUR FRUMPLED, FRAZZLED LOOK HIDES ONE OF THE KEENEST TECHNICAL LEGAL MINDS HE'S EVER MET!
WHAT PEOPLE SEE ISN'T WHAT THEY GET-- AND YOU ARE ITS MASTER!
MAYBE SOME DAY I'LL BE HALF AS GOOD AS YOU!
AND SPEAKING OF HALF...
NOT SURE WHEN YOU'LL HEAR THIS, MATT!
RICHARDS IS THE SMARTEST MAN ON THE PLANET, BUT NOT THE MOST ORGANIZED! BY THE TIME YOU GET THIS EVERYONE WILL PROBABLY HAVE JET-PACKS...
...AND NELSON AND MURDOCK WILL BE THE TOP LAW FIRM IN THE COUNTRY!
Nelson and Murdock are no longer accepting or advising any clients. If you need legal assistance, please contact: Jennifer Walters at J_Walters@shehulk.net
IF THERE'S ANY JUSTICE!

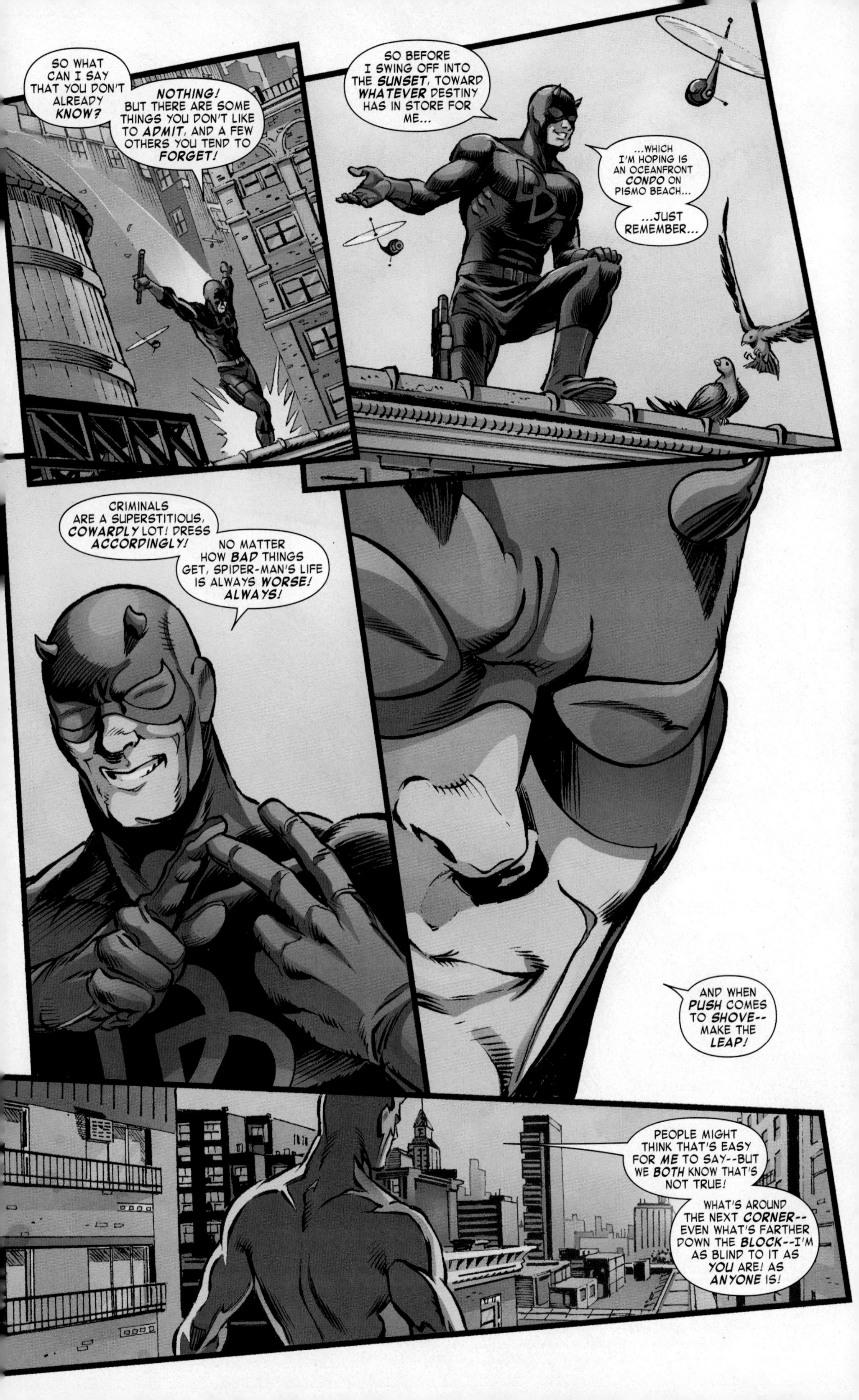

SO WHAT CAN I SAY THAT YOU DON'T ALREADY KNOW?
NOTHING! BUT THERE ARE SOME THINGS YOU DON'T LIKE TO ADMIT, AND A FEW OTHERS YOU TEND TO FORGET!
SO BEFORE I SWING OFF INTO THE SUNSET, TOWARD WHATEVER DESTINY HAS IN STORE FOR ME...
...WHICH I'M HOPING IS AN OCEANFRONT CONDO ON PISMO BEACH...
...JUST REMEMBER...
CRIMINALS ARE A SUPERSTITIOUS, COWARDLY LOT! DRESS ACCORDINGLY!
NO MATTER HOW BAD THINGS GET, SPIDER-MAN'S LIFE IS ALWAYS WORSE! ALWAYS!
AND WHEN PUSH COMES TO SHOVE--MAKE THE LEAP!
PEOPLE MIGHT THINK THAT'S EASY FOR ME TO SAY--BUT WE BOTH KNOW THAT'S NOT TRUE!
WHAT'S AROUND THE NEXT CORNER--EVEN WHAT'S FARTHER DOWN THE BLOCK--I'M AS BLIND TO IT AS YOU ARE! AS ANYONE IS!

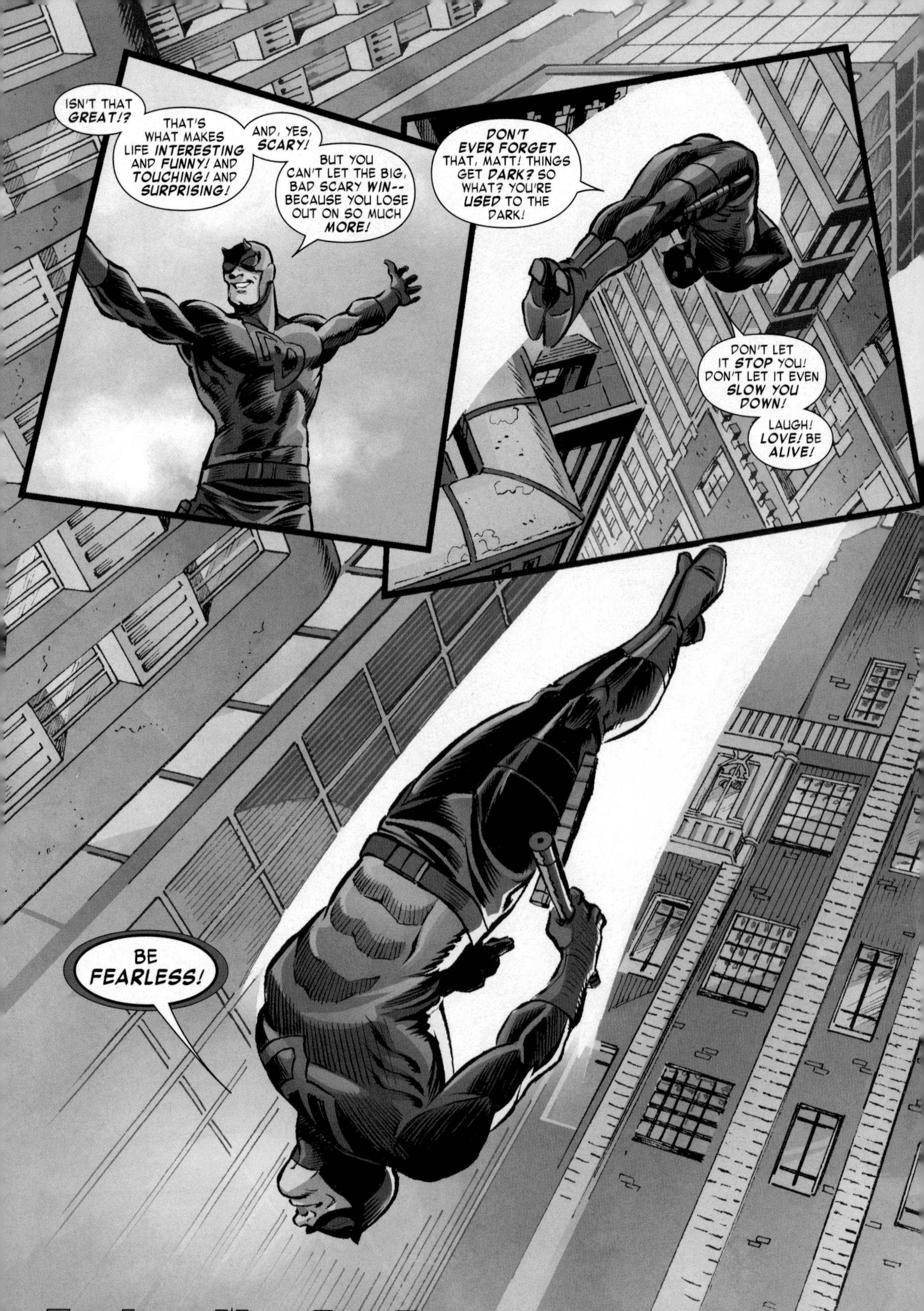
ISN'T THAT GREAT!?
THAT'S WHAT MAKES LIFE INTERESTING AND FUNNY! AND TOUCHING! AND SURPRISING!
AND, YES, SCARY!
BUT YOU CAN'T LET THE BIG, BAD SCARY WIN-- BECAUSE YOU LOSE OUT ON SO MUCH MORE!
DON'T EVER FORGET THAT, MATT! THINGS GET DARK? SO WHAT? YOU'RE USED TO THE DARK!
DON'T LET IT STOP YOU! DON'T LET IT EVEN SLOW YOU DOWN!
LAUGH! LOVE! BE ALIVE!
BE FEARLESS!

THE LAST WILL AND TESTAMENT OF MIKE MURDOCK

WRITTEN & PENCILED BY THE "DOUBLE-TROUBLE TWINS" *KARL & KURT KESEL*
INKED BY *"TITANIC" TOM PALMER* COLORED BY *"AMAZING" GRACE ALLISON*
LETTERED BY VC'S *"JAMMIN'" JOE CARAMAGNA* EDITED BY *THE FEARLESS, PEERLESS ELLIE PYLE*
ALEX ALONSO, JOE QUESADA, DAN BUCKLEY, & ALAN FINE - STILL THINK MATT AND MIKE MURDOCK ARE DIFFERENT PEOPLE.
DEDICATED TO *STAN LEE & GENE COLAN* - WHO MADE DAREDEVIL A FUN, FRANTIC, FEARLESS AND UNFORGETTABLE BOOK.

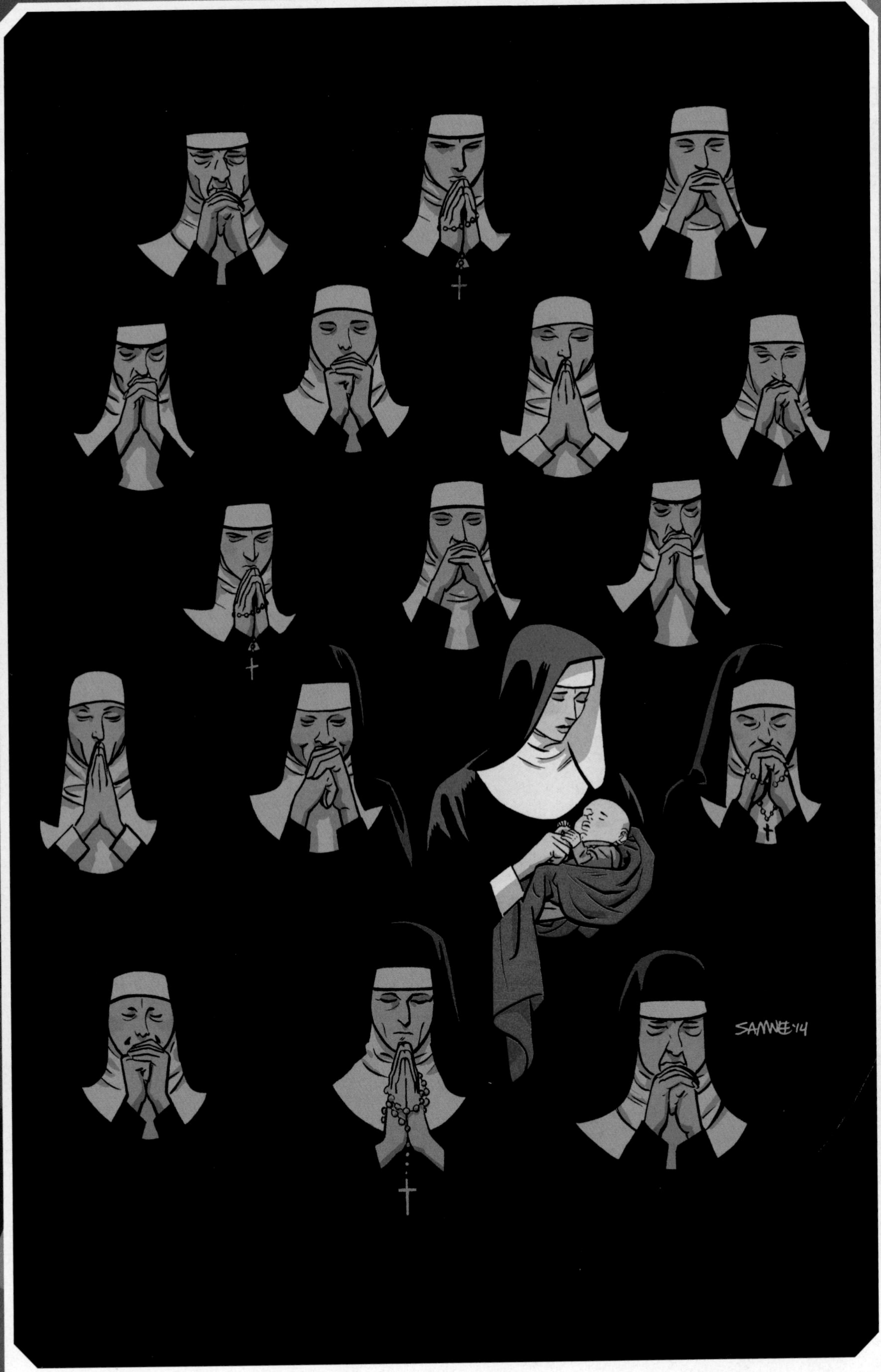
SAMNEE '14

DAREDEVIL #6

NEW YORK CITY BULLETIN

F**INAL**

SINCE 1907

$1.00 (in NYC)
$1.50 (outside city)

BLIND MAN SEES?

People caught in the blast radius of the most recent super human incident are reporting strange, revealing visions of long buried secrets. Could this be linked to the murder of a rumored cosmic being known as The Watcher? Numerous super heroes were on the scene including Daredevil, whose alter ego, the blind lawyer Matt Murdock, moved to San Francisco after being disbarred in the state of New York following his admission under oath that he is the masked hero.

SISTERS ACT!

A local convent recently celebrated a day of service by marking the opening of a food and clothing pantry for the local community. Led by Sister Maggie (pictured here) who is known for her good works in the Hell's Kitchen area... (story continued inside)

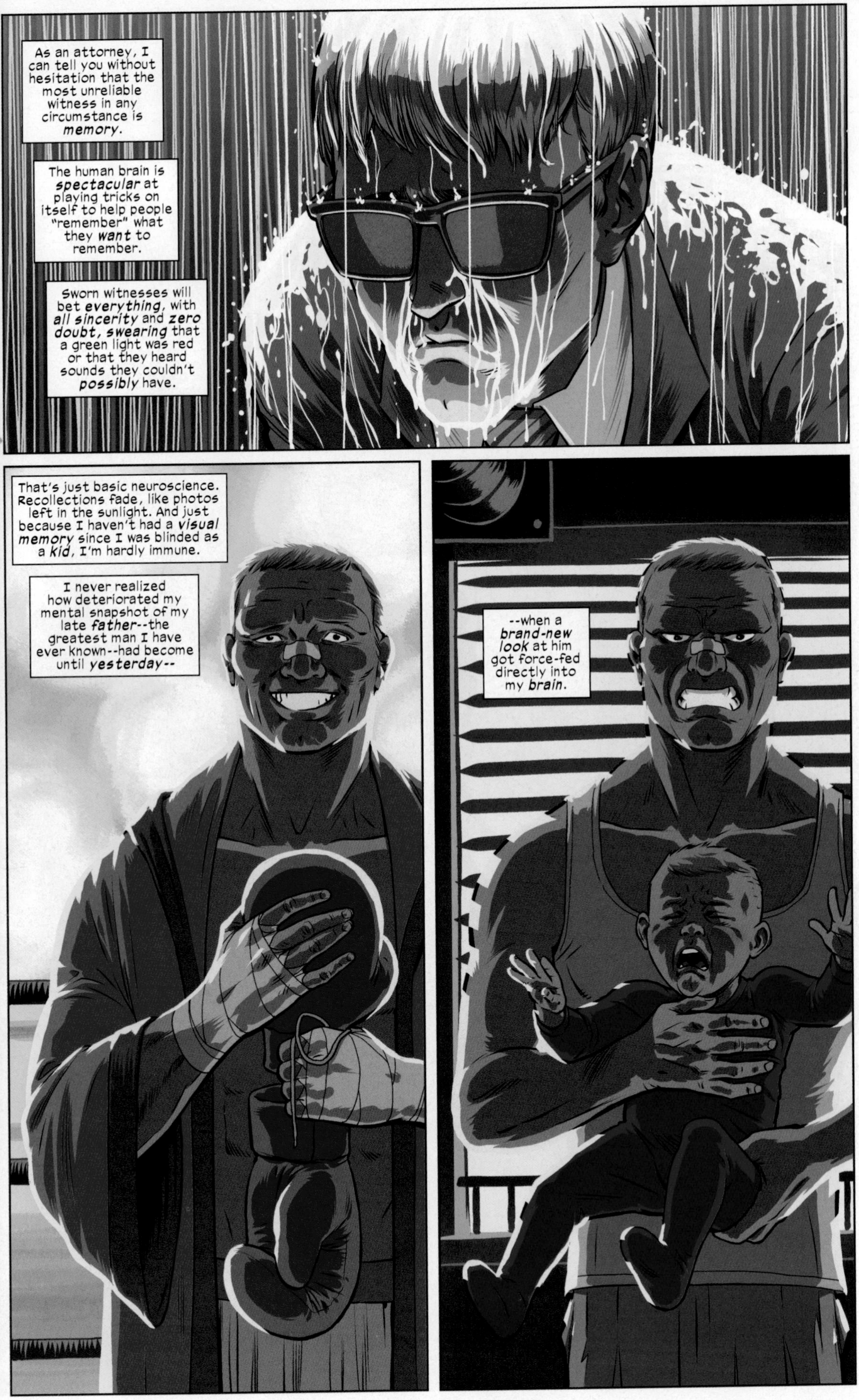
As an attorney, I can tell you without hesitation that the most unreliable witness in any circumstance is *memory*.
The human brain is *spectacular* at playing tricks on itself to help people "remember" what they *want* to remember.
Sworn witnesses will bet *everything*, with *all sincerity* and *zero doubt*, *swearing* that a green light was red or that they heard sounds they couldn't *possibly* have.
That's just basic neuroscience. Recollections fade, like photos left in the sunlight. And just because I haven't had a *visual memory* since I was blinded as a *kid*, I'm hardly immune.
I never realized how deteriorated my mental snapshot of my late *father*--the greatest man I have ever known--had become until *yesterday*--
--when a *brand-new look* at him got force-fed directly into my *brain*.

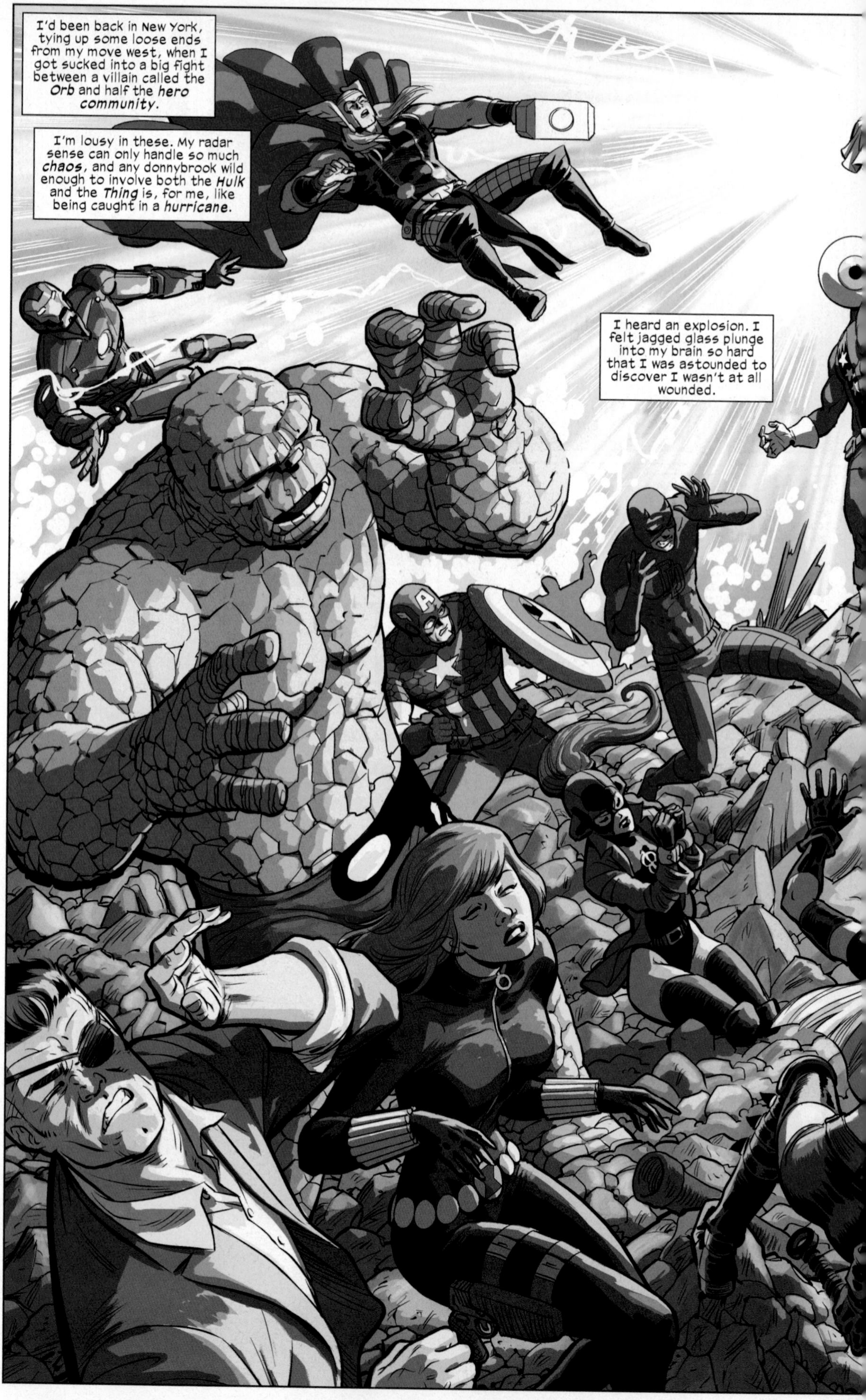
I'd been back in New York, tying up some loose ends from my move west, when I got sucked into a big fight between a villain called the *Orb* and half the *hero community*.
I'm lousy in these. My radar sense can only handle so much *chaos*, and any donnybrook wild enough to involve both the *Hulk* and the *Thing* is, for me, like being caught in a *hurricane*.
I heard an explosion. I felt jagged glass plunge into my brain so hard that I was astounded to discover I wasn't at all wounded.

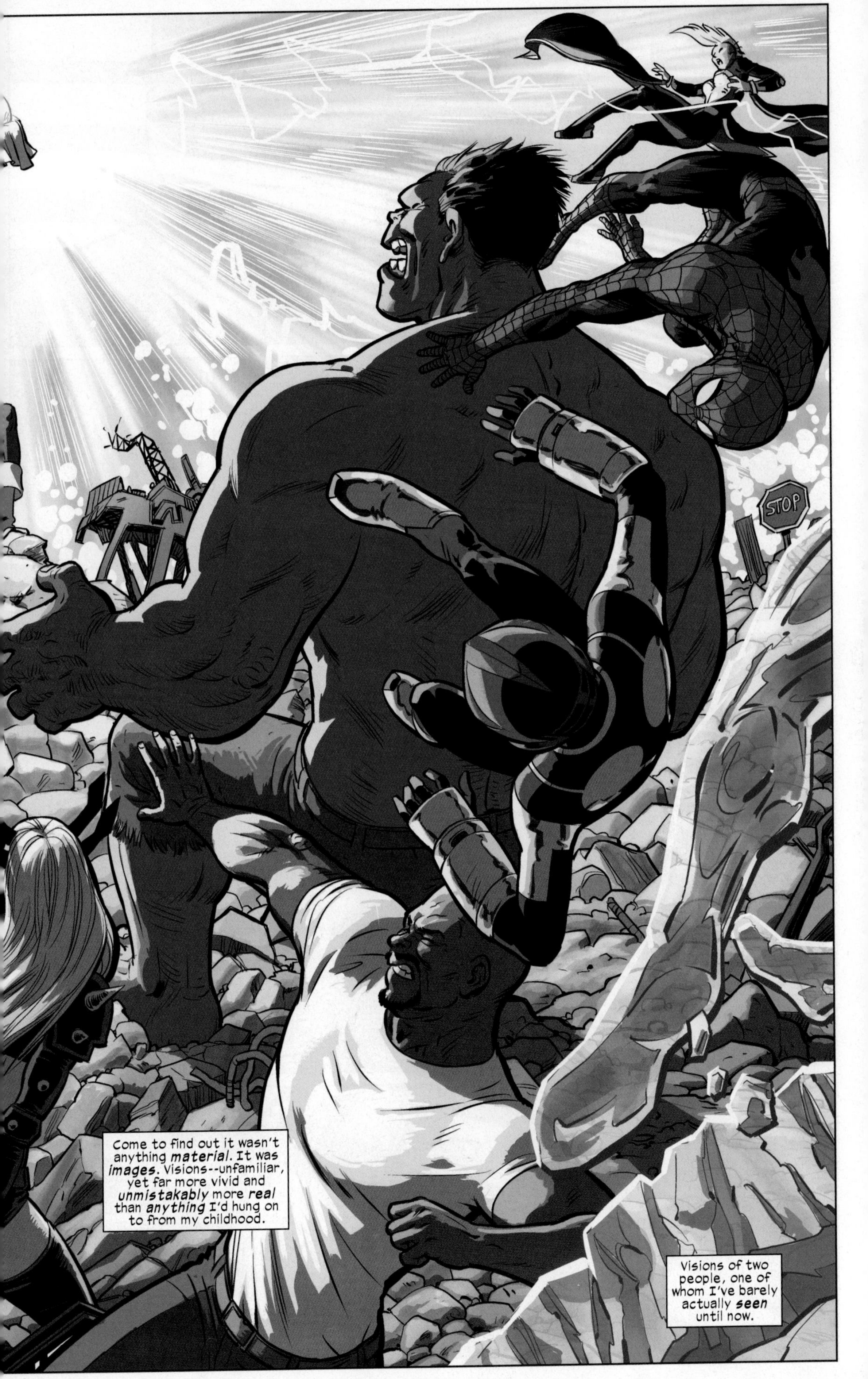
STOP
Come to find out it wasn't anything *material*. It was *images*. Visions--unfamiliar, yet far more vivid and *unmistakably* more *real* than *anything* I'd hung on to from my childhood.
Visions of two people, one of whom I've barely actually *seen* until now.

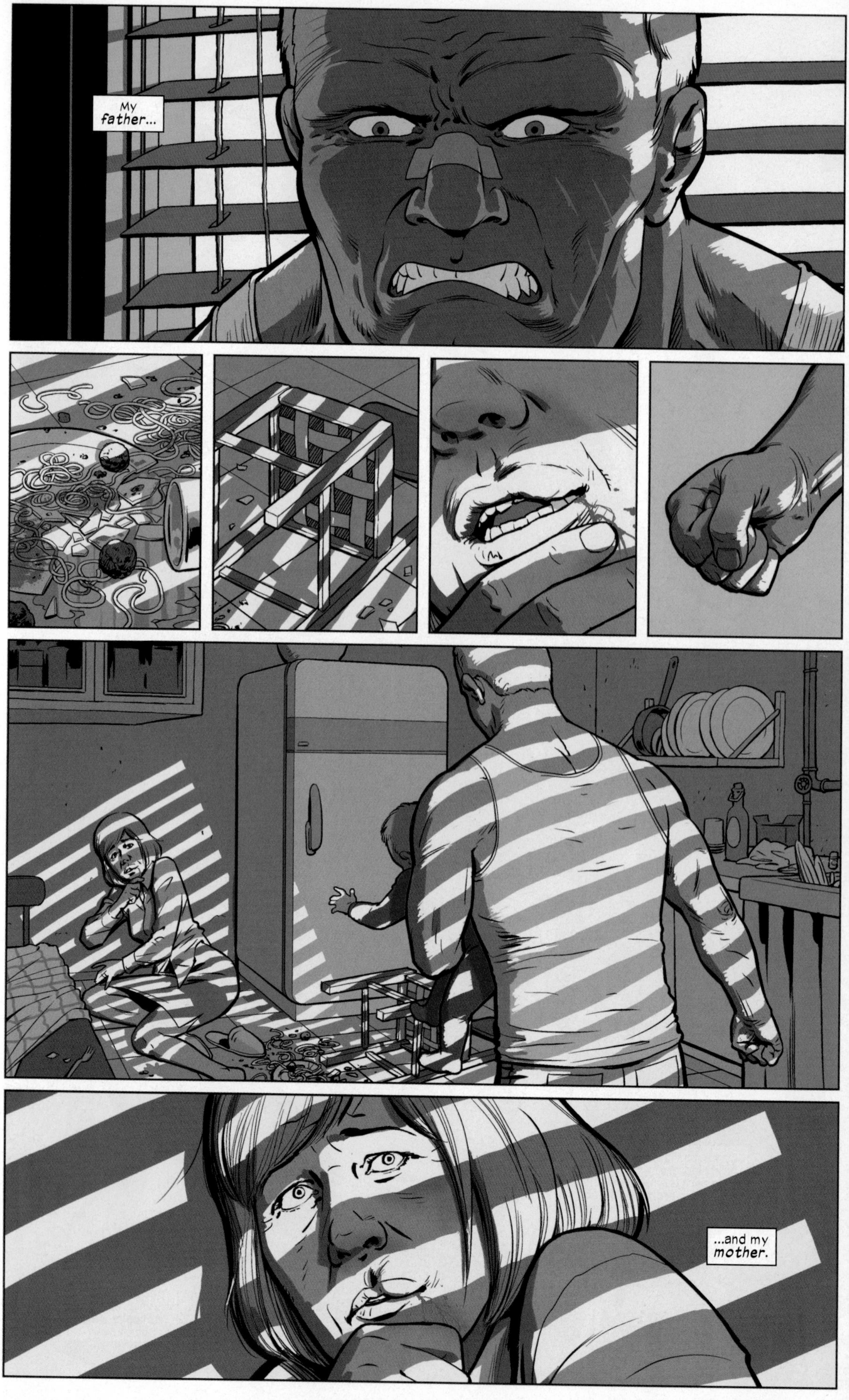
My *father*...
...and my *mother*.

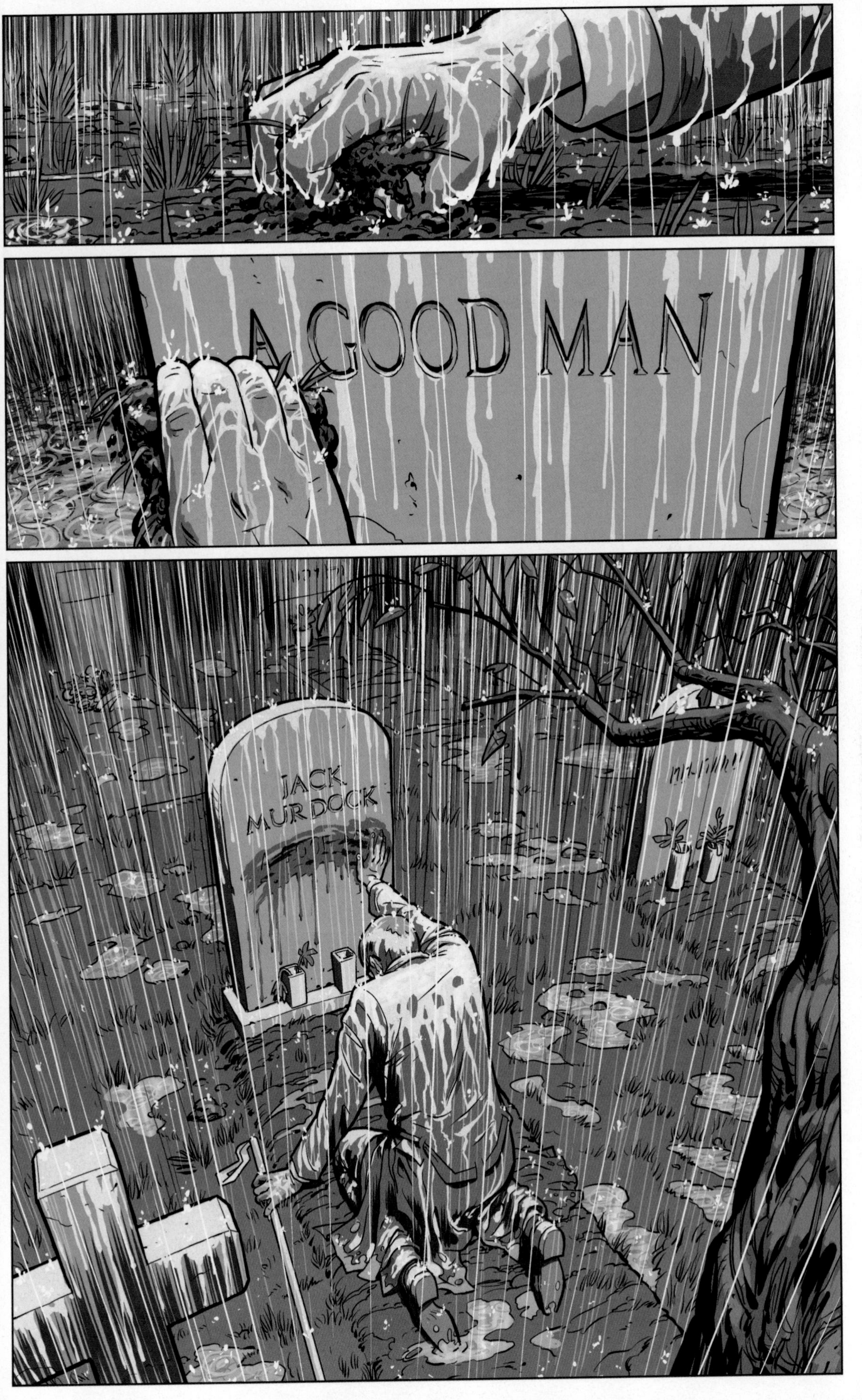
A GOOD MAN
JACK MURDOCK

To call that memory *crystal clear* would be selling it short. It wasn't just fragments of *pictures* in my head. It was *real*.

It was the smell of our old apartment. The familiar clanging of the radiator and the taste of spaghetti--Dad's favorite--in the air.

Before I went back home, I had to know for sure just how *delusional* I'd been about Jack Murdock all my life. How flawed my *own* worship of my father really was.

If you knew me, you'd understand why that would become an instant obsession.

My mother would have the answers.

Her name was *GRACE*.

But I never knew her as a boy. She'd left my dad, who *never* talked about her.

Only in the last few years did I discover what had become of her. She'd joined a *convent* and had been watching me from a *distance* under a *different name*.

FATHER, WHERE CAN I FIND SISTER MAGGIE?

A FRIEND.

YOU'RE...?

His heart rate spikes as if I'd asked him where I could hide a *bloody axe*.

Why on *earth*...?

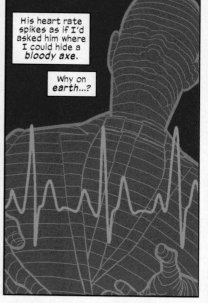

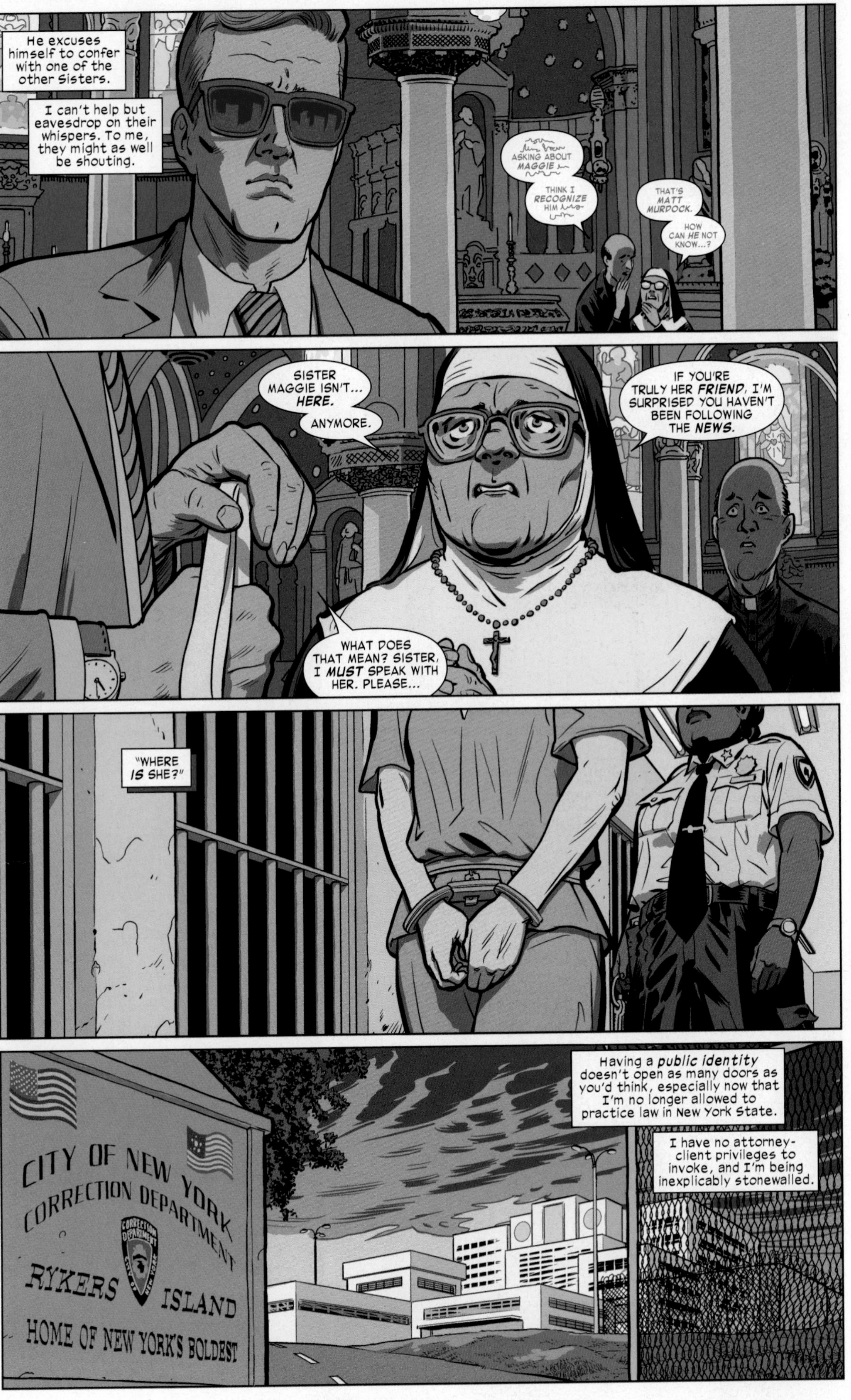
He excuses himself to confer with one of the other Sisters.
I can't help but eavesdrop on their whispers. To me, they might as well be shouting.
ASKING ABOUT MAGGIE
THINK I RECOGNIZE HIM
THAT'S MATT MURDOCK.
HOW CAN HE NOT KNOW...?
SISTER MAGGIE ISN'T... HERE.
ANYMORE.
IF YOU'RE TRULY HER FRIEND, I'M SURPRISED YOU HAVEN'T BEEN FOLLOWING THE NEWS.
WHAT DOES THAT MEAN? SISTER, I MUST SPEAK WITH HER. PLEASE...
"WHERE IS SHE?"
Having a public identity doesn't open as many doors as you'd think, especially now that I'm no longer allowed to practice law in New York State.
I have no attorney-client privileges to invoke, and I'm being inexplicably stonewalled.
CITY OF NEW YORK
CORRECTION DEPARTMENT
RYKERS ISLAND
HOME OF NEW YORK'S BOLDEST

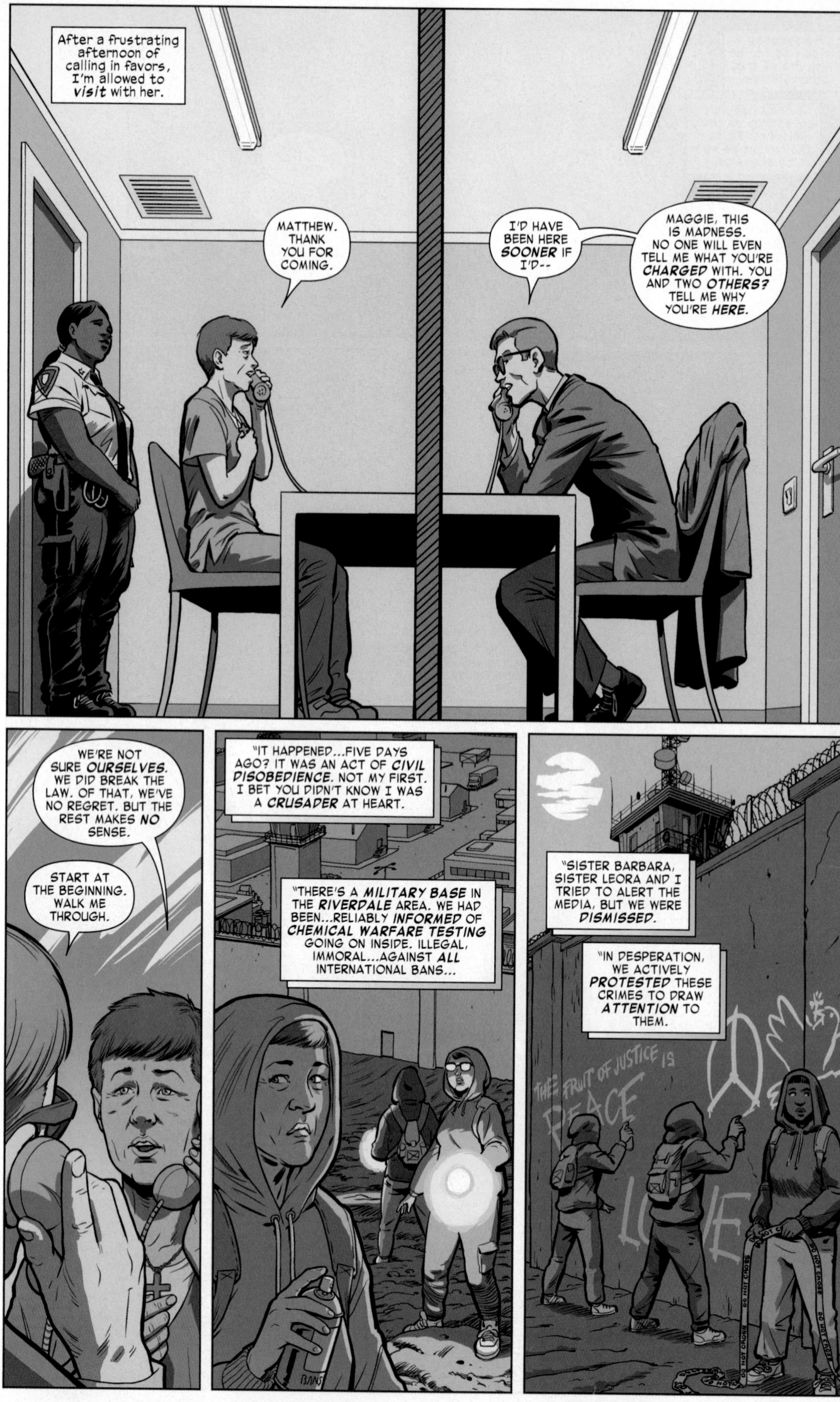
After a frustrating afternoon of calling in favors, I'm allowed to visit with her.
MATTHEW. THANK YOU FOR COMING.
I'D HAVE BEEN HERE SOONER IF I'D--
MAGGIE, THIS IS MADNESS. NO ONE WILL EVEN TELL ME WHAT YOU'RE CHARGED WITH. YOU AND TWO OTHERS? TELL ME WHY YOU'RE HERE.
WE'RE NOT SURE OURSELVES. WE DID BREAK THE LAW. OF THAT, WE'VE NO REGRET. BUT THE REST MAKES NO SENSE.
START AT THE BEGINNING. WALK ME THROUGH.
"IT HAPPENED...FIVE DAYS AGO? IT WAS AN ACT OF CIVIL DISOBEDIENCE. NOT MY FIRST. I BET YOU DIDN'T KNOW I WAS A CRUSADER AT HEART.
"THERE'S A MILITARY BASE IN THE RIVERDALE AREA. WE HAD BEEN...RELIABLY INFORMED OF CHEMICAL WARFARE TESTING GOING ON INSIDE. ILLEGAL, IMMORAL...AGAINST ALL INTERNATIONAL BANS...
"SISTER BARBARA, SISTER LEORA AND I TRIED TO ALERT THE MEDIA, BUT WE WERE DISMISSED.
"IN DESPERATION, WE ACTIVELY PROTESTED THESE CRIMES TO DRAW ATTENTION TO THEM.
THE FRUIT OF JUSTICE IS PEACE
LOVE
DO NOT CROSS

"WE KNEW THE RISKS. SURE ENOUGH, WE WERE JAILED. BUT EVERYTHING AFTER THAT WAS A *SHOCK.*

"THERE WAS NO READING OF RIGHTS, NO LEGAL COUNSEL, NO PRELIMINARY HEARING.

"WITHIN 24 HOURS, WE HAD BEEN PARADED BEFORE A MILITARY TRIBUNAL, FACING JUDGES WHO REFUSED TO *IDENTIFY* THEMSELVES...

"...AND WERE TOLD THAT, FOR OUR *CRIMES,* WE WERE BEING *EXTRADITED* TO THE NATION OF *WAKANDA.*"

WHAT?

FOR *VANDALISM?* ON WHAT *GROUNDS?* ON WHAT *CHARGES?*

THEY WON'T TELL US.

THEY *HAVE* TO! THIS IS *AMERICA!* IT'S HOW THE SYSTEM *WORKS!* THEY *CAN'T NOT—* ⟩KLIK⟨

TIME'S UP.

MATTHEW, IT'LL BE ALL RIGHT.

THE LORD WATCHES OVER US.

HAVE FAITH.

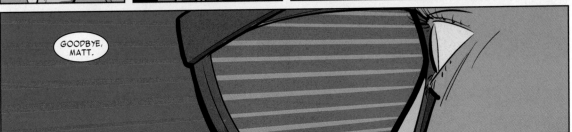

GOODBYE, MATT.

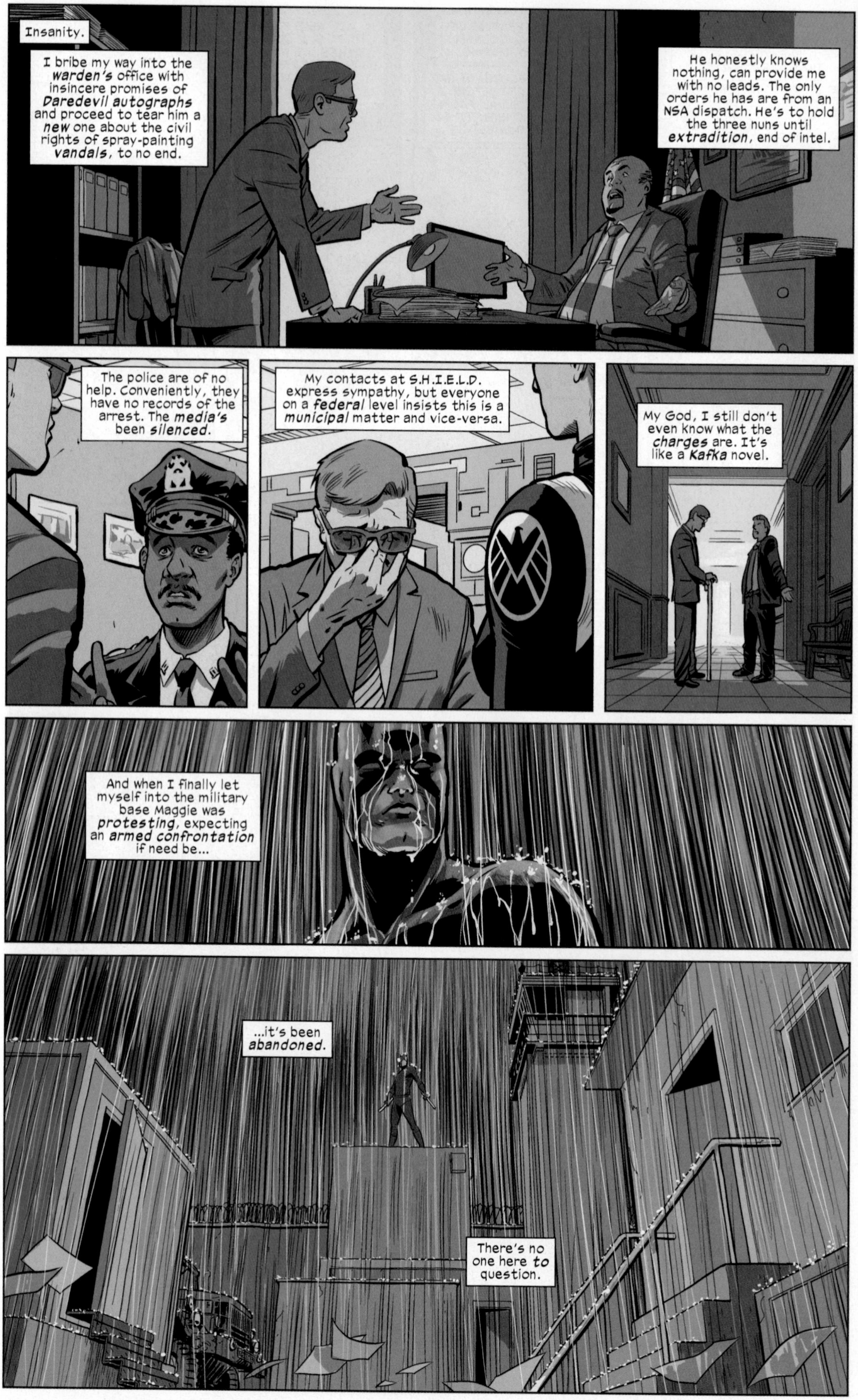
Insanity.
I bribe my way into the warden's office with insincere promises of Daredevil autographs and proceed to tear him a new one about the civil rights of spray-painting vandals, to no end.
He honestly knows nothing, can provide me with no leads. The only orders he has are from an NSA dispatch. He's to hold the three nuns until extradition, end of intel.
The police are of no help. Conveniently, they have no records of the arrest. The media's been silenced.
My contacts at S.H.I.E.L.D. express sympathy, but everyone on a federal level insists this is a municipal matter and vice-versa.
My God, I still don't even know what the charges are. It's like a Kafka novel.
And when I finally let myself into the military base Maggie was protesting, expecting an armed confrontation if need be...
...it's been abandoned.
There's no one here to question.

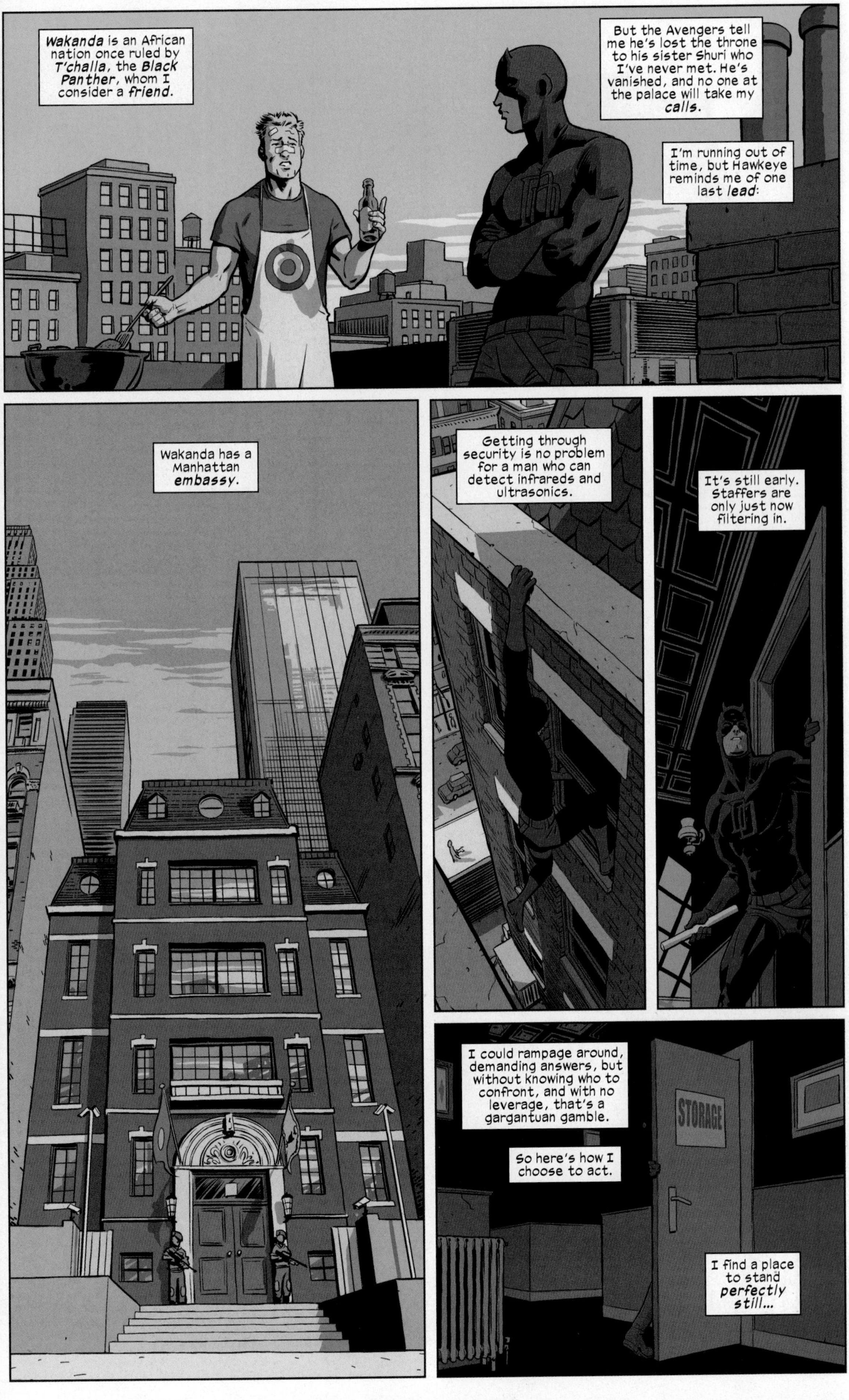

Wakanda is an African nation once ruled by T'challa, the Black Panther, whom I consider a friend.
But the Avengers tell me he's lost the throne to his sister Shuri who I've never met. He's vanished, and no one at the palace will take my calls.
I'm running out of time, but Hawkeye reminds me of one last lead:
Wakanda has a Manhattan embassy.
Getting through security is no problem for a man who can detect infrareds and ultrasonics.
It's still early. Staffers are only just now filtering in.
I could rampage around, demanding answers, but without knowing who to confront, and with no leverage, that's a gargantuan gamble.
STORAGE
So here's how I choose to act.
I find a place to stand perfectly still...

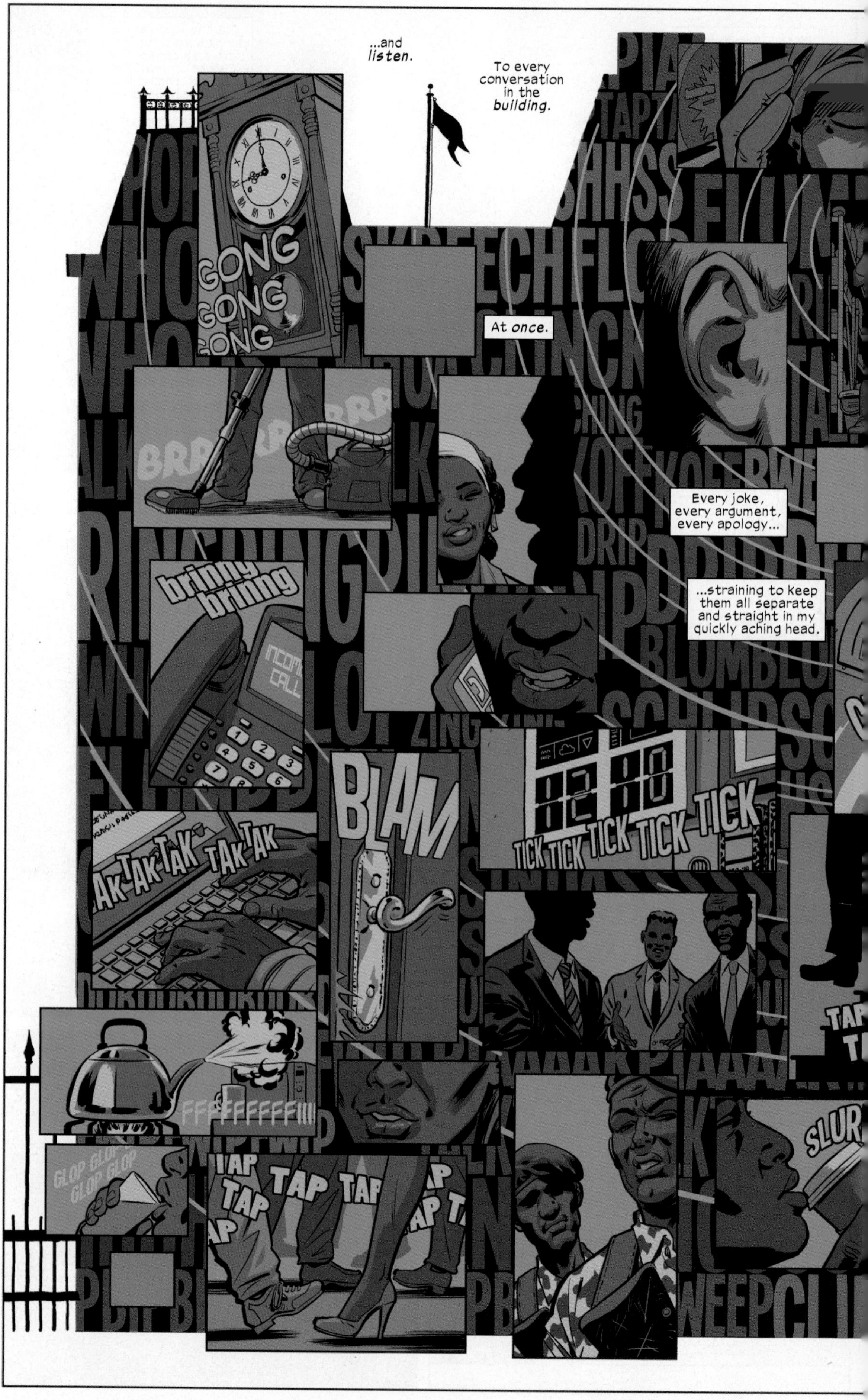

...and *listen*.
To every conversation in the *building*.
GONG
GONG
BRRR
At *once*.
Every joke, every argument, every apology...
brinng brinng
...straining to keep them all separate and straight in my quickly aching head.
BLAM
TICK TICK TICK TICK TICK
TAK TAK TAK TAK TAK
FFFFFFFF!!!
GLOP GLOP GLOP GLOP
TAP TAP TAP TAP

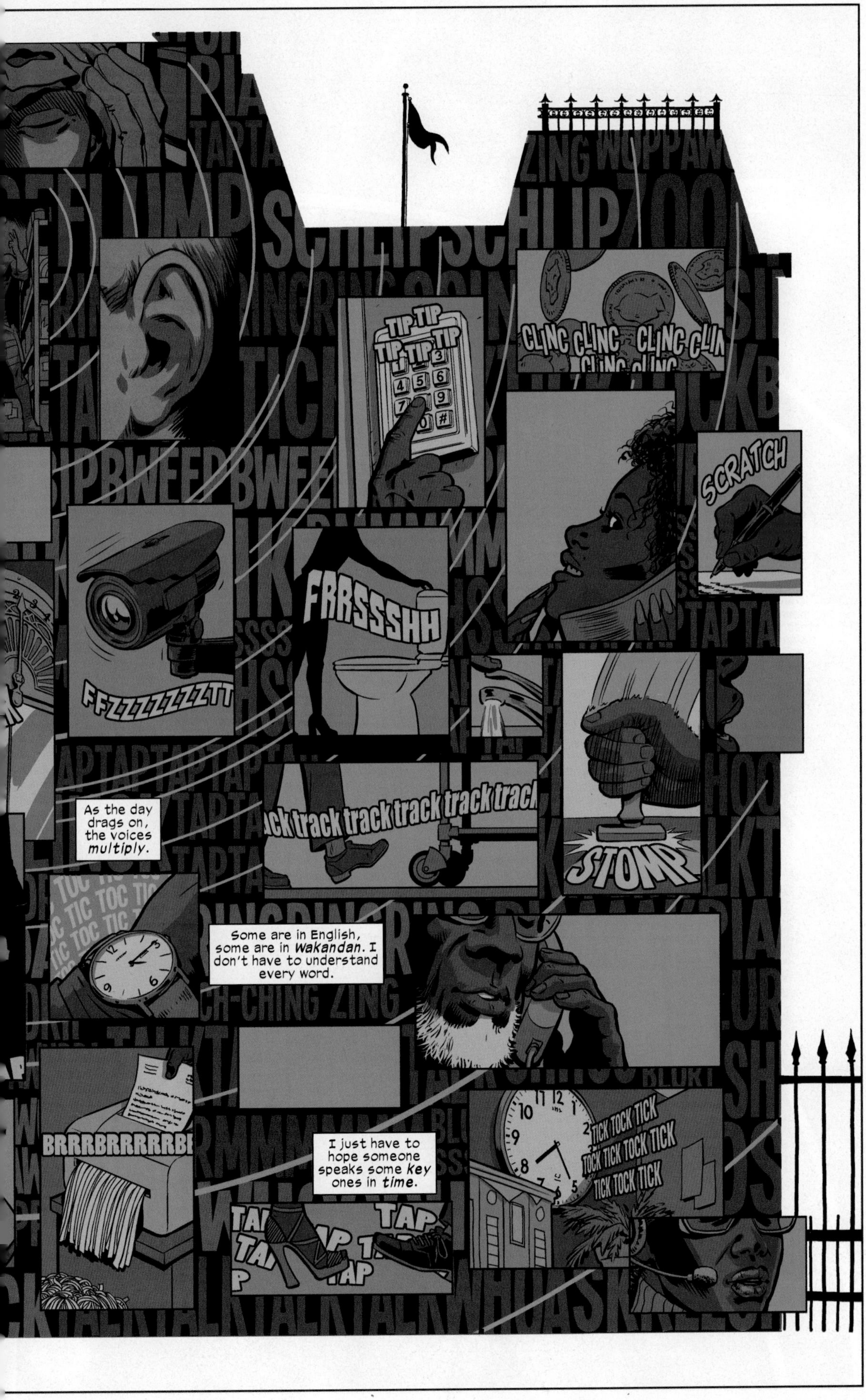

TIP TIP TIP TIP TIP
CLINC CLINC CLINC CLIN
SCRATCH
FFZZZZZZZZTT
FRRSSSHH
track track track track track
STOMP
As the day drags on, the voices *multiply*.
TIC TOC TIC TOC TIC
Some are in English, some are in *Wakandan*. I don't have to understand every word.
CH-CHING ZING
I just have to hope someone speaks some *key* ones in *time*.
TICK TOCK TICK
TOCK TICK TOCK TICK
TICK TOCK TICK
TAP TAP TAP

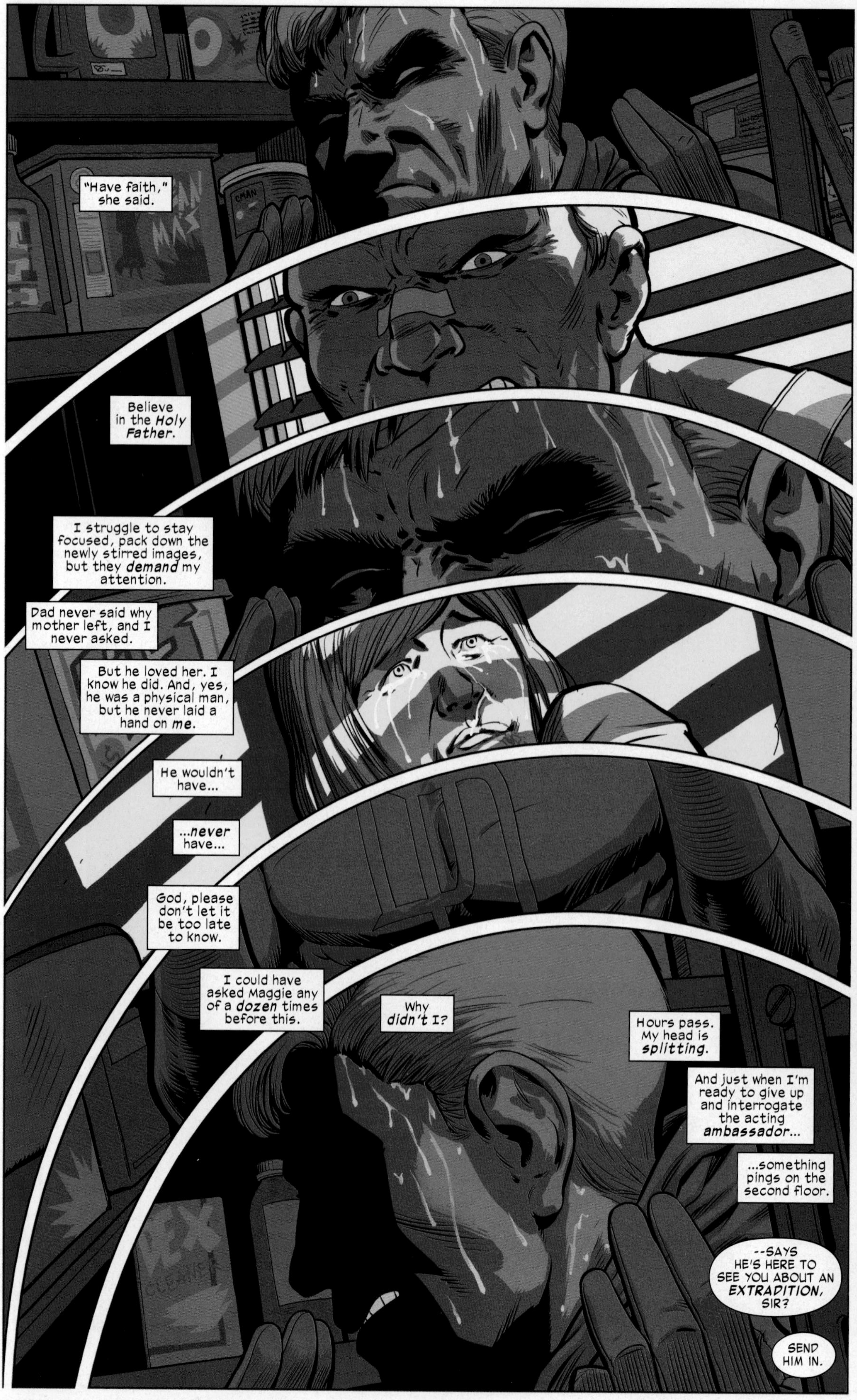
"Have faith," she said.
Believe in the Holy Father.
I struggle to stay focused, pack down the newly stirred images, but they demand my attention.
Dad never said why mother left, and I never asked.
But he loved her. I know he did. And, yes, he was a physical man, but he never laid a hand on me.
He wouldn't have...
...never have...
God, please don't let it be too late to know.
I could have asked Maggie any of a dozen times before this.
Why didn't I?
Hours pass. My head is splitting.
And just when I'm ready to give up and interrogate the acting ambassador...
...something pings on the second floor.
--SAYS HE'S HERE TO SEE YOU ABOUT AN EXTRADITION, SIR?
SEND HIM IN.

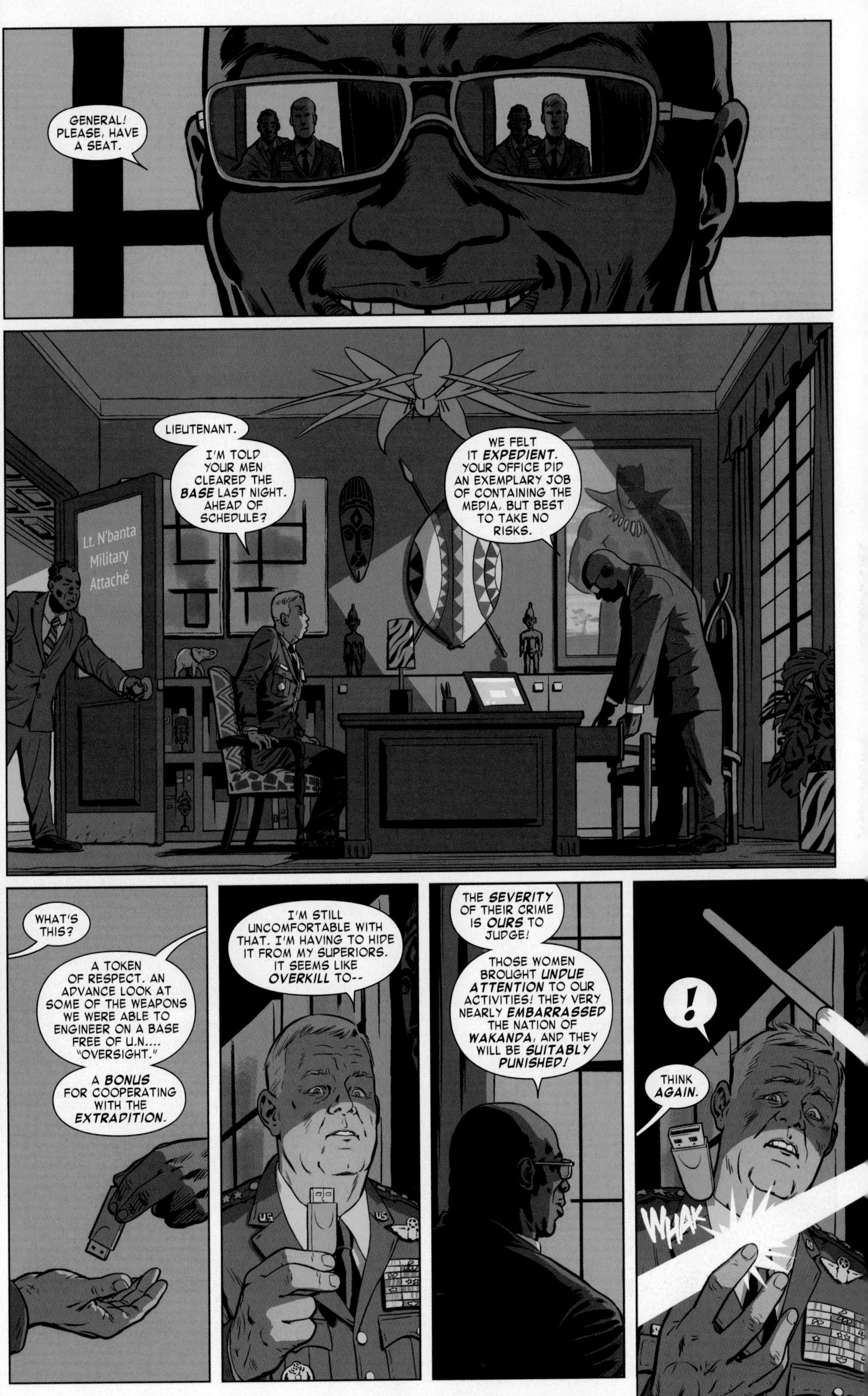
GENERAL! PLEASE, HAVE A SEAT.
LIEUTENANT.
I'M TOLD YOUR MEN CLEARED THE BASE LAST NIGHT. AHEAD OF SCHEDULE?
Lt. N'banta Military Attaché
WE FELT IT EXPEDIENT. YOUR OFFICE DID AN EXEMPLARY JOB OF CONTAINING THE MEDIA, BUT BEST TO TAKE NO RISKS.
WHAT'S THIS?
A TOKEN OF RESPECT. AN ADVANCE LOOK AT SOME OF THE WEAPONS WE WERE ABLE TO ENGINEER ON A BASE FREE OF U.N.... "OVERSIGHT."
A BONUS FOR COOPERATING WITH THE EXTRADITION.
I'M STILL UNCOMFORTABLE WITH THAT. I'M HAVING TO HIDE IT FROM MY SUPERIORS. IT SEEMS LIKE OVERKILL TO--
THE SEVERITY OF THEIR CRIME IS OURS TO JUDGE!
THOSE WOMEN BROUGHT UNDUE ATTENTION TO OUR ACTIVITIES! THEY VERY NEARLY EMBARRASSED THE NATION OF WAKANDA, AND THEY WILL BE SUITABLY PUNISHED!
!
THINK AGAIN.
WHAK

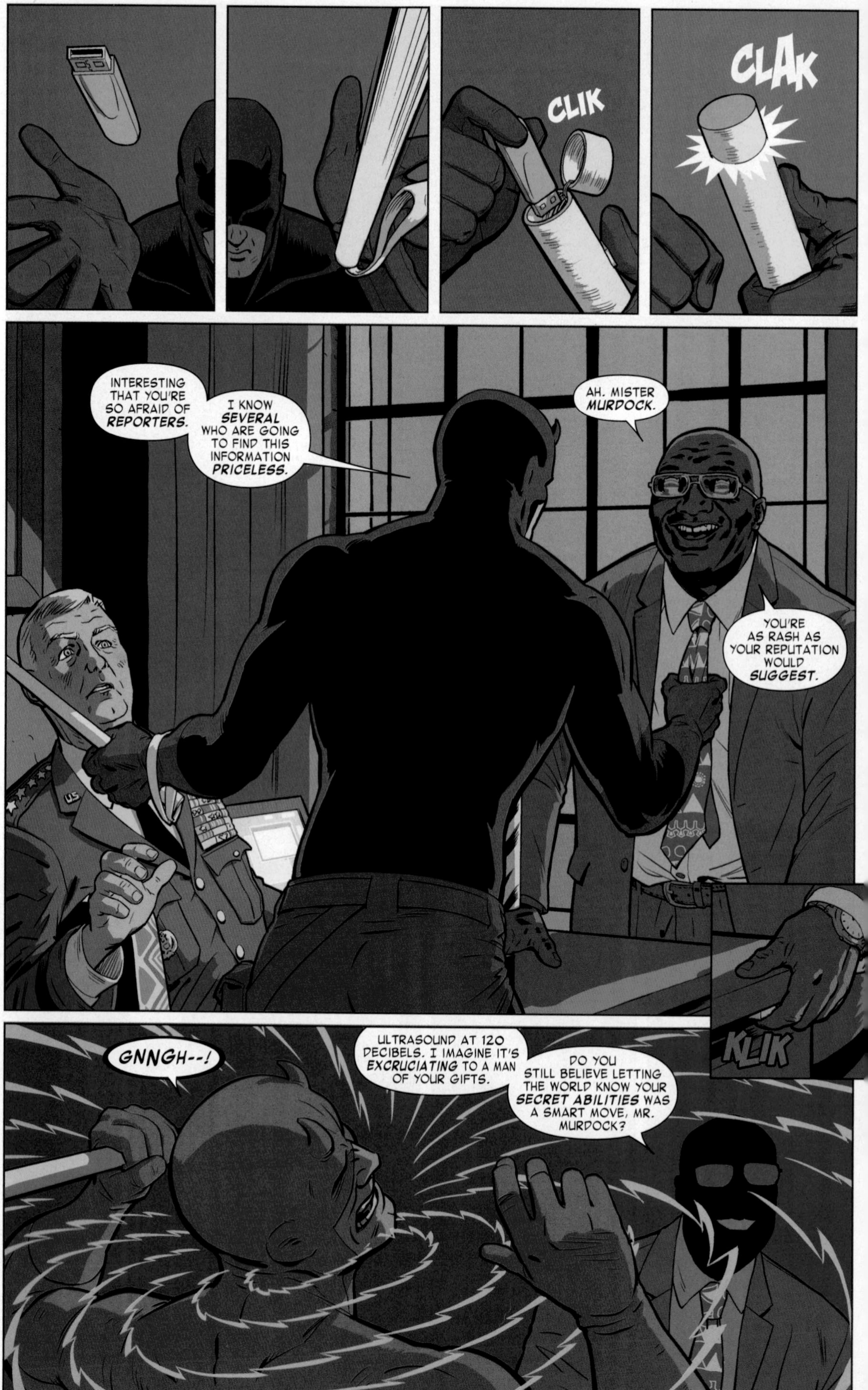
CLIK
CLAK
INTERESTING THAT YOU'RE SO AFRAID OF REPORTERS.
I KNOW SEVERAL WHO ARE GOING TO FIND THIS INFORMATION PRICELESS.
AH. MISTER MURDOCK.
YOU'RE AS RASH AS YOUR REPUTATION WOULD SUGGEST.
KLIK
GNNGH--!
ULTRASOUND AT 120 DECIBELS. I IMAGINE IT'S EXCRUCIATING TO A MAN OF YOUR GIFTS.
DO YOU STILL BELIEVE LETTING THE WORLD KNOW YOUR SECRET ABILITIES WAS A SMART MOVE, MR. MURDOCK?

YOU...WERE EXPECTING...?

WAKANDA IS THE MOST TECHNOLOGICALLY ADVANCED NATION ON *EARTH*, SIR. IT TOOK *NOTHING* FOR US TO MINE EVERY *SCRAP* OF DATA ON THOSE THREE NUNS.

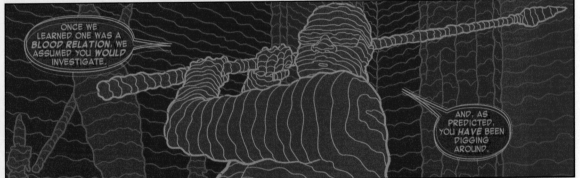

ONCE WE LEARNED ONE WAS A *BLOOD RELATION*, WE ASSUMED YOU *WOULD* INVESTIGATE.

AND, AS PREDICTED, YOU *HAVE* BEEN DIGGING AROUND.

OF *COURSE* YOU'D WIND UP IN MY OFFICE.

Get your *guard* up, Matt--he's taking *another*--

HNNGH!

...

Stupid. *Stupid.*

I've been up 36 hours. Sonics are like *shrapnel* in my ears. I'm exhausted, physically *and* mentally.

I didn't expect a *fight.*

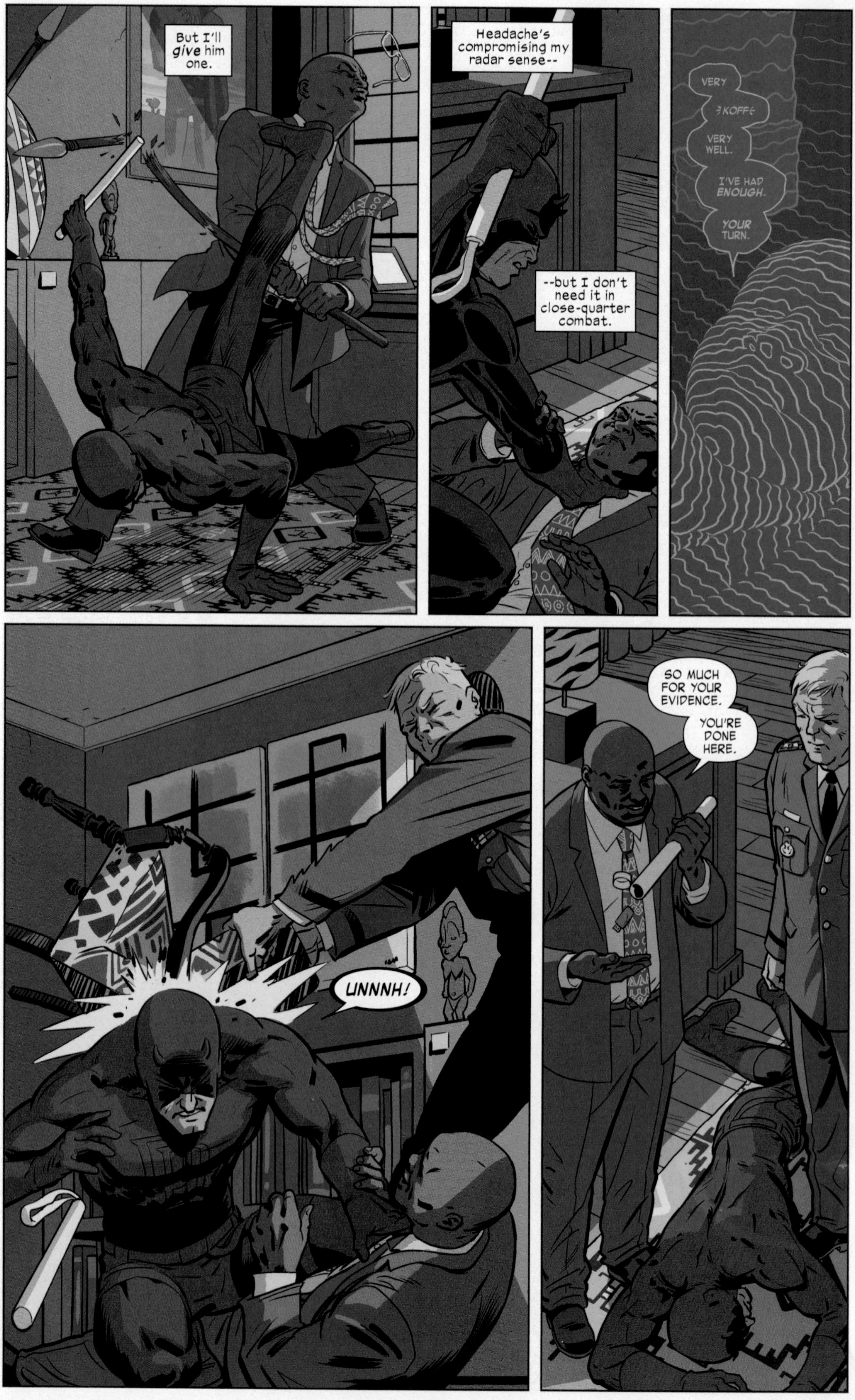
But I'll *give* him one.
Headache's compromising my radar sense--
--but I don't need it in close-quarter combat.
VERY
KOFF
VERY WELL.
I'VE HAD *ENOUGH.*
YOUR TURN.
UNNNH!
SO MUCH FOR YOUR EVIDENCE.
YOU'RE DONE HERE.

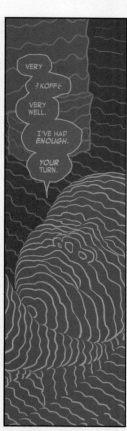

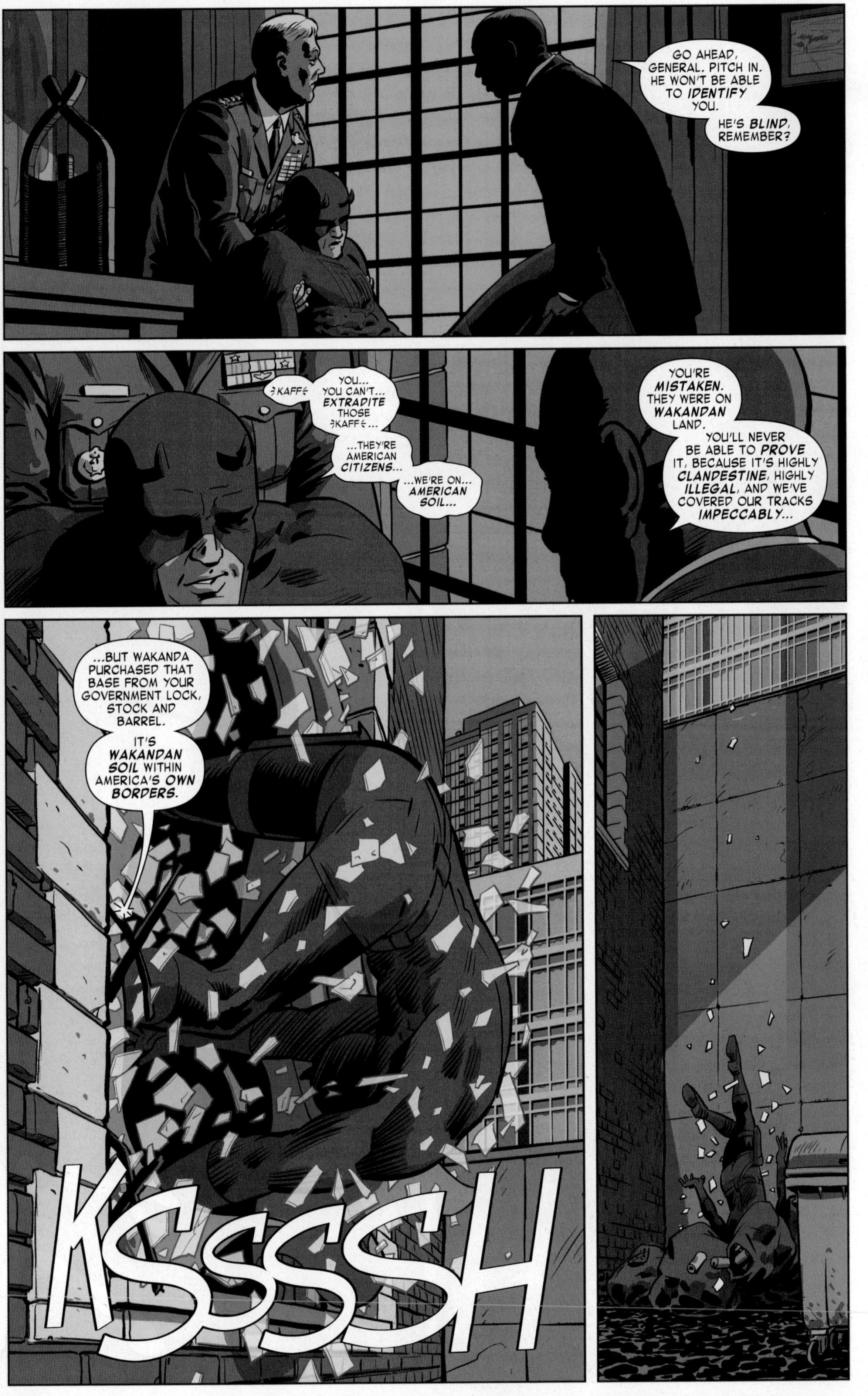
GO AHEAD, GENERAL. PITCH IN. HE WON'T BE ABLE TO IDENTIFY YOU.
HE'S BLIND, REMEMBER?
KAFF
YOU... YOU CAN'T... EXTRADITE THOSE KAFF...
...THEY'RE AMERICAN CITIZENS...
...WE'RE ON... AMERICAN SOIL...
YOU'RE MISTAKEN. THEY WERE ON WAKANDAN LAND.
YOU'LL NEVER BE ABLE TO PROVE IT, BECAUSE IT'S HIGHLY CLANDESTINE, HIGHLY ILLEGAL, AND WE'VE COVERED OUR TRACKS IMPECCABLY...
...BUT WAKANDA PURCHASED THAT BASE FROM YOUR GOVERNMENT LOCK, STOCK AND BARREL.
IT'S WAKANDAN SOIL WITHIN AMERICA'S OWN BORDERS.
KSSSH

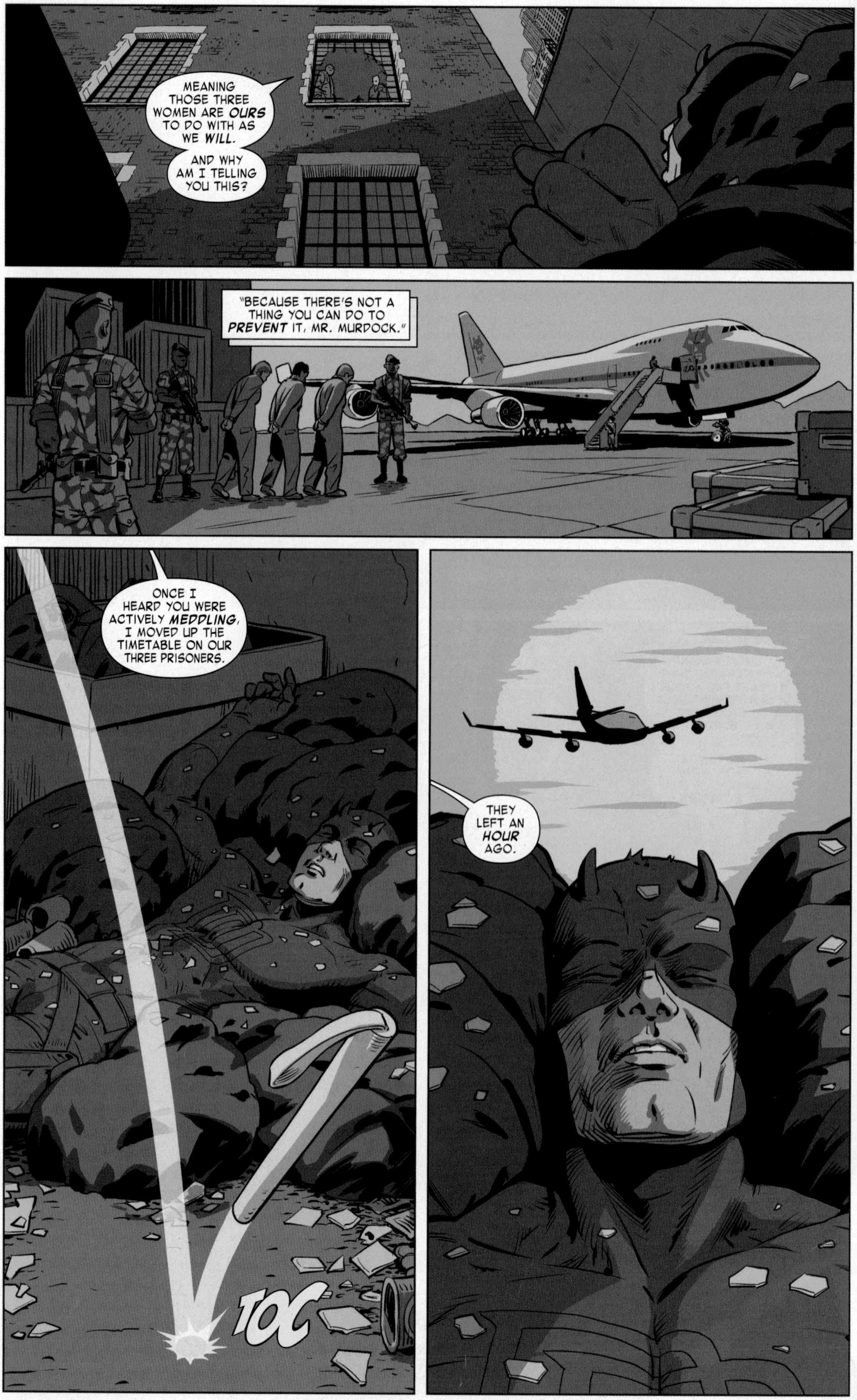
MEANING THOSE THREE WOMEN ARE OURS TO DO WITH AS WE WILL.
AND WHY AM I TELLING YOU THIS?
"BECAUSE THERE'S NOT A THING YOU CAN DO TO PREVENT IT, MR. MURDOCK."
ONCE I HEARD YOU WERE ACTIVELY MEDDLING, I MOVED UP THE TIMETABLE ON OUR THREE PRISONERS.
TOC
THEY LEFT AN HOUR AGO.

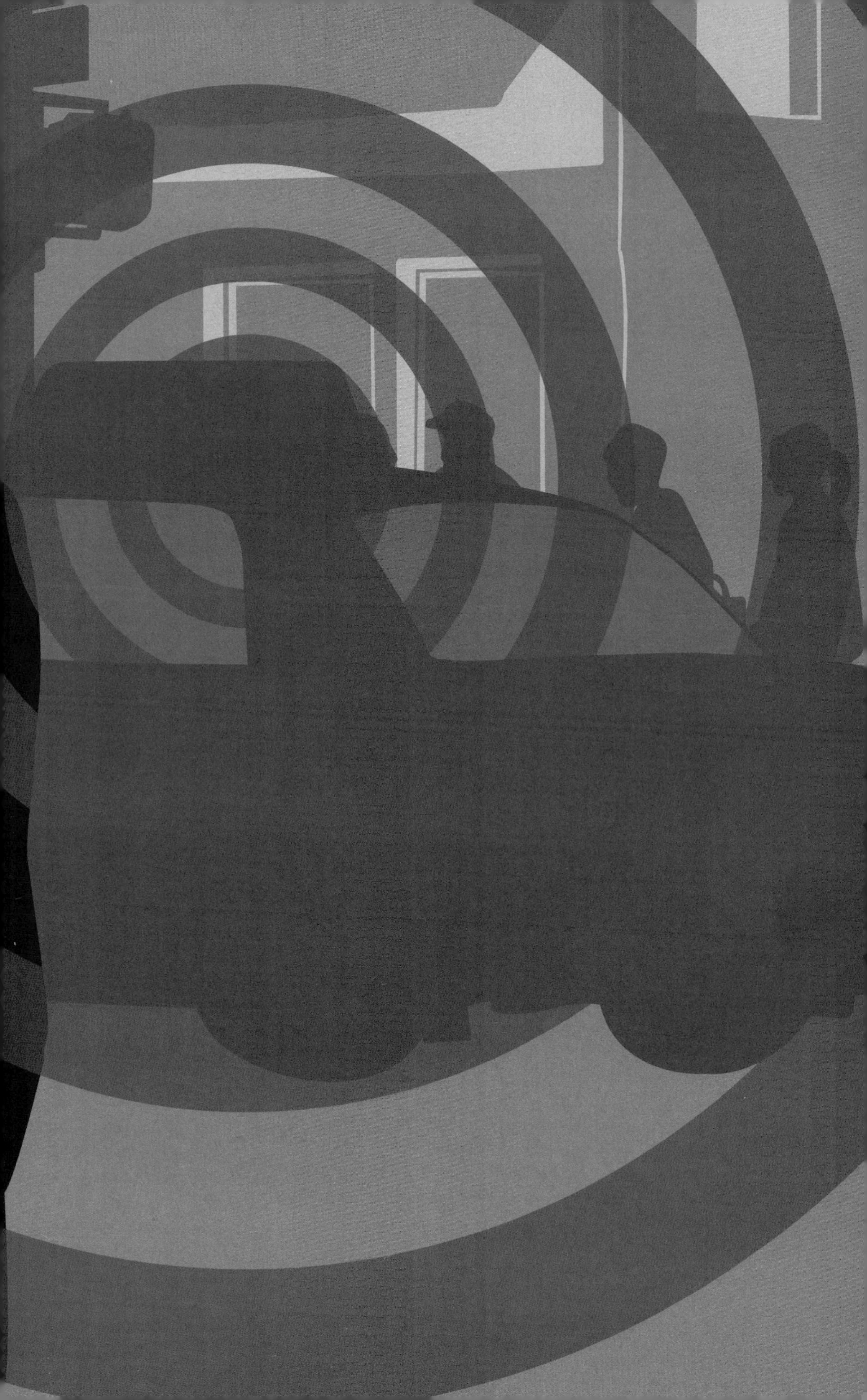

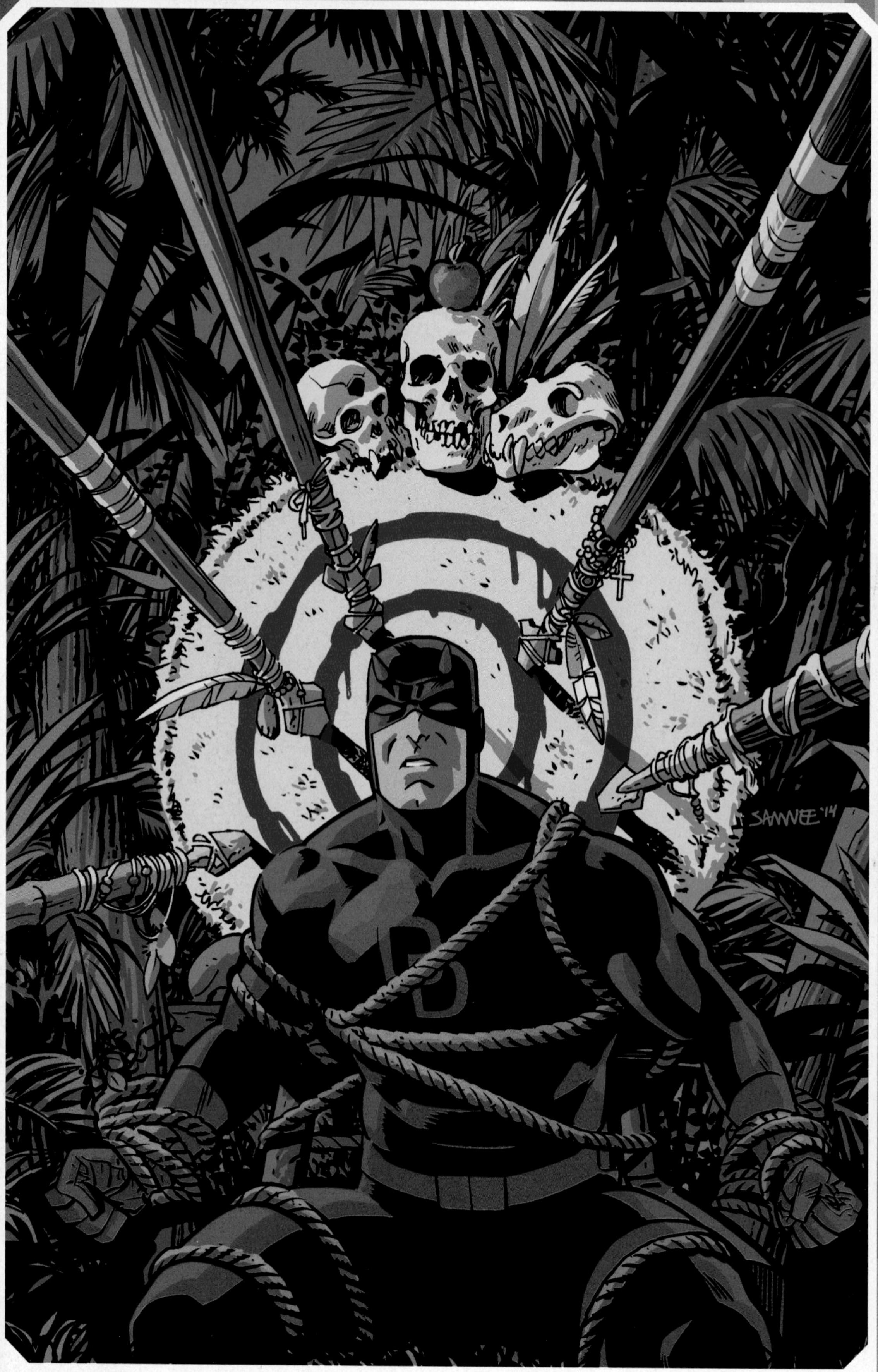
SAMNEE '14

DAREDEVIL #7

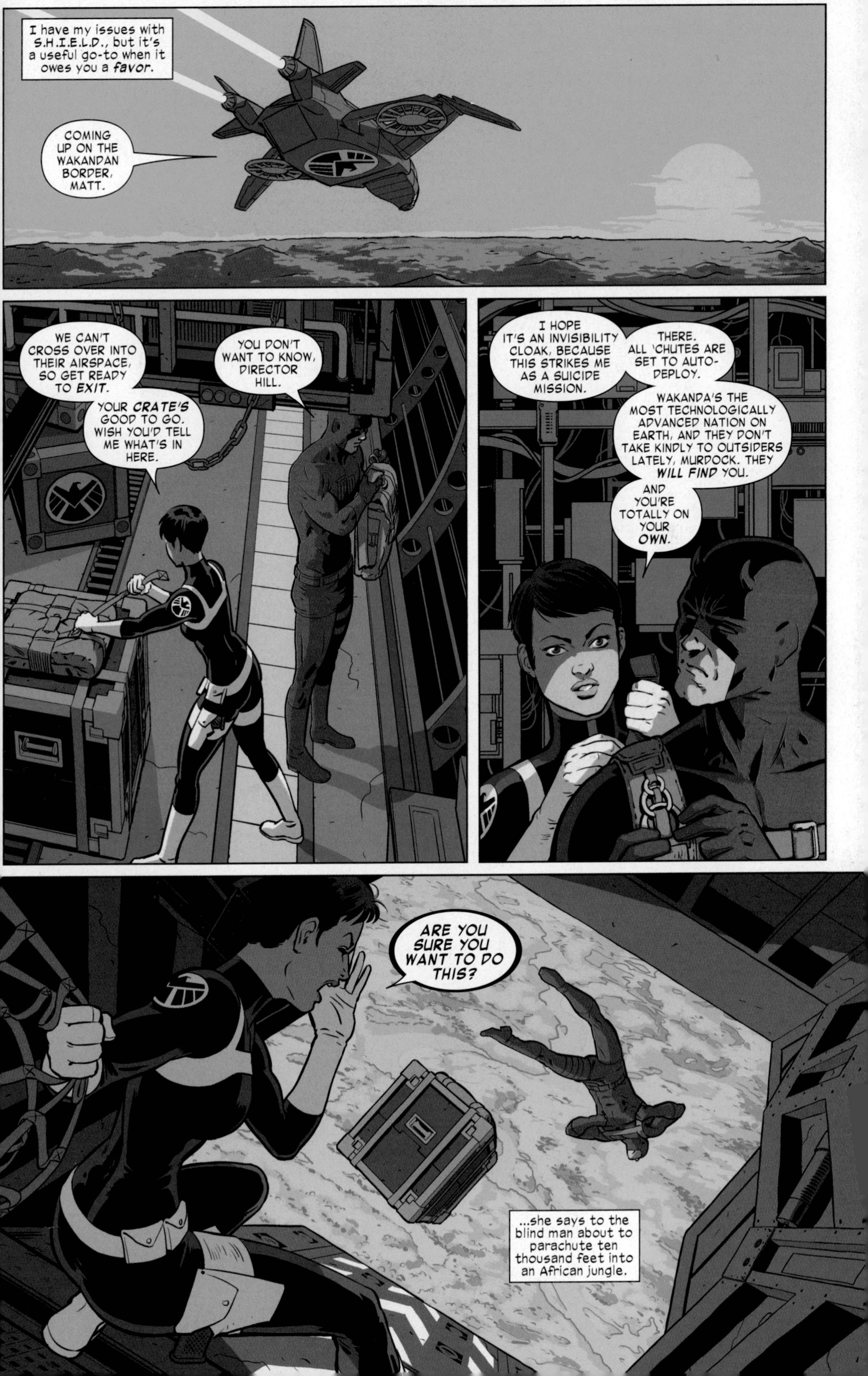
I have my issues with S.H.I.E.L.D., but it's a useful go-to when it owes you a *favor*.
COMING UP ON THE WAKANDAN BORDER, MATT.
WE CAN'T CROSS OVER INTO THEIR AIRSPACE, SO GET READY TO *EXIT*.
YOUR *CRATE'S* GOOD TO GO. WISH YOU'D TELL ME WHAT'S IN HERE.
YOU DON'T WANT TO KNOW, DIRECTOR HILL.
I HOPE IT'S AN INVISIBILITY CLOAK, BECAUSE THIS STRIKES ME AS A SUICIDE MISSION.
THERE. ALL 'CHUTES ARE SET TO AUTO-DEPLOY.
WAKANDA'S THE MOST TECHNOLOGICALLY ADVANCED NATION ON EARTH, AND THEY DON'T TAKE KINDLY TO OUTSIDERS LATELY, MURDOCK. THEY *WILL FIND* YOU.
AND YOU'RE TOTALLY ON YOUR *OWN*.
ARE YOU SURE YOU WANT TO DO THIS?
...she says to the blind man about to parachute ten thousand feet into an African jungle.

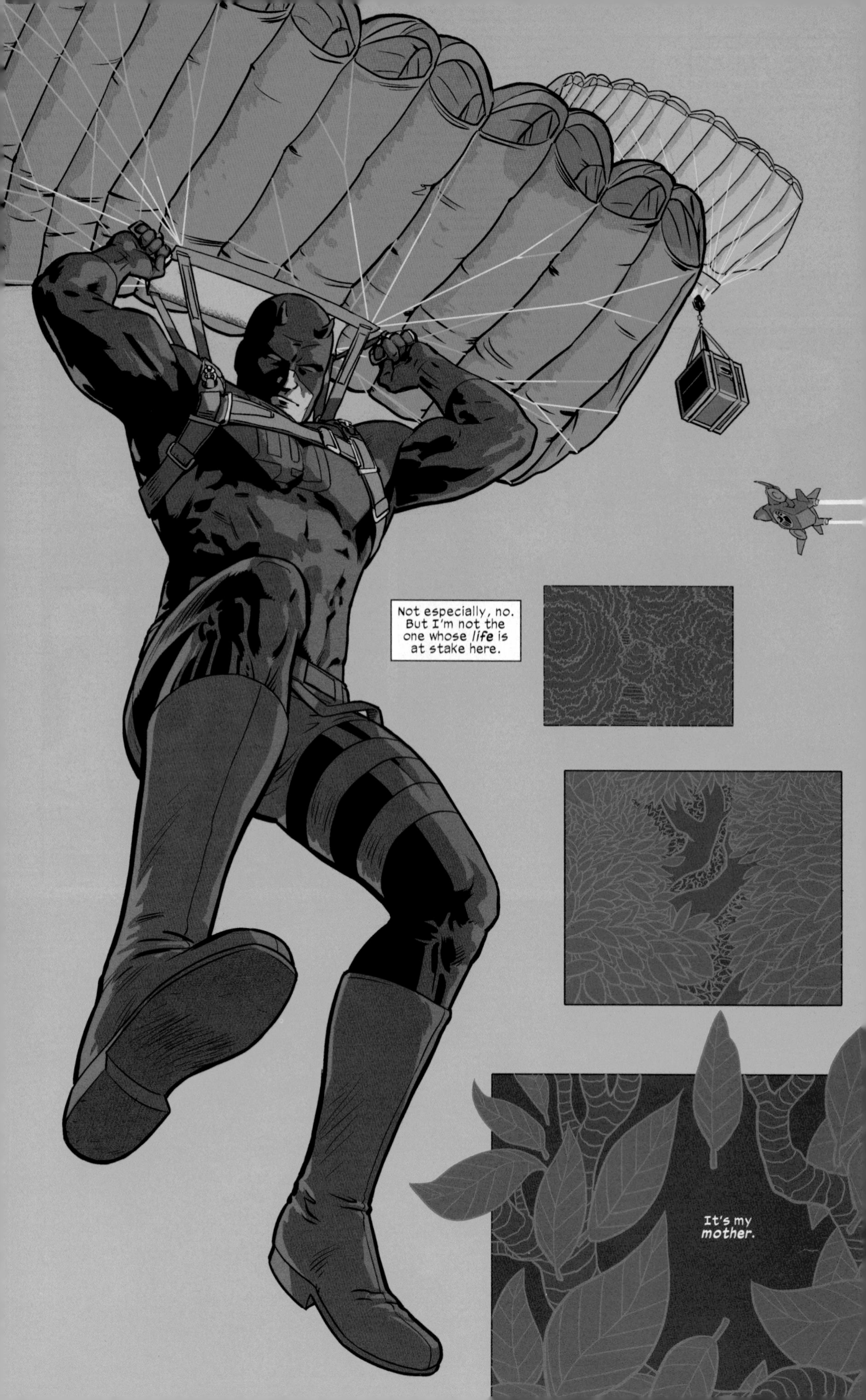
Not especially, no. But I'm not the one whose *life* is at stake here.
It's my *mother*.

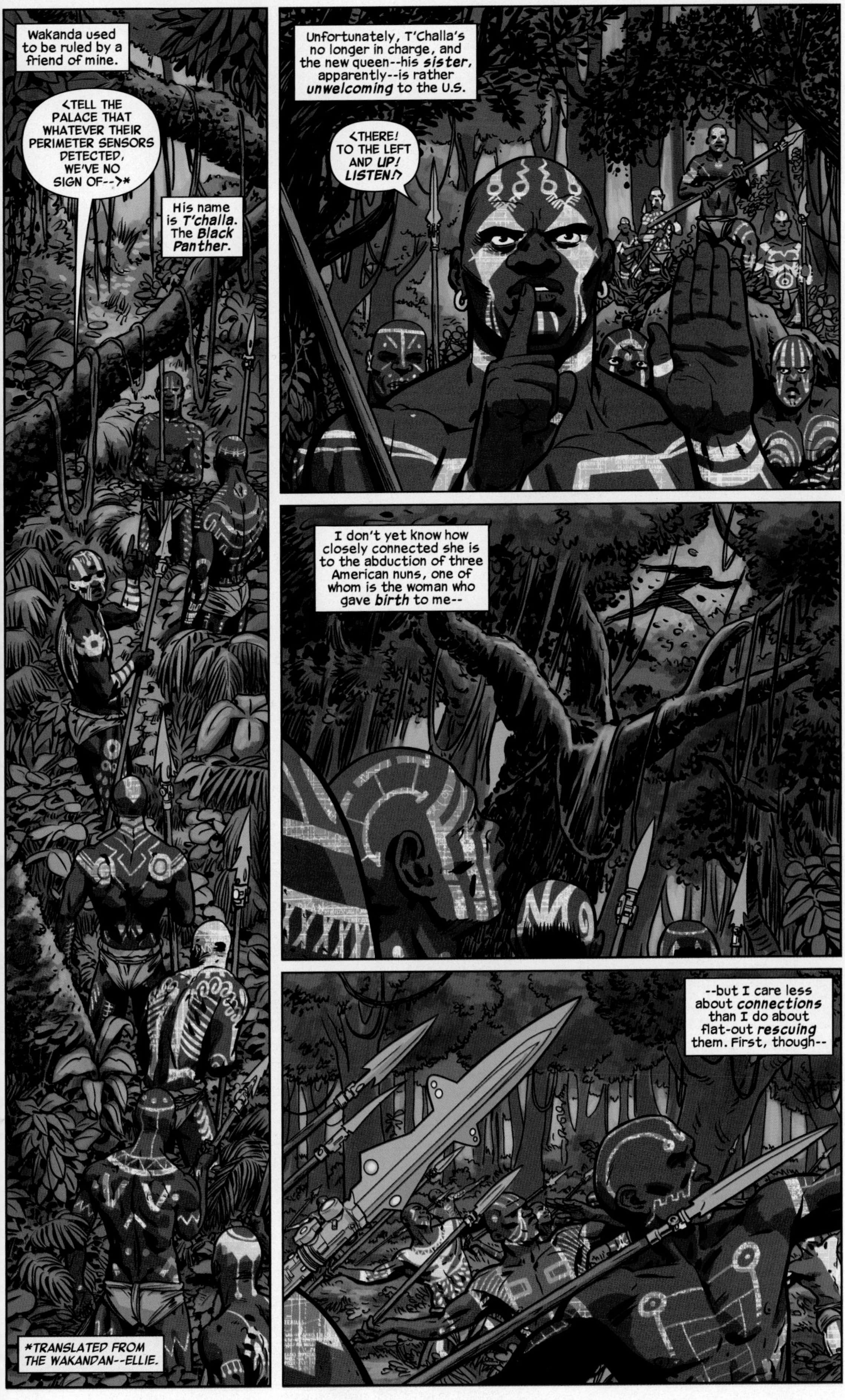
Wakanda used to be ruled by a friend of mine.
<TELL THE PALACE THAT WHATEVER THEIR PERIMETER SENSORS DETECTED, WE'VE NO SIGN OF-->*
His name is *T'challa*. The *Black Panther*.
*TRANSLATED FROM THE WAKANDAN--ELLIE.
Unfortunately, T'Challa's no longer in charge, and the new queen--his *sister*, apparently--is rather *unwelcoming* to the U.S.
<THERE! TO THE LEFT AND *UP! LISTEN!*>
I don't yet know how closely connected she is to the abduction of three American nuns, one of whom is the woman who gave *birth* to me--
--but I care less about *connections* than I do about flat-out *rescuing* them. First, though--

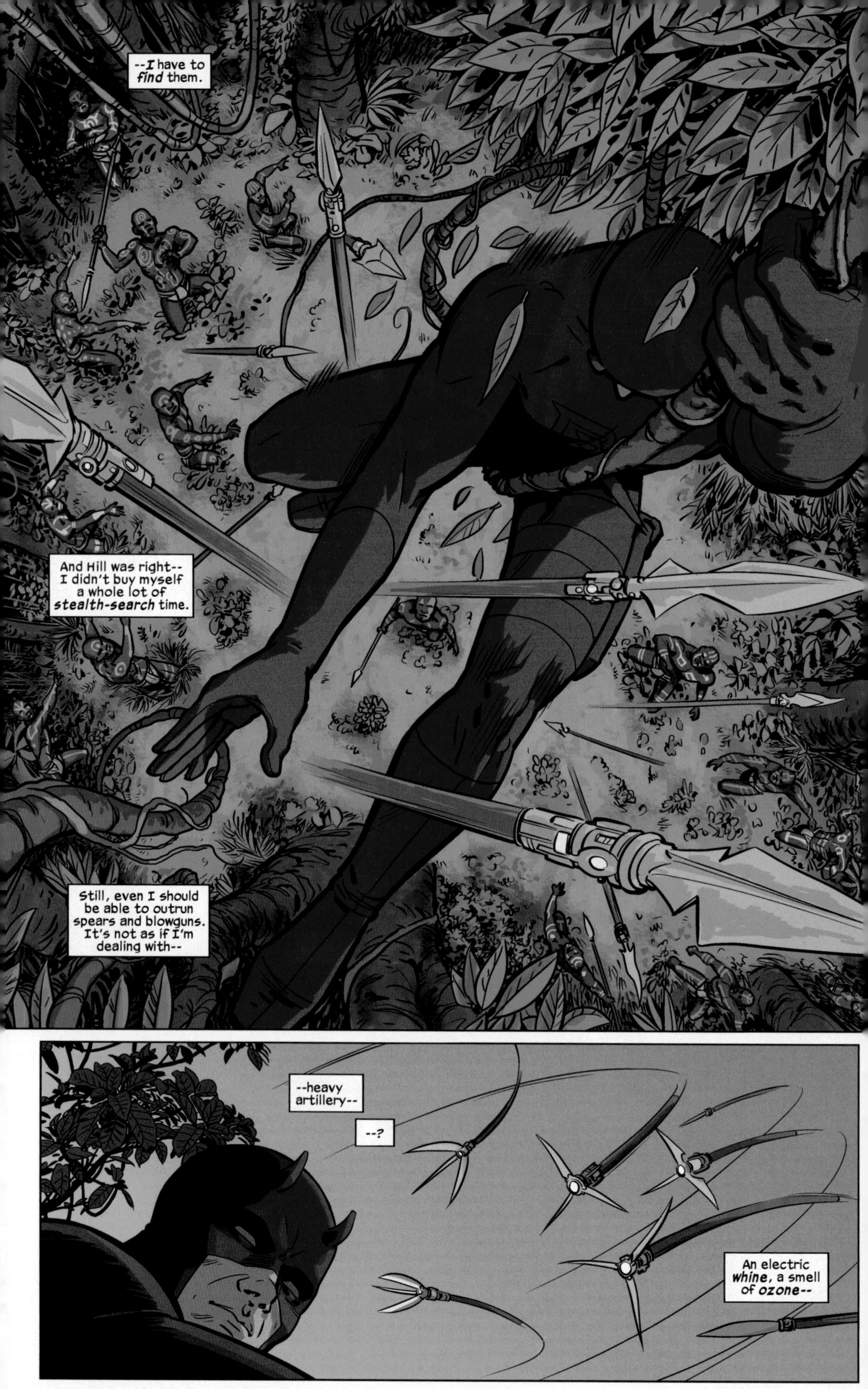
--*I* have to *find* them.
And Hill was right-- I didn't buy myself a whole lot of *stealth-search* time.
Still, even I should be able to outrun spears and blowguns. It's not as if I'm dealing with--
--heavy artillery--
--?
An electric *whine*, a smell of *ozone*--

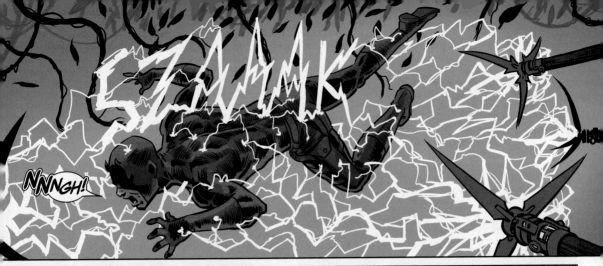

NNNGH!

<DAREDEVIL-- AS THE QUEEN PREDICTED.>

<SHE WILL BE *PLEASED* WITH US. *SEIZE HIM!*>

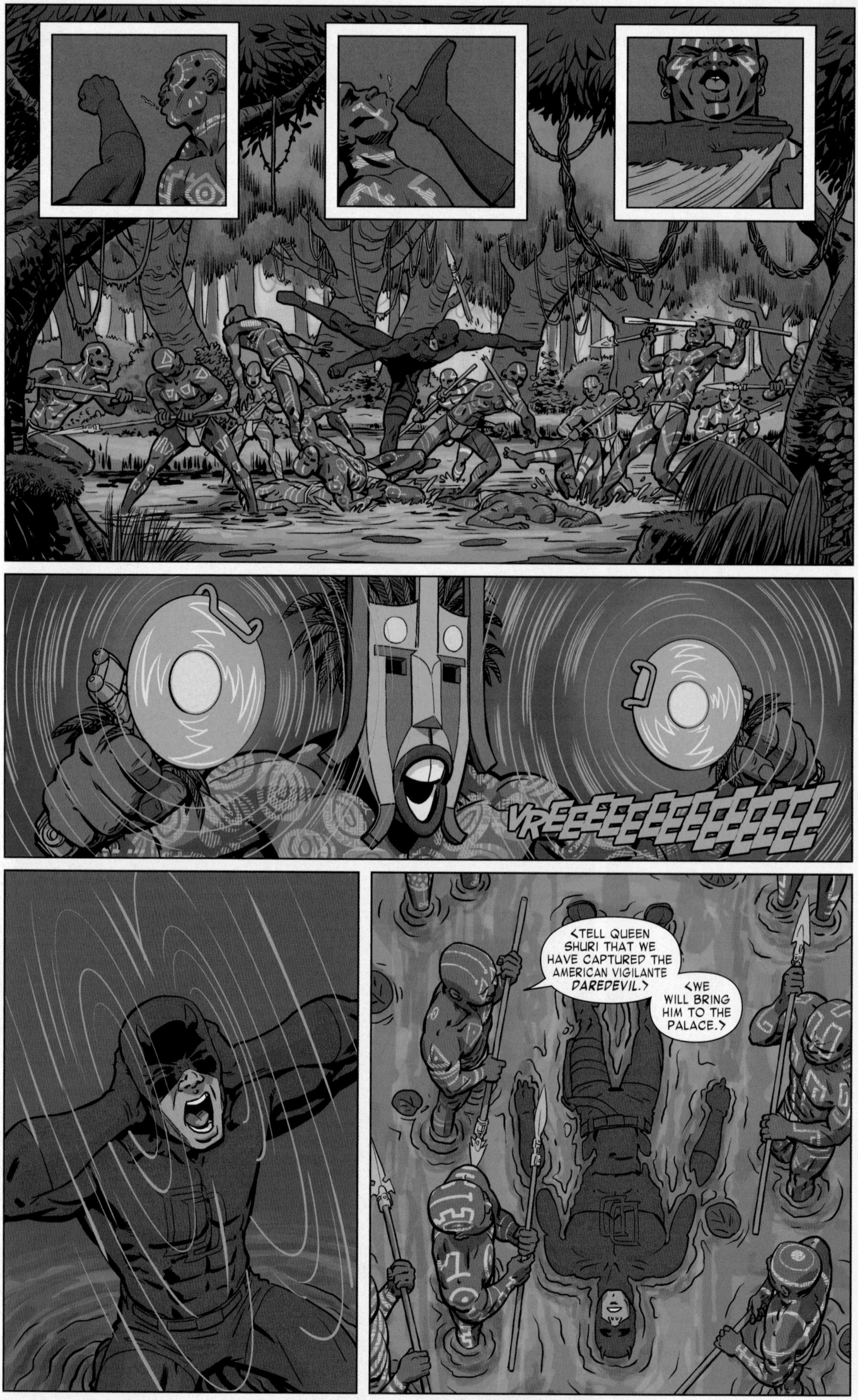
VREEEEEEEEEEEEEEEEE
<TELL QUEEN SHURI THAT WE HAVE CAPTURED THE AMERICAN VIGILANTE DAREDEVIL.>
<WE WILL BRING HIM TO THE PALACE.>

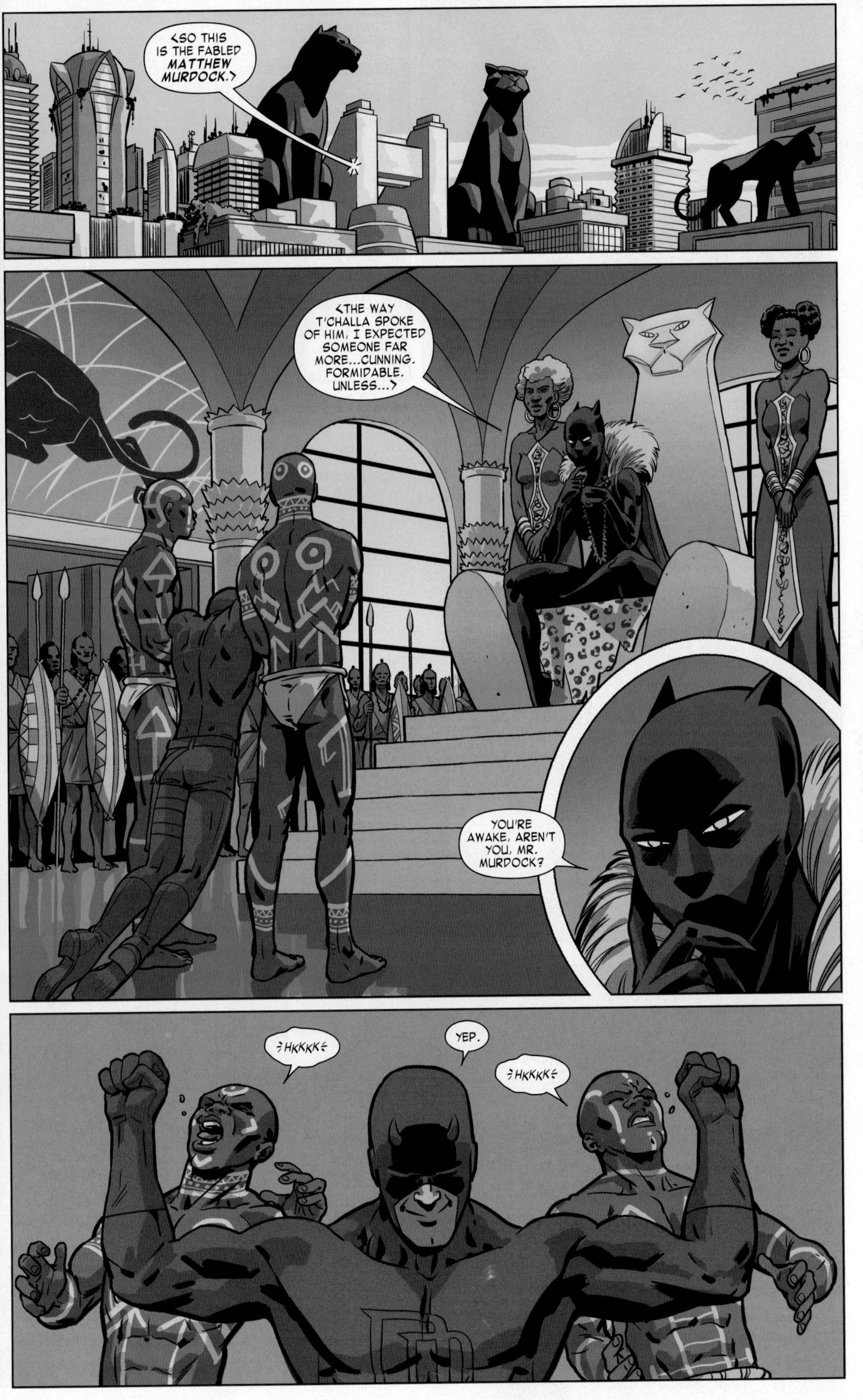

<SO THIS IS THE FABLED MATTHEW MURDOCK.>
<THE WAY T'CHALLA SPOKE OF HIM, I EXPECTED SOMEONE FAR MORE...CUNNING. FORMIDABLE. UNLESS...>
YOU'RE AWAKE, AREN'T YOU, MR. MURDOCK?
HKKKK
YEP.
HKKKK

I *wanted* to get captured. What was I going to do--

--radar-sense my way through miles of jungle in hopes of stumbling onto the prisoners I'm here to rescue?

She's *strong* and *fast*, like T'Challa.

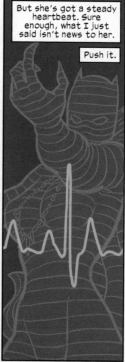

But she's got a steady heartbeat. Sure enough, what I just said isn't news to her.

Push it.

YOU BARGAINED WITH EAGLEMORE TO CONDUCT WEAPONS RESEARCH ON AMERICAN SOIL IN DEFIANCE OF INTERNATIONAL LAW.

THEN HAD THREE WOMEN SECRETLY *"EXTRADITED"* FOR THE *"CRIME"* OF DRAWING *ATTENTION* TO YOUR OPERATION.

DON'T BE ABSURD. I'M NOT *IRON MAN*, NOR AM I *STUPID*.

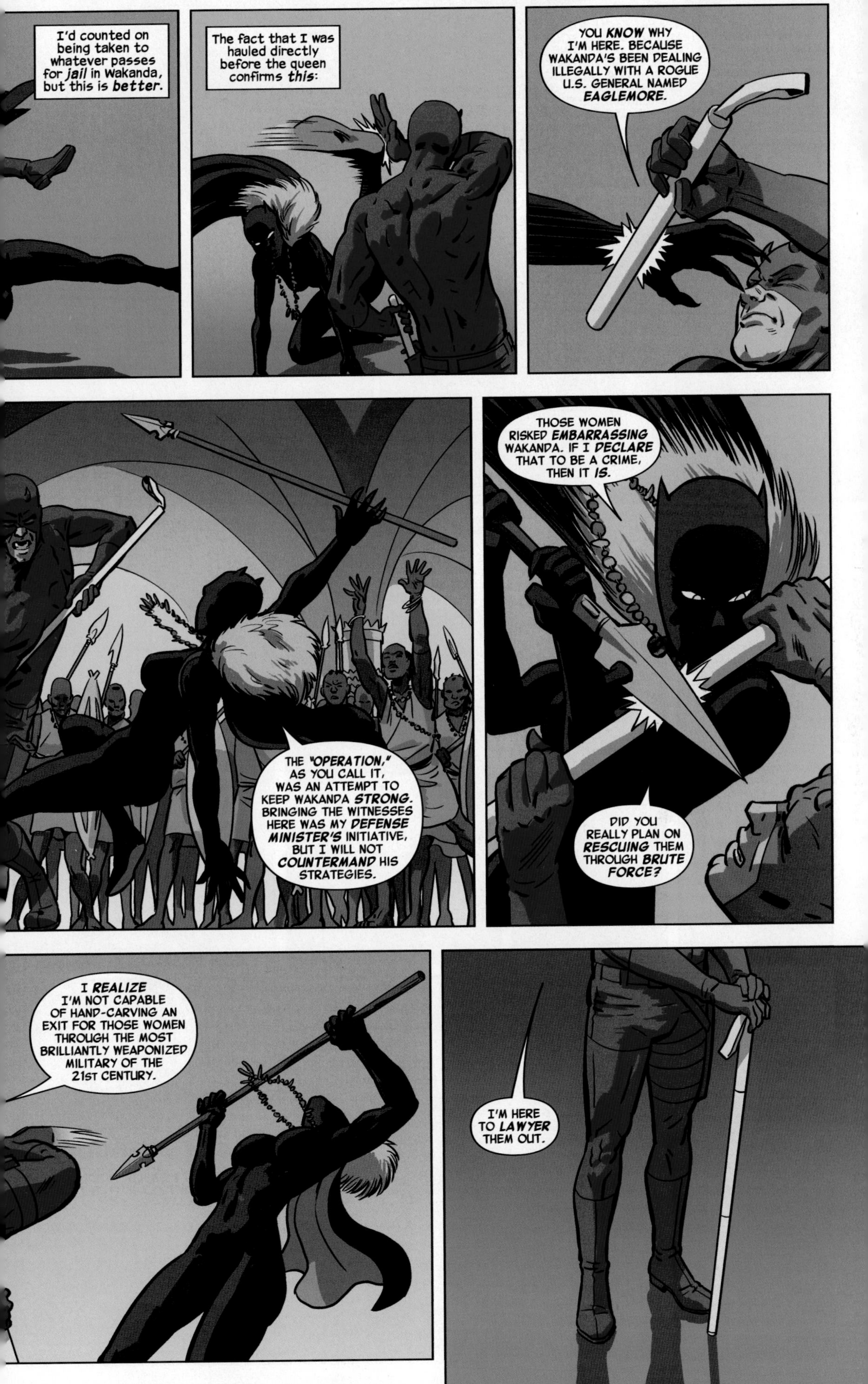
I'd counted on being taken to whatever passes for jail in Wakanda, but this is better.
The fact that I was hauled directly before the queen confirms this:
YOU KNOW WHY I'M HERE. BECAUSE WAKANDA'S BEEN DEALING ILLEGALLY WITH A ROGUE U.S. GENERAL NAMED EAGLEMORE.
THE "OPERATION," AS YOU CALL IT, WAS AN ATTEMPT TO KEEP WAKANDA STRONG. BRINGING THE WITNESSES HERE WAS MY DEFENSE MINISTER'S INITIATIVE, BUT I WILL NOT COUNTERMAND HIS STRATEGIES.
THOSE WOMEN RISKED EMBARRASSING WAKANDA. IF I DECLARE THAT TO BE A CRIME, THEN IT IS.
DID YOU REALLY PLAN ON RESCUING THEM THROUGH BRUTE FORCE?
I REALIZE I'M NOT CAPABLE OF HAND-CARVING AN EXIT FOR THOSE WOMEN THROUGH THE MOST BRILLIANTLY WEAPONIZED MILITARY OF THE 21ST CENTURY.
I'M HERE TO LAWYER THEM OUT.

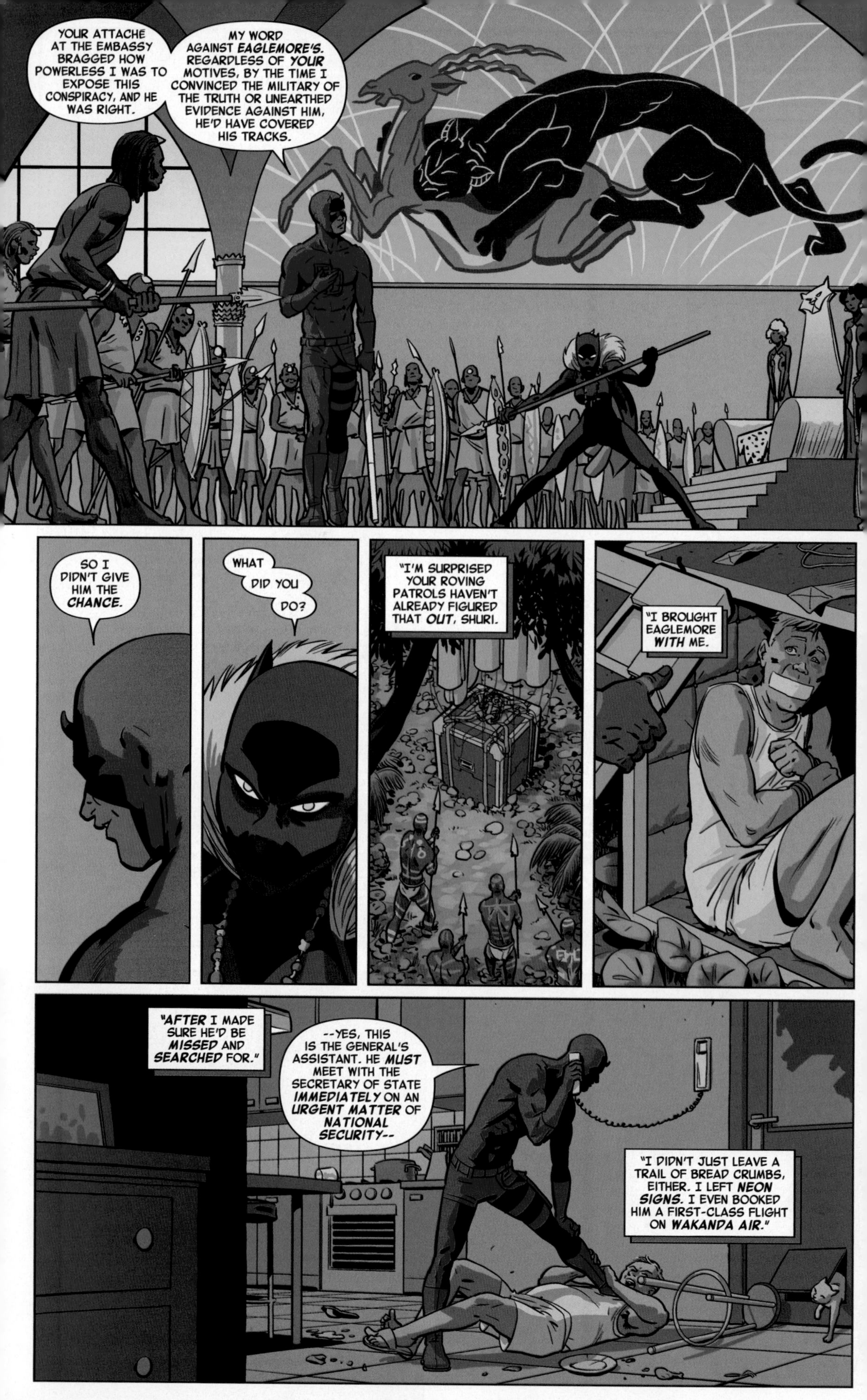
YOUR ATTACHE AT THE EMBASSY BRAGGED HOW POWERLESS I WAS TO EXPOSE THIS CONSPIRACY, AND HE WAS RIGHT.
MY WORD AGAINST EAGLEMORE'S. REGARDLESS OF YOUR MOTIVES, BY THE TIME I CONVINCED THE MILITARY OF THE TRUTH OR UNEARTHED EVIDENCE AGAINST HIM, HE'D HAVE COVERED HIS TRACKS.
SO I DIDN'T GIVE HIM THE CHANCE.
WHAT DID YOU DO?
"I'M SURPRISED YOUR ROVING PATROLS HAVEN'T ALREADY FIGURED THAT OUT, SHURI.
"I BROUGHT EAGLEMORE WITH ME.
"AFTER I MADE SURE HE'D BE MISSED AND SEARCHED FOR."
--YES, THIS IS THE GENERAL'S ASSISTANT. HE MUST MEET WITH THE SECRETARY OF STATE IMMEDIATELY ON AN URGENT MATTER OF NATIONAL SECURITY--
"I DIDN'T JUST LEAVE A TRAIL OF BREAD CRUMBS, EITHER. I LEFT NEON SIGNS. I EVEN BOOKED HIM A FIRST-CLASS FLIGHT ON WAKANDA AIR."

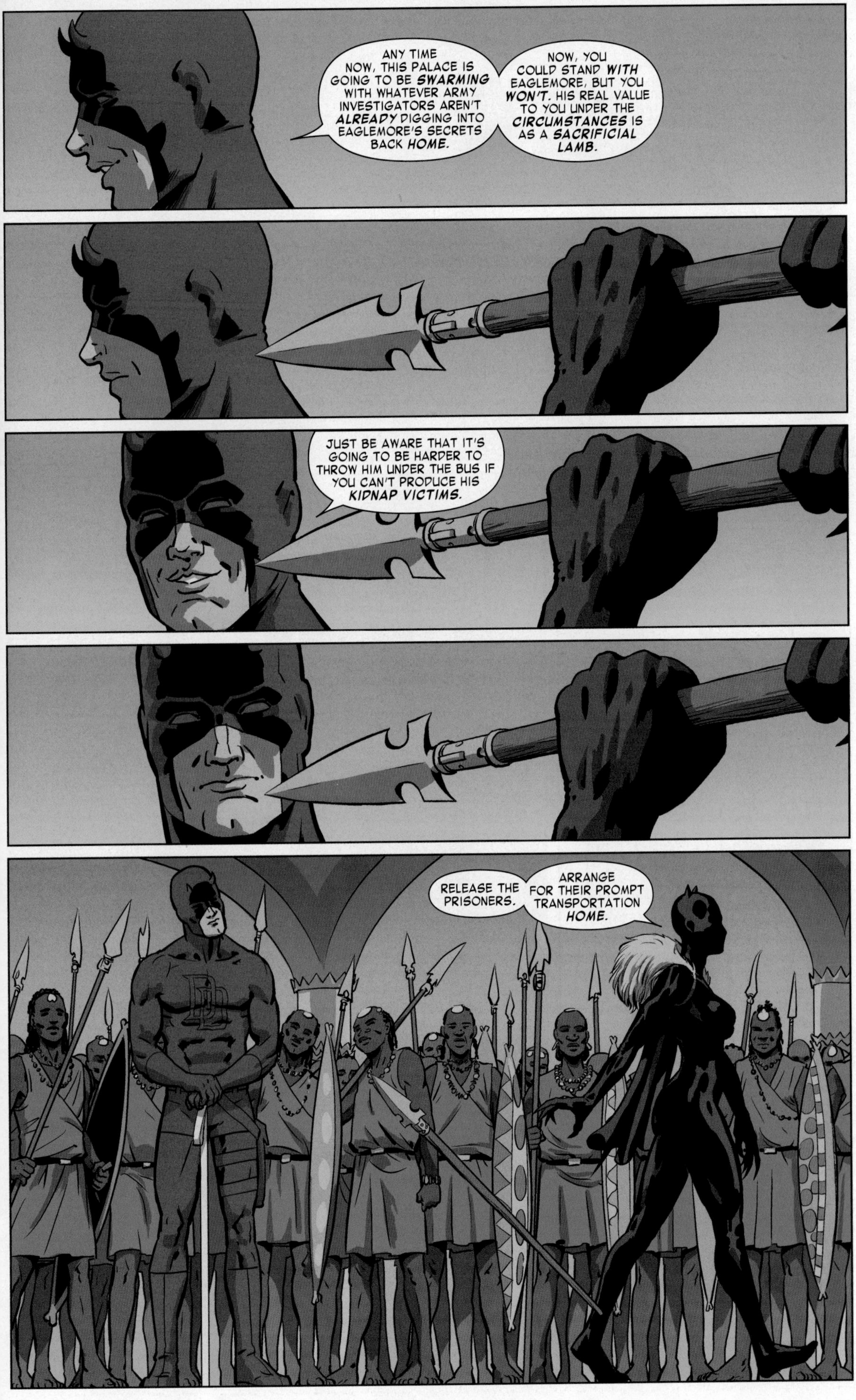
ANY TIME NOW, THIS PALACE IS GOING TO BE SWARMING WITH WHATEVER ARMY INVESTIGATORS AREN'T ALREADY DIGGING INTO EAGLEMORE'S SECRETS BACK HOME.
NOW, YOU COULD STAND WITH EAGLEMORE, BUT YOU WON'T. HIS REAL VALUE TO YOU UNDER THE CIRCUMSTANCES IS AS A SACRIFICIAL LAMB.
JUST BE AWARE THAT IT'S GOING TO BE HARDER TO THROW HIM UNDER THE BUS IF YOU CAN'T PRODUCE HIS KIDNAP VICTIMS.
RELEASE THE PRISONERS.
ARRANGE FOR THEIR PROMPT TRANSPORTATION HOME.

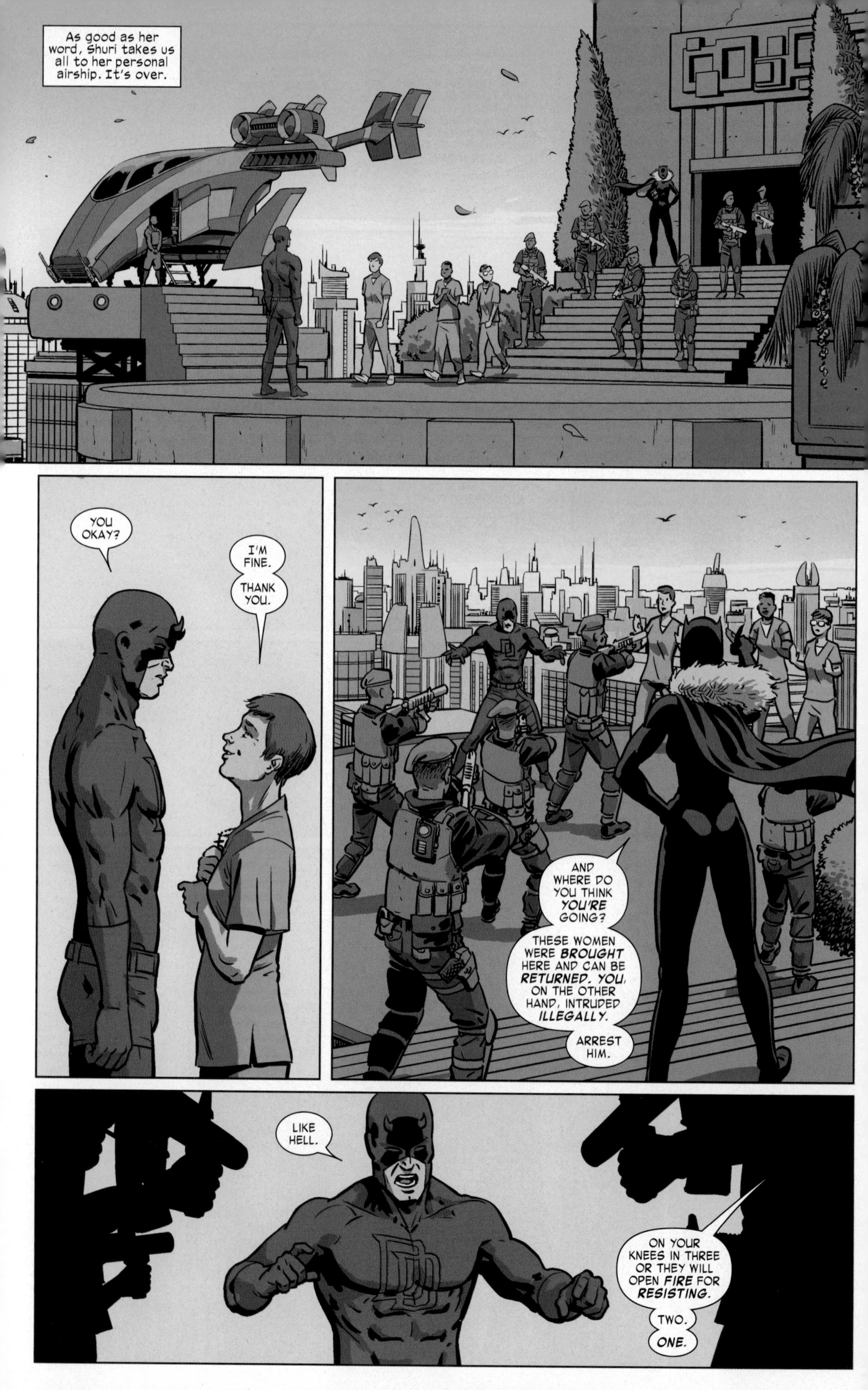
As good as her word, Shuri takes us all to her personal airship. It's over.
YOU OKAY?
I'M FINE.
THANK YOU.
AND WHERE DO YOU THINK YOU'RE GOING?
THESE WOMEN WERE BROUGHT HERE AND CAN BE RETURNED. YOU, ON THE OTHER HAND, INTRUDED ILLEGALLY.
ARREST HIM.
LIKE HELL.
ON YOUR KNEES IN THREE OR THEY WILL OPEN FIRE FOR RESISTING.
TWO.
ONE.

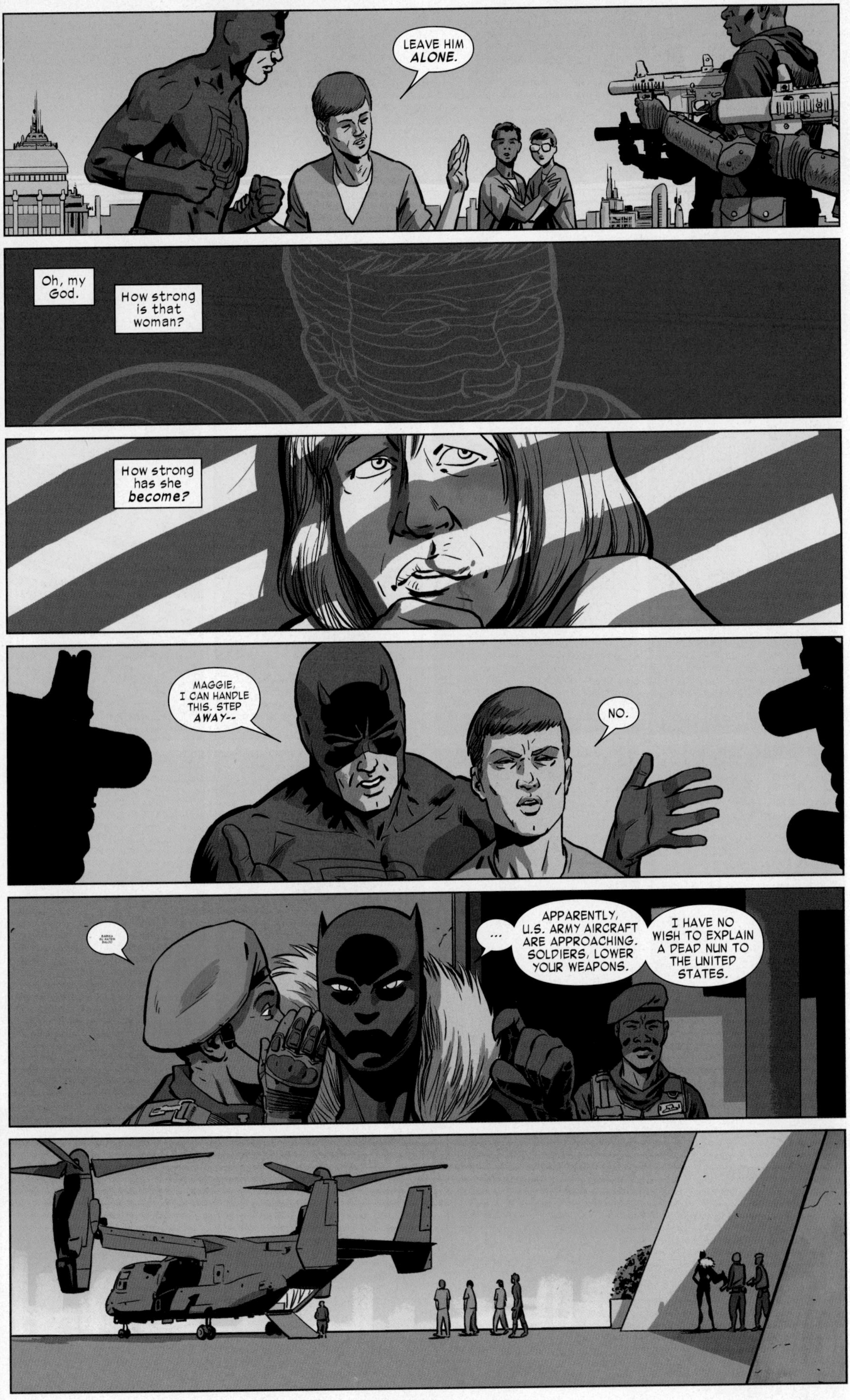

LEAVE HIM *ALONE.*
Oh, my God.
How strong is that woman?
How strong has she *become?*
MAGGIE, I CAN HANDLE THIS. STEP *AWAY--*
NO.
...
APPARENTLY, U.S. ARMY AIRCRAFT ARE APPROACHING. SOLDIERS, LOWER YOUR WEAPONS.
I HAVE NO WISH TO EXPLAIN A DEAD NUN TO THE UNITED STATES.

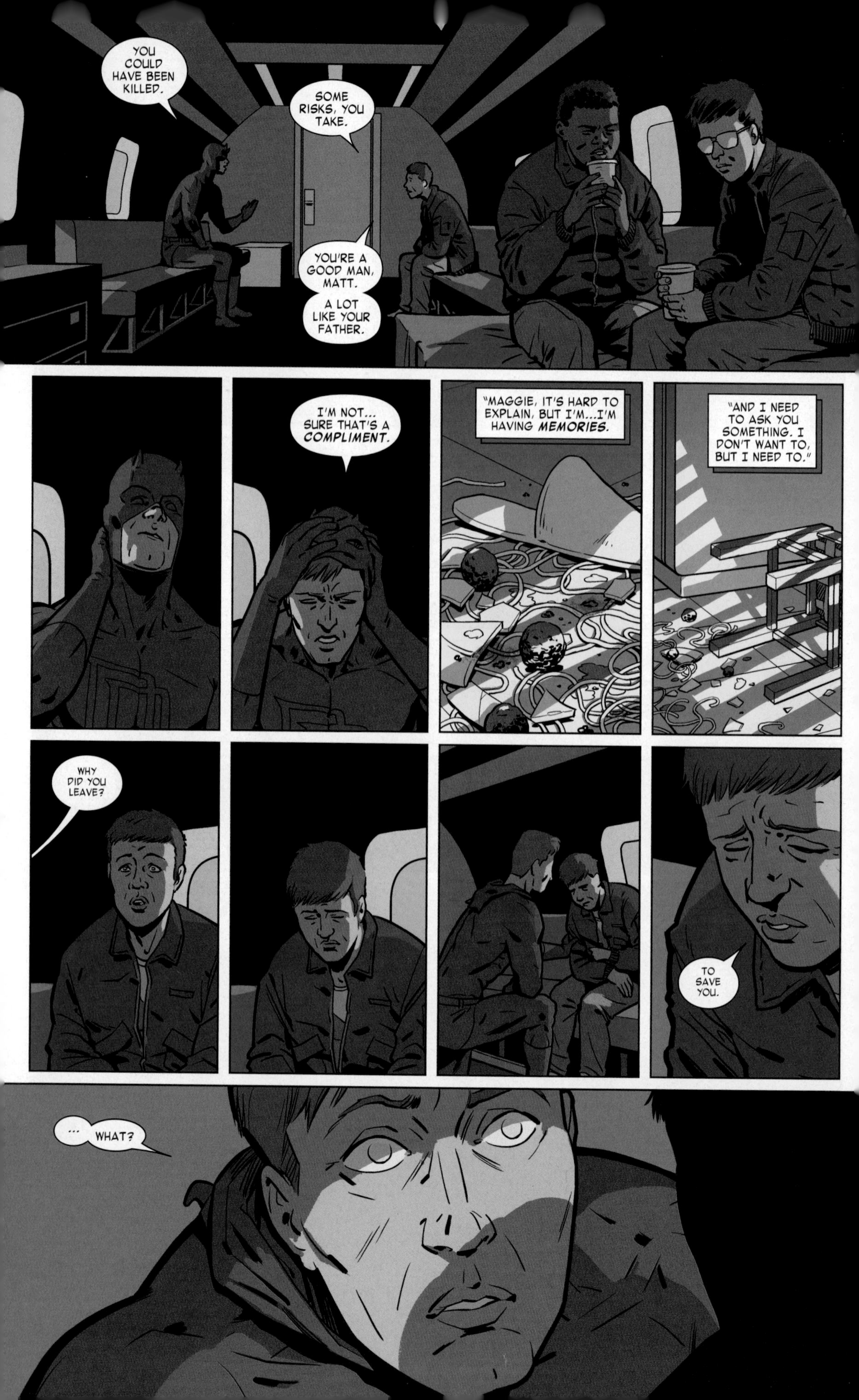
YOU COULD HAVE BEEN KILLED.
SOME RISKS, YOU TAKE.
YOU'RE A GOOD MAN, MATT.
A LOT LIKE YOUR FATHER.
I'M NOT... SURE THAT'S A COMPLIMENT.
"MAGGIE, IT'S HARD TO EXPLAIN, BUT I'M...I'M HAVING MEMORIES.
"AND I NEED TO ASK YOU SOMETHING. I DON'T WANT TO, BUT I NEED TO."
WHY DID YOU LEAVE?
TO SAVE YOU.
...
WHAT?

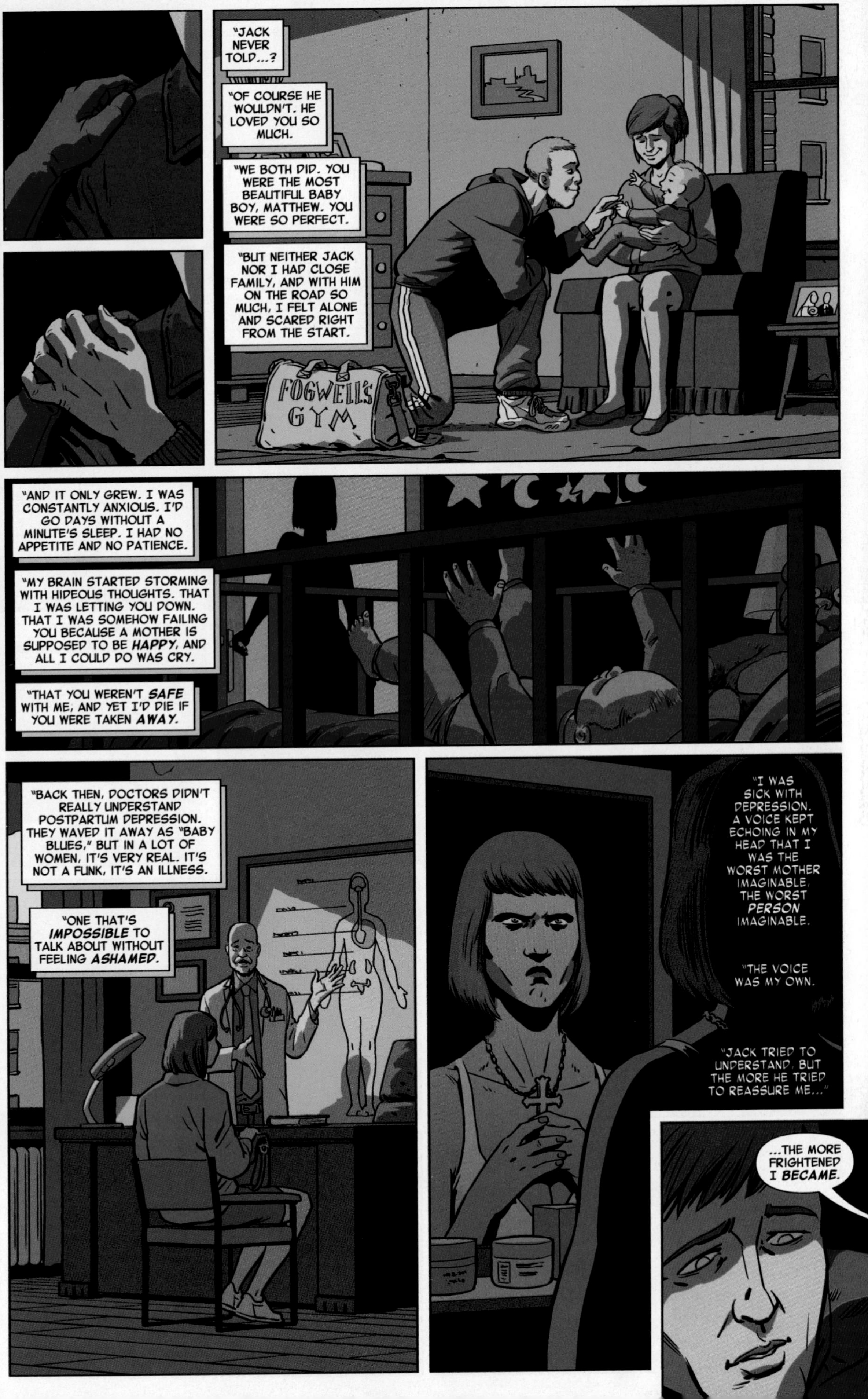

"JACK NEVER TOLD...?
"OF COURSE HE WOULDN'T. HE LOVED YOU SO MUCH.
"WE BOTH DID. YOU WERE THE MOST BEAUTIFUL BABY BOY, MATTHEW. YOU WERE SO PERFECT.
"BUT NEITHER JACK NOR I HAD CLOSE FAMILY, AND WITH HIM ON THE ROAD SO MUCH, I FELT ALONE AND SCARED RIGHT FROM THE START.
FOGWELL'S GYM
"AND IT ONLY GREW. I WAS CONSTANTLY ANXIOUS. I'D GO DAYS WITHOUT A MINUTE'S SLEEP. I HAD NO APPETITE AND NO PATIENCE.
"MY BRAIN STARTED STORMING WITH HIDEOUS THOUGHTS. THAT I WAS LETTING YOU DOWN. THAT I WAS SOMEHOW FAILING YOU BECAUSE A MOTHER IS SUPPOSED TO BE *HAPPY*, AND ALL I COULD DO WAS CRY.
"THAT YOU WEREN'T *SAFE* WITH ME, AND YET I'D DIE IF YOU WERE TAKEN *AWAY*.
"BACK THEN, DOCTORS DIDN'T REALLY UNDERSTAND POSTPARTUM DEPRESSION. THEY WAVED IT AWAY AS "BABY BLUES," BUT IN A LOT OF WOMEN, IT'S VERY REAL. IT'S NOT A FUNK, IT'S AN ILLNESS.
"ONE THAT'S *IMPOSSIBLE* TO TALK ABOUT WITHOUT FEELING *ASHAMED*.
"I WAS SICK WITH DEPRESSION. A VOICE KEPT ECHOING IN MY HEAD THAT I WAS THE WORST MOTHER IMAGINABLE, THE WORST *PERSON* IMAGINABLE.
"THE VOICE WAS MY OWN.
"JACK TRIED TO UNDERSTAND, BUT THE MORE HE TRIED TO REASSURE ME..."
...THE MORE FRIGHTENED I *BECAME*.

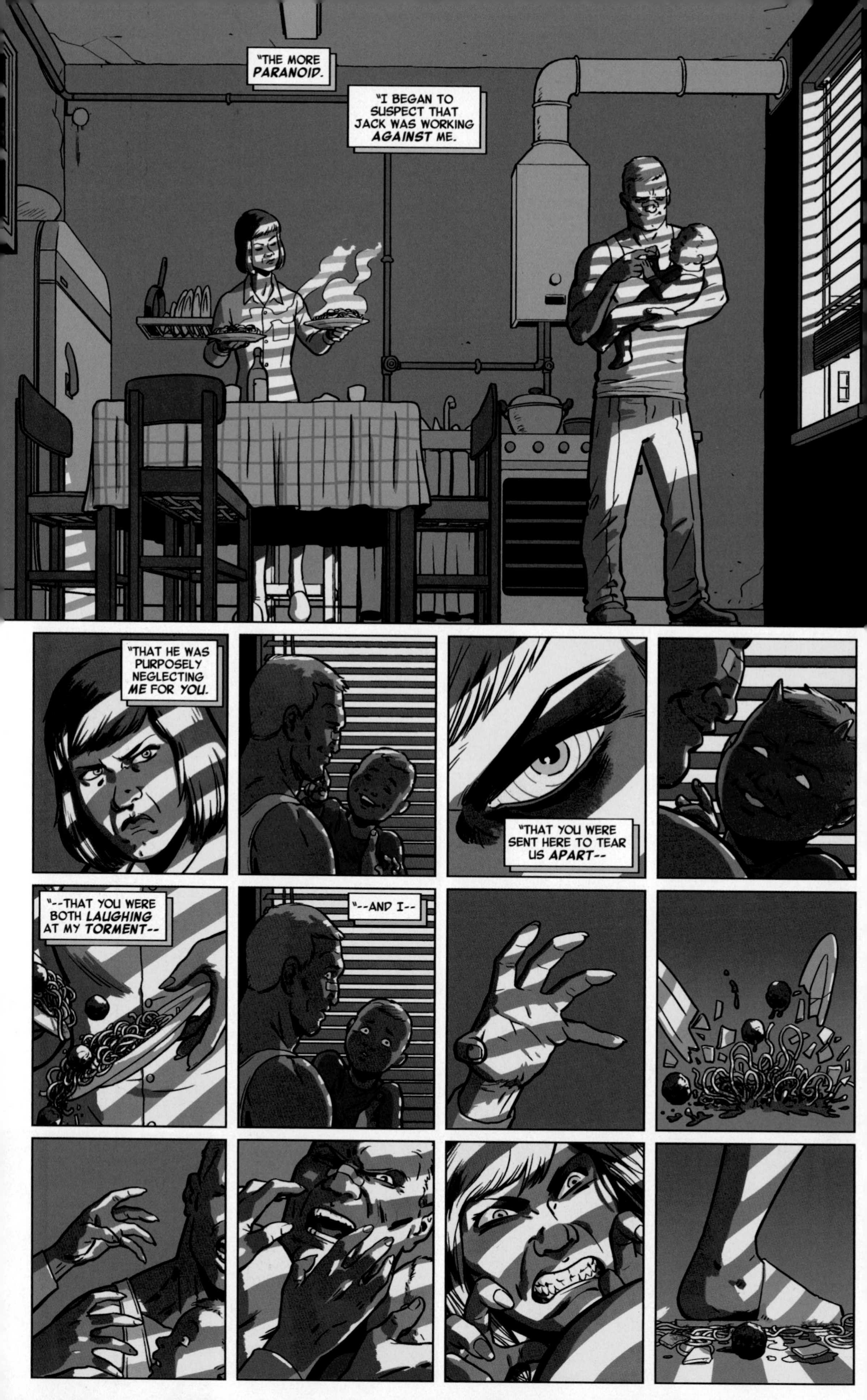
"THE MORE PARANOID.
"I BEGAN TO SUSPECT THAT JACK WAS WORKING AGAINST ME.
"THAT HE WAS PURPOSELY NEGLECTING ME FOR YOU.
"THAT YOU WERE SENT HERE TO TEAR US APART--
"--THAT YOU WERE BOTH LAUGHING AT MY TORMENT--
"--AND I--

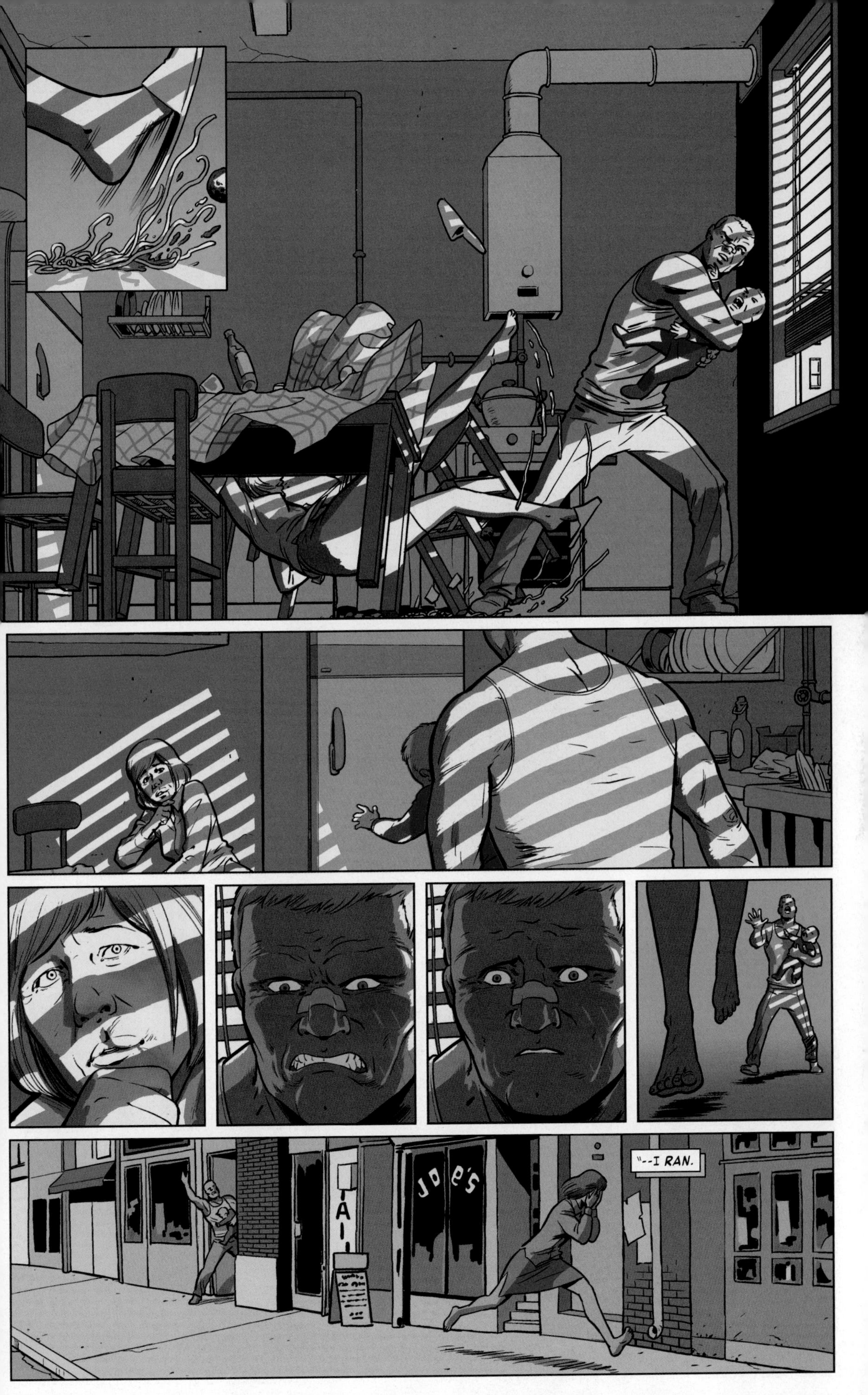

JOE'S
"--I RAN.

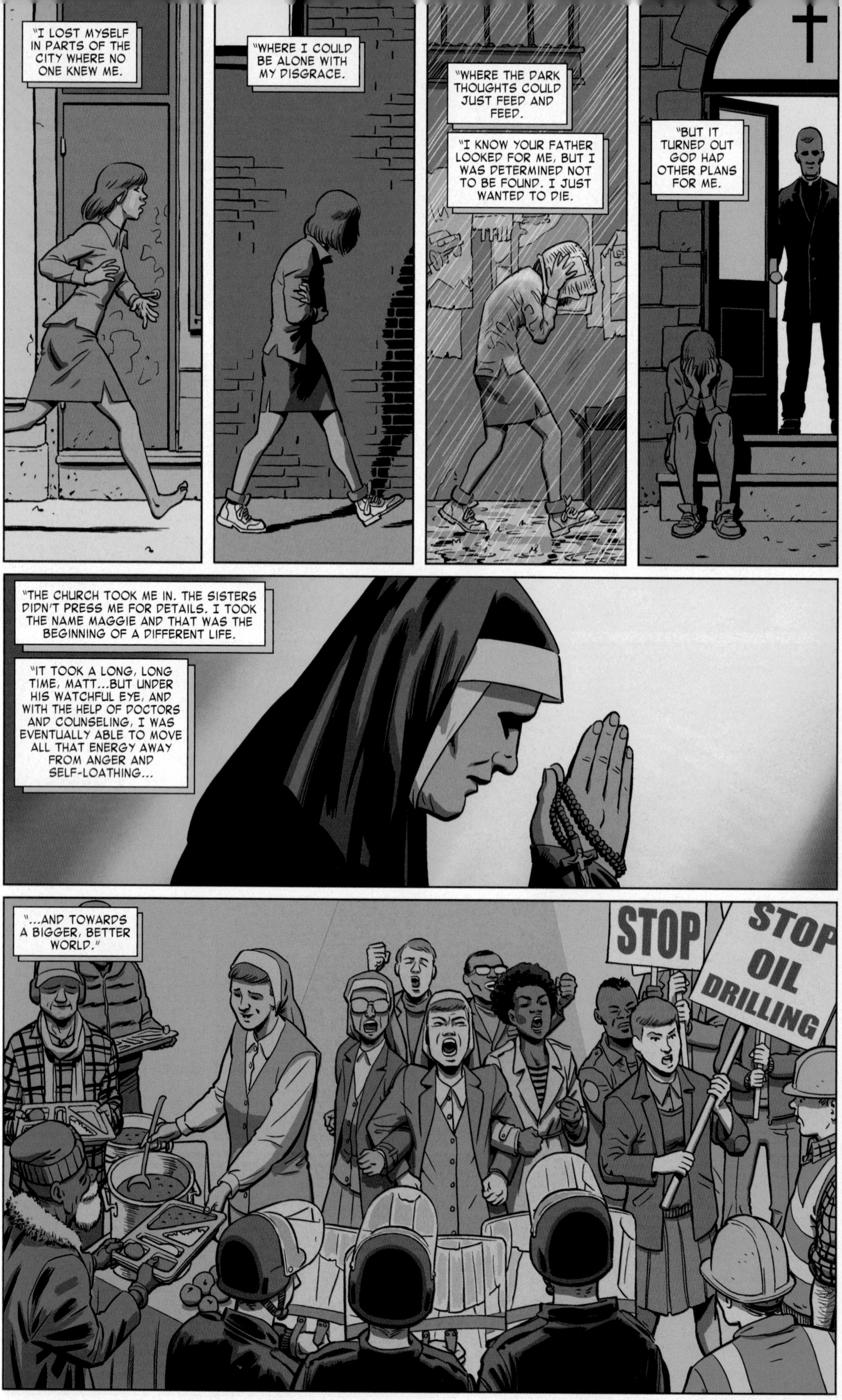
"I LOST MYSELF IN PARTS OF THE CITY WHERE NO ONE KNEW ME.
"WHERE I COULD BE ALONE WITH MY DISGRACE.
"WHERE THE DARK THOUGHTS COULD JUST FEED AND FEED.
"I KNOW YOUR FATHER LOOKED FOR ME, BUT I WAS DETERMINED NOT TO BE FOUND. I JUST WANTED TO DIE.
"BUT IT TURNED OUT GOD HAD OTHER PLANS FOR ME.
"THE CHURCH TOOK ME IN. THE SISTERS DIDN'T PRESS ME FOR DETAILS. I TOOK THE NAME MAGGIE AND THAT WAS THE BEGINNING OF A DIFFERENT LIFE.
"IT TOOK A LONG, LONG TIME, MATT...BUT UNDER HIS WATCHFUL EYE, AND WITH THE HELP OF DOCTORS AND COUNSELING, I WAS EVENTUALLY ABLE TO MOVE ALL THAT ENERGY AWAY FROM ANGER AND SELF-LOATHING...
"...AND TOWARDS A BIGGER, BETTER WORLD."
STOP
STOP OIL DRILLING

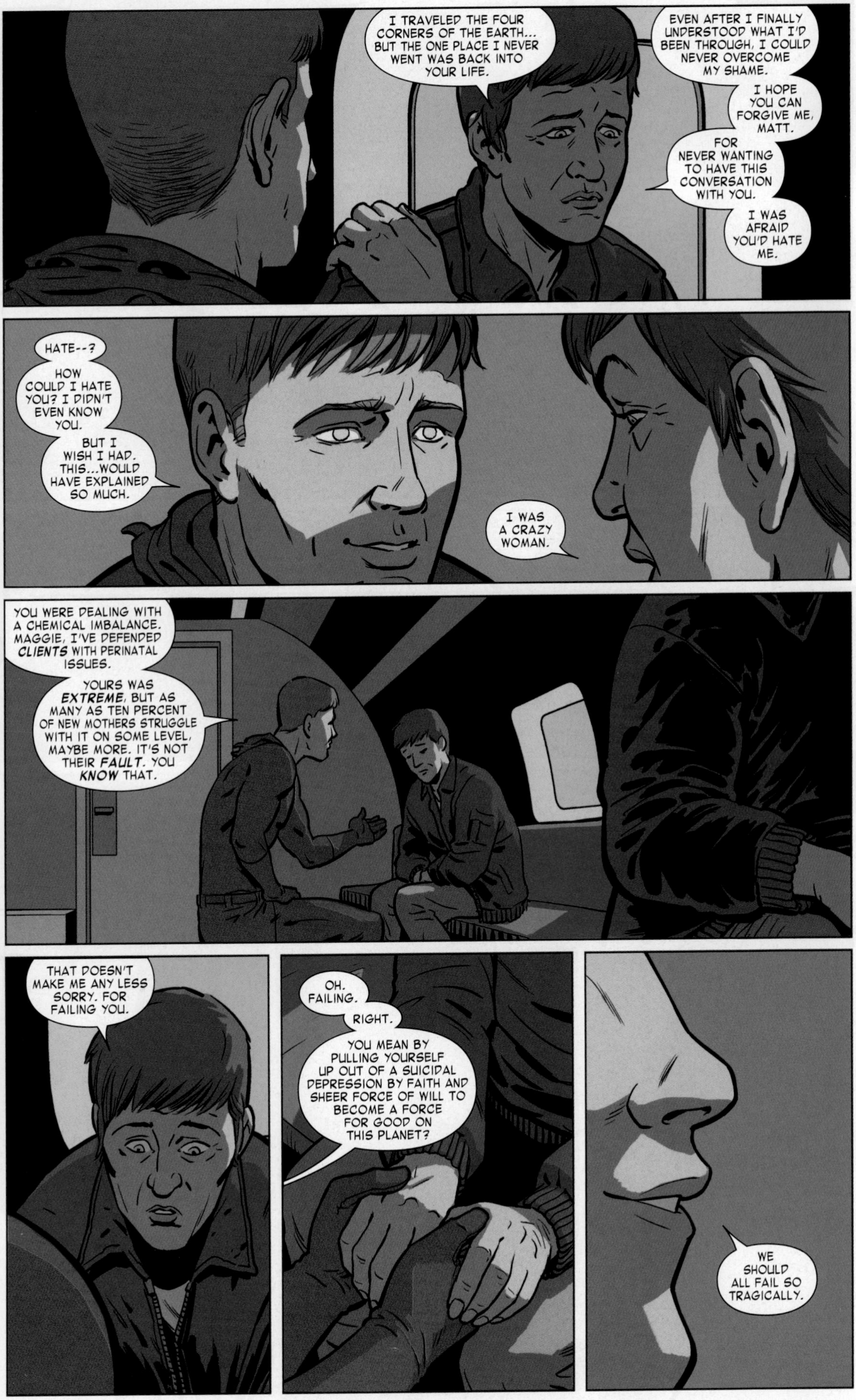
I TRAVELED THE FOUR CORNERS OF THE EARTH... BUT THE ONE PLACE I NEVER WENT WAS BACK INTO YOUR LIFE.
EVEN AFTER I FINALLY UNDERSTOOD WHAT I'D BEEN THROUGH, I COULD NEVER OVERCOME MY SHAME.
I HOPE YOU CAN FORGIVE ME, MATT.
FOR NEVER WANTING TO HAVE THIS CONVERSATION WITH YOU.
I WAS AFRAID YOU'D HATE ME.
HATE--?
HOW COULD I HATE YOU? I DIDN'T EVEN KNOW YOU.
BUT I WISH I HAD. THIS...WOULD HAVE EXPLAINED SO MUCH.
I WAS A CRAZY WOMAN.
YOU WERE DEALING WITH A CHEMICAL IMBALANCE. MAGGIE, I'VE DEFENDED *CLIENTS* WITH PERINATAL ISSUES.
YOURS WAS *EXTREME*, BUT AS MANY AS TEN PERCENT OF NEW MOTHERS STRUGGLE WITH IT ON SOME LEVEL, MAYBE MORE. IT'S NOT THEIR *FAULT*. YOU *KNOW* THAT.
THAT DOESN'T MAKE ME ANY LESS SORRY. FOR FAILING YOU.
OH. FAILING.
RIGHT.
YOU MEAN BY PULLING YOURSELF UP OUT OF A SUICIDAL DEPRESSION BY FAITH AND SHEER FORCE OF WILL TO BECOME A FORCE FOR GOOD ON THIS PLANET?
WE SHOULD ALL FAIL SO TRAGICALLY.

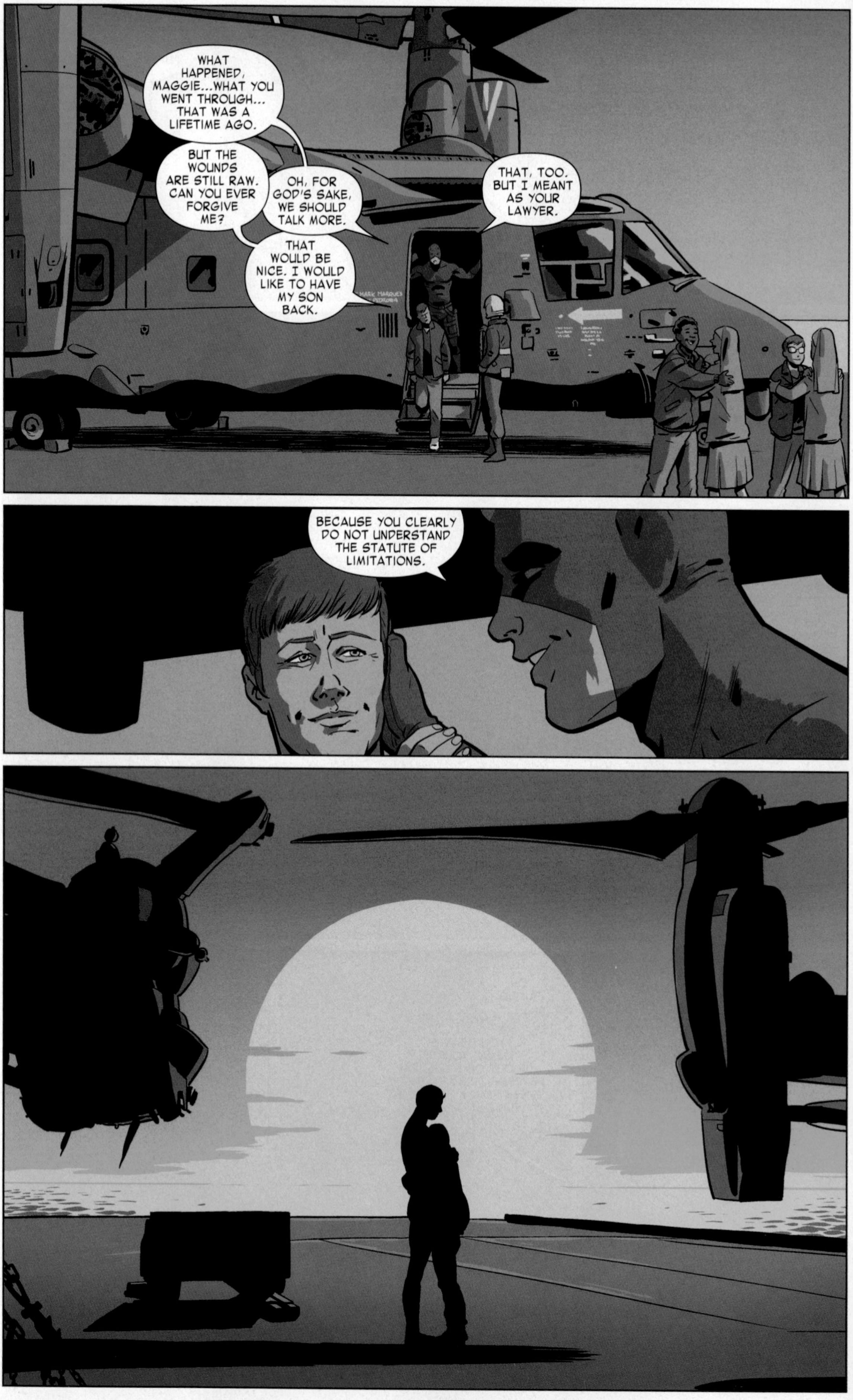
WHAT HAPPENED, MAGGIE...WHAT YOU WENT THROUGH... THAT WAS A LIFETIME AGO.
BUT THE WOUNDS ARE STILL RAW. CAN YOU EVER FORGIVE ME?
OH, FOR GOD'S SAKE, WE SHOULD TALK MORE.
THAT WOULD BE NICE. I WOULD LIKE TO HAVE MY SON BACK.
THAT, TOO. BUT I MEANT AS YOUR LAWYER.
BECAUSE YOU CLEARLY DO NOT UNDERSTAND THE STATUTE OF LIMITATIONS.

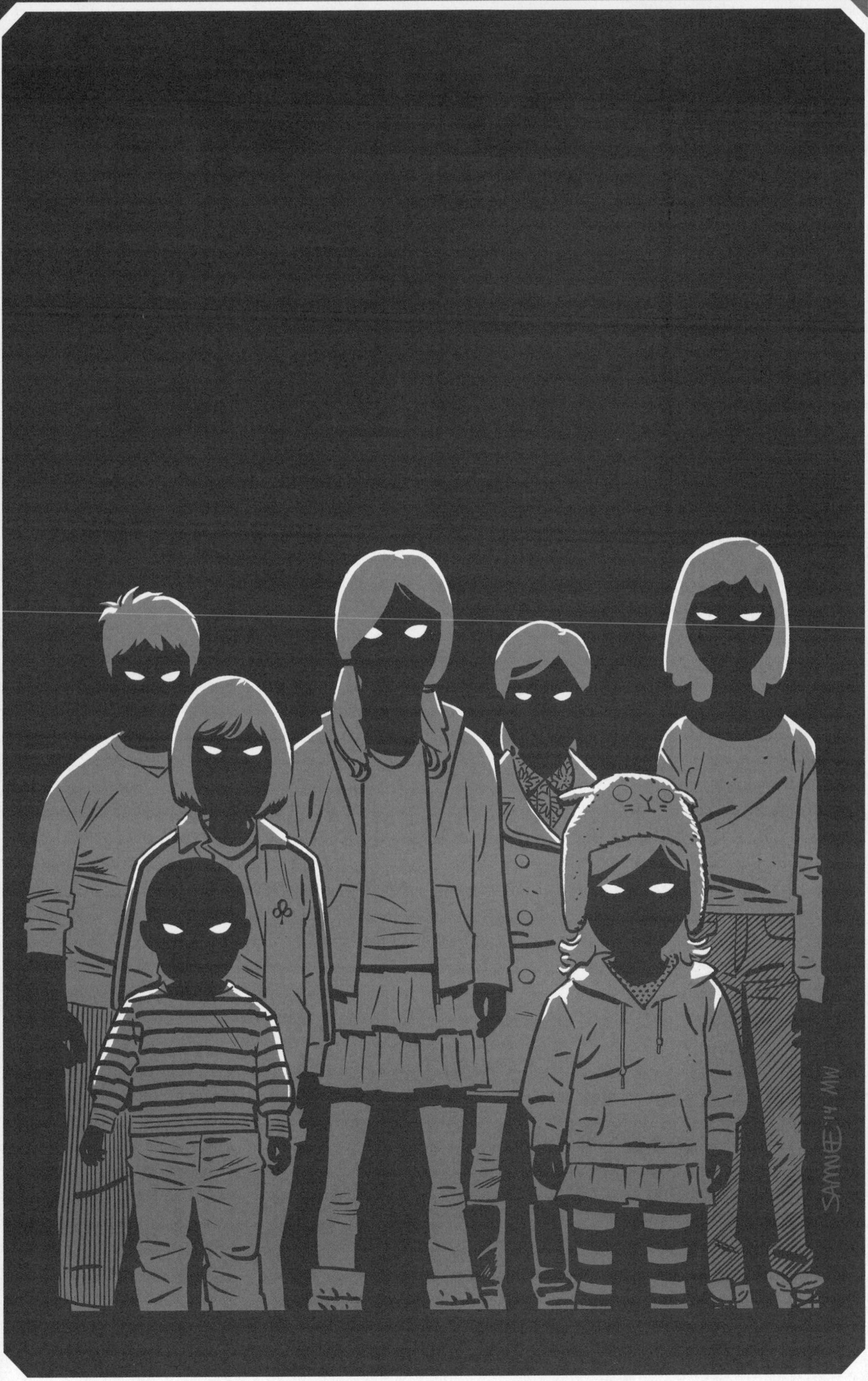

DAREDEVIL #8

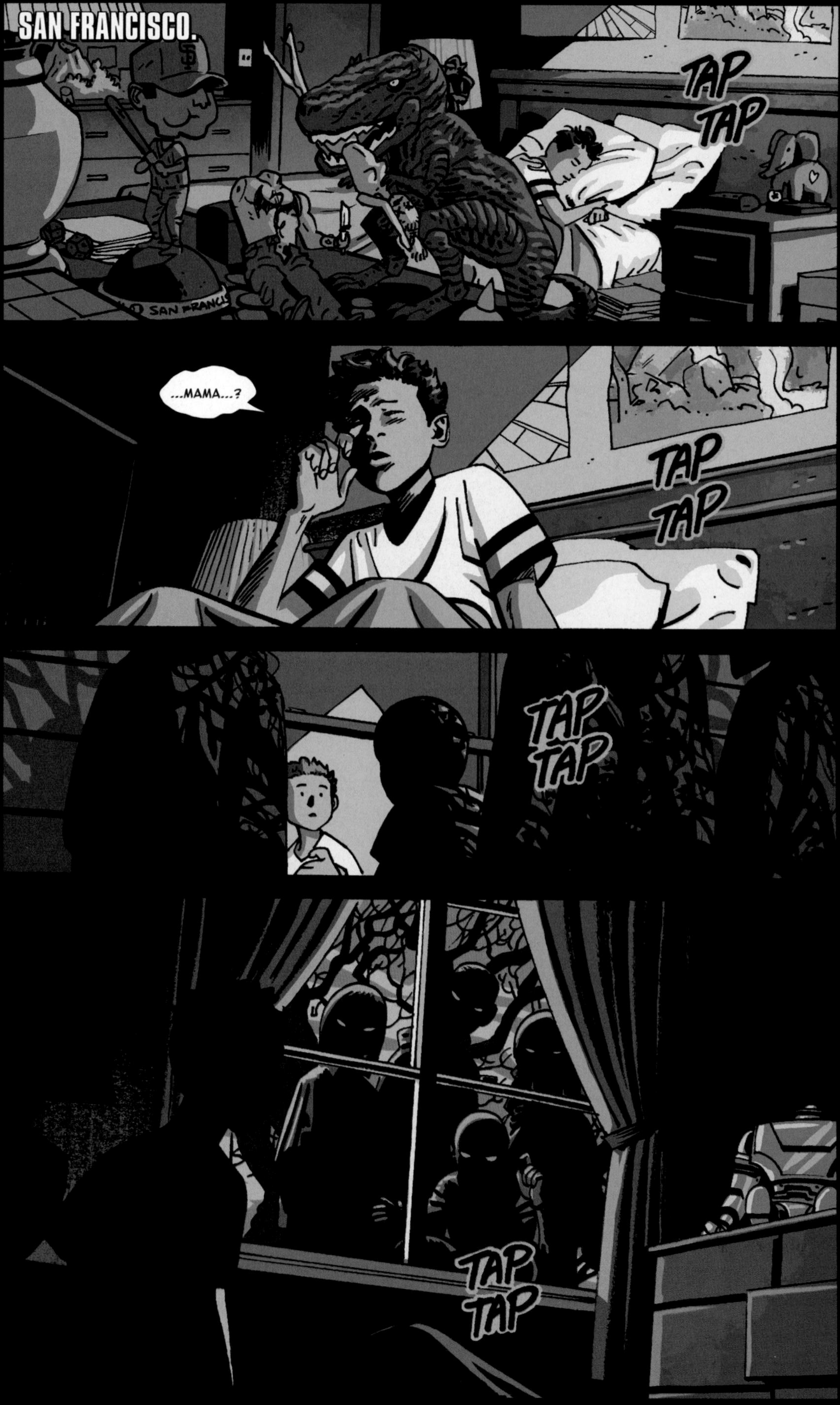
SAN FRANCISCO.
SAN FRANCIS
TAP
TAP
...MAMA...?
TAP
TAP
TAP
TAP
TAP
TAP

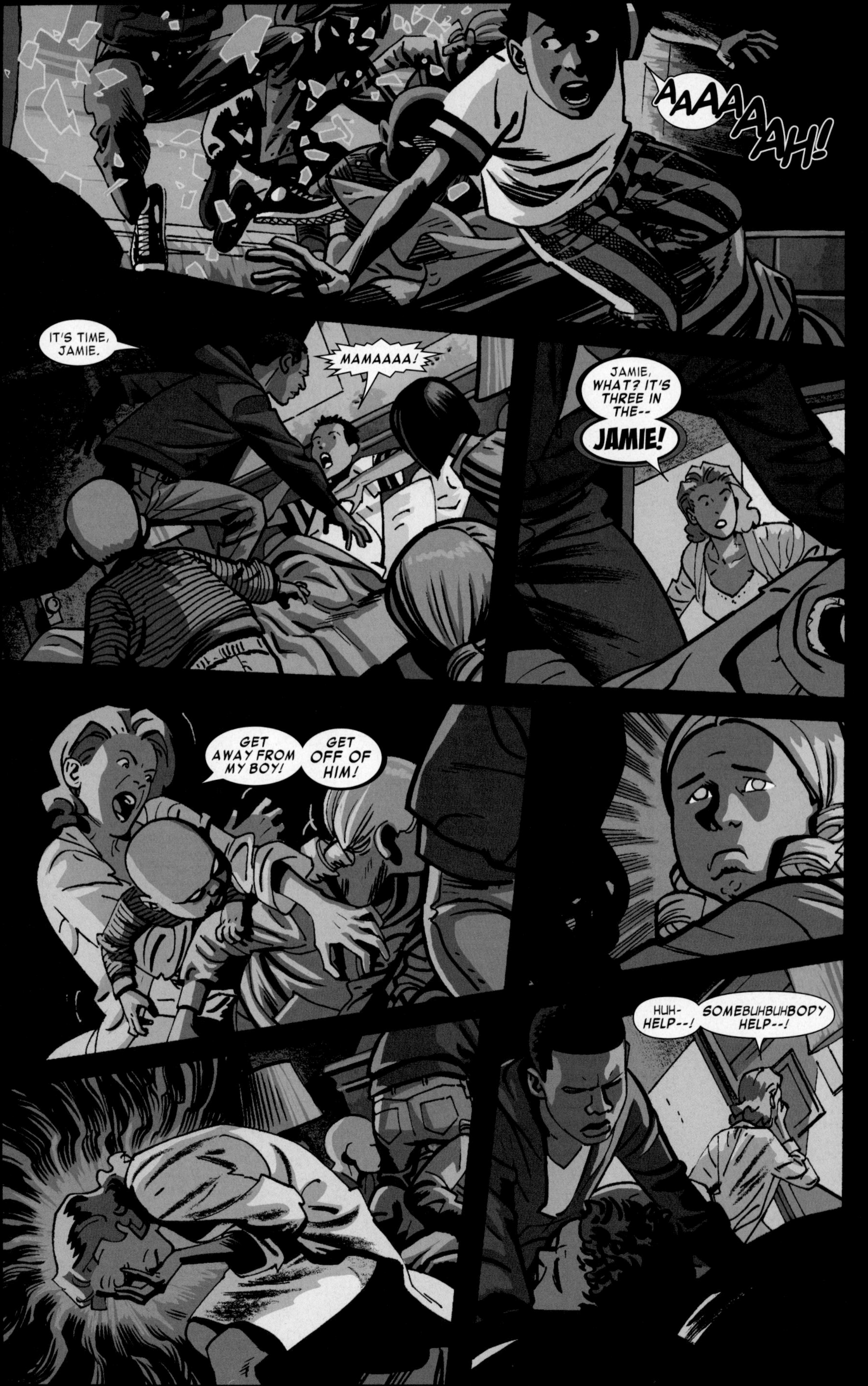
AAAAAAAH!
IT'S TIME, JAMIE.
MAMAAAA!
JAMIE, WHAT? IT'S THREE IN THE--
JAMIE!
GET AWAY FROM MY BOY!
GET OFF OF HIM!
HUH-HELP--!
SOMEBUHBUHBODY HELP--!

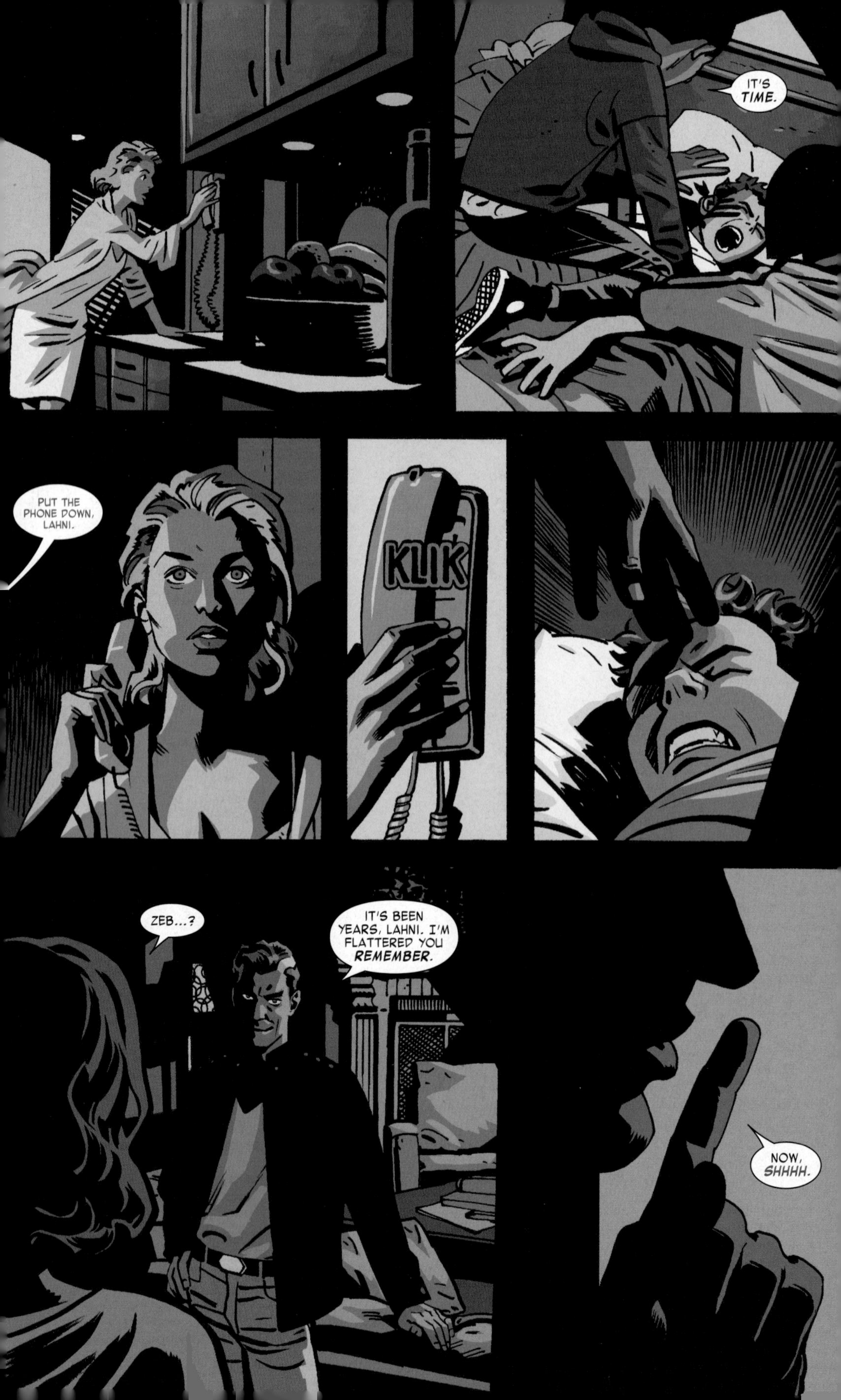
IT'S TIME.
PUT THE PHONE DOWN, LAHNI.
KLIK
ZEB...?
IT'S BEEN YEARS, LAHNI. I'M FLATTERED YOU REMEMBER.
NOW, SHHHH.

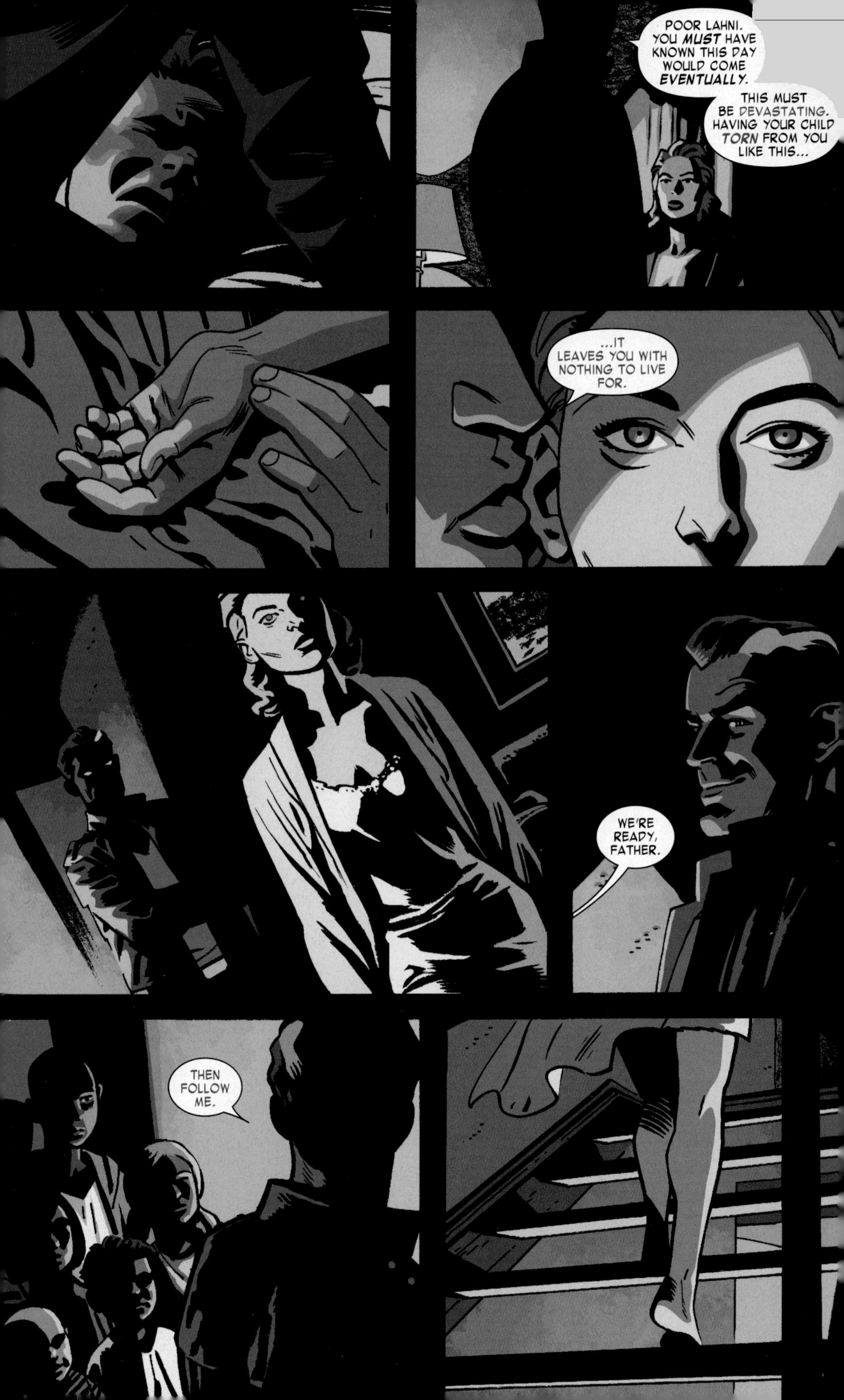
POOR LAHNI. YOU MUST HAVE KNOWN THIS DAY WOULD COME EVENTUALLY.
THIS MUST BE DEVASTATING. HAVING YOUR CHILD TORN FROM YOU LIKE THIS...
...IT LEAVES YOU WITH NOTHING TO LIVE FOR.
WE'RE READY, FATHER.
THEN FOLLOW ME.

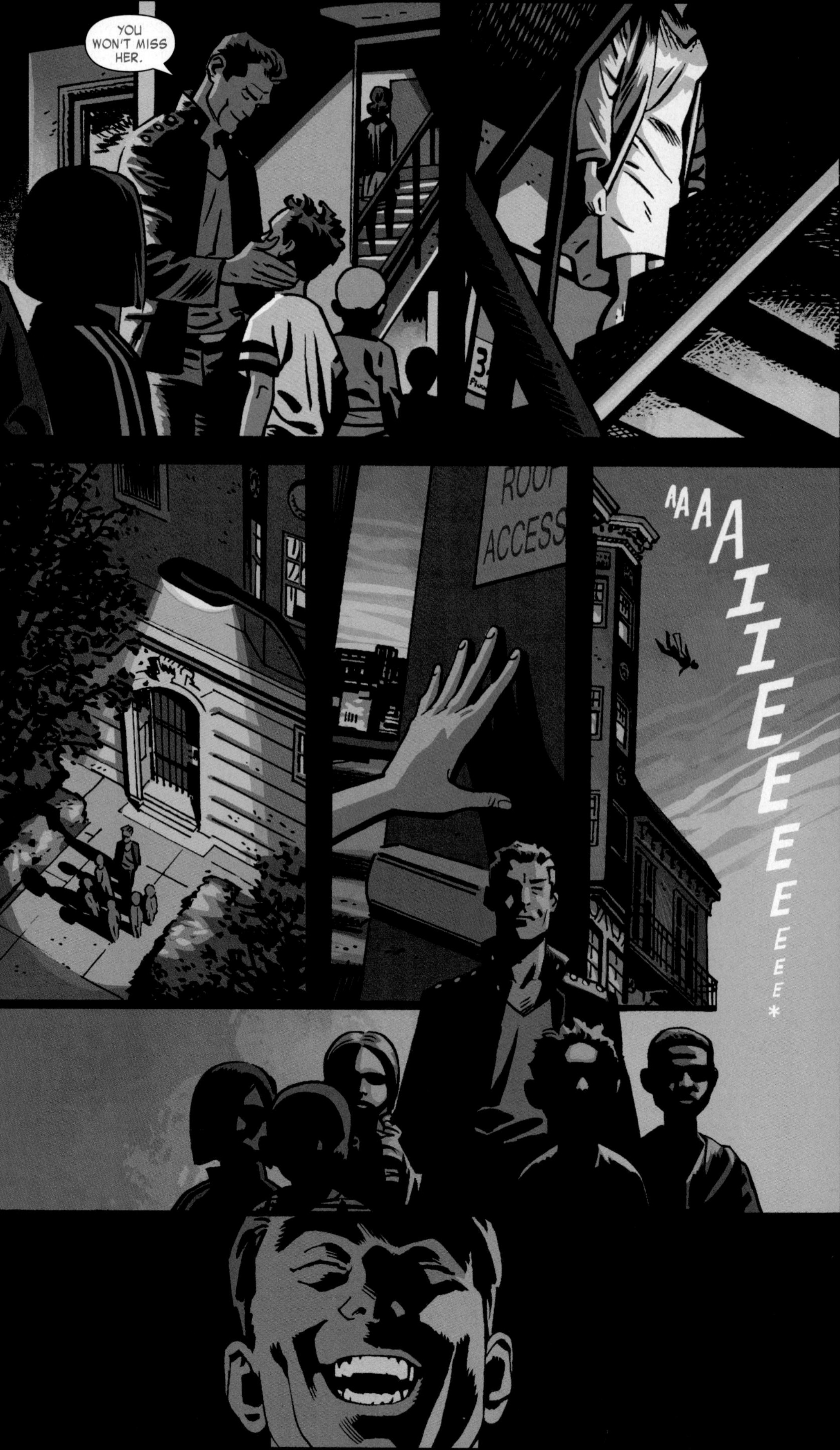
YOU WON'T MISS HER.
ROOF ACCESS
AAAAIIEEEEEEE*

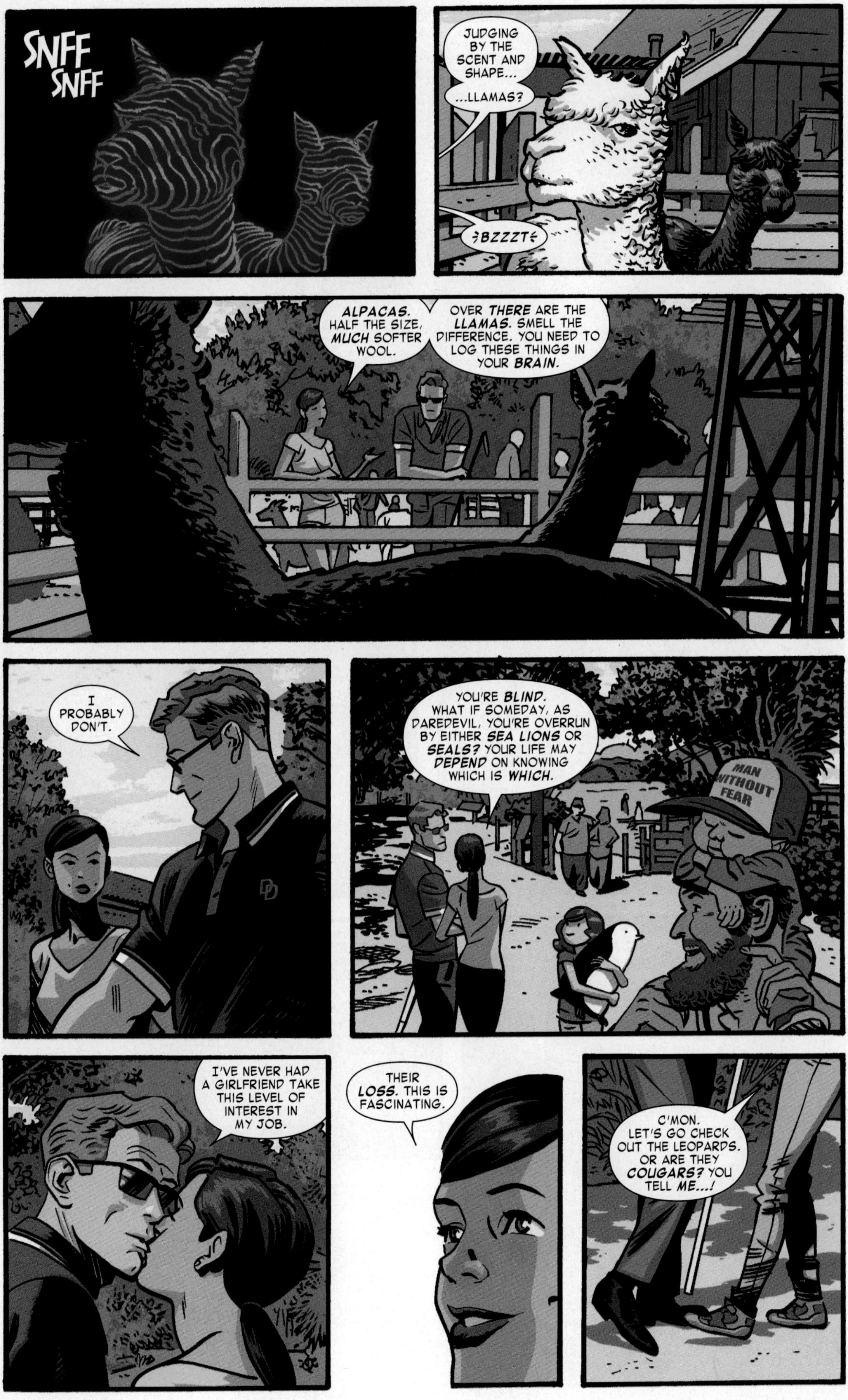
SNFF SNFF
JUDGING BY THE SCENT AND SHAPE...
...LLAMAS?
BZZZT
ALPACAS. HALF THE SIZE, MUCH SOFTER WOOL.
OVER THERE ARE THE LLAMAS. SMELL THE DIFFERENCE. YOU NEED TO LOG THESE THINGS IN YOUR BRAIN.
I PROBABLY DON'T.
YOU'RE BLIND. WHAT IF SOMEDAY, AS DAREDEVIL, YOU'RE OVERRUN BY EITHER SEA LIONS OR SEALS? YOUR LIFE MAY DEPEND ON KNOWING WHICH IS WHICH.
MAN WITHOUT FEAR
I'VE NEVER HAD A GIRLFRIEND TAKE THIS LEVEL OF INTEREST IN MY JOB.
THEIR LOSS. THIS IS FASCINATING.
C'MON. LET'S GO CHECK OUT THE LEOPARDS. OR ARE THEY COUGARS? YOU TELL ME...!

Kirsten McDuffie is the best thing that's happened to me in a long while.

I got disbarred in New York. My best friend's dealing with cancer. I had to move *cross-country* once I publicly outed myself as *Daredevil*.

And she's been with me every step of the way.

We even set up a *law practice* together.

DOES IT REALLY NOT BOTHER YOU THAT MOST OF OUR CLIENTS ASK FOR *ME*?

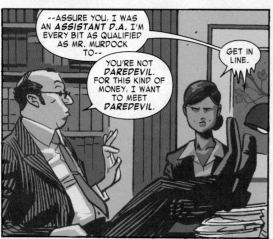

--ASSURE YOU, I WAS AN *ASSISTANT D.A.* I'M EVERY BIT AS QUALIFIED AS MR. MURDOCK TO--

GET IN LINE.

YOU'RE NOT *DAREDEVIL*. FOR THIS KIND OF MONEY, I WANT TO MEET *DAREDEVIL*.

NOPE.

Liar.

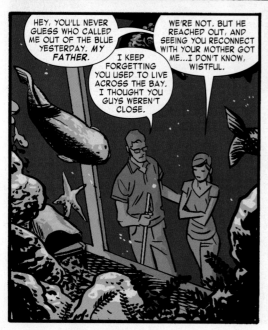

HEY, YOU'LL NEVER GUESS WHO CALLED ME OUT OF THE BLUE YESTERDAY. *MY FATHER*.

I KEEP FORGETTING YOU USED TO LIVE ACROSS THE BAY. I THOUGHT YOU GUYS WEREN'T CLOSE.

WE'RE NOT. BUT HE REACHED OUT, AND SEEING YOU RECONNECT WITH YOUR MOTHER GOT ME...I DON'T KNOW, WISTFUL.

HE AND THE PIECE-OF-WORK *BARRACUDA* HE MARRIED INVITED US OUT FOR AN AFTERNOON *SAIL*. YOU GAME?

"*BARRACUDA*"?

TRUST ME. YOU WILL *HATE* HER.

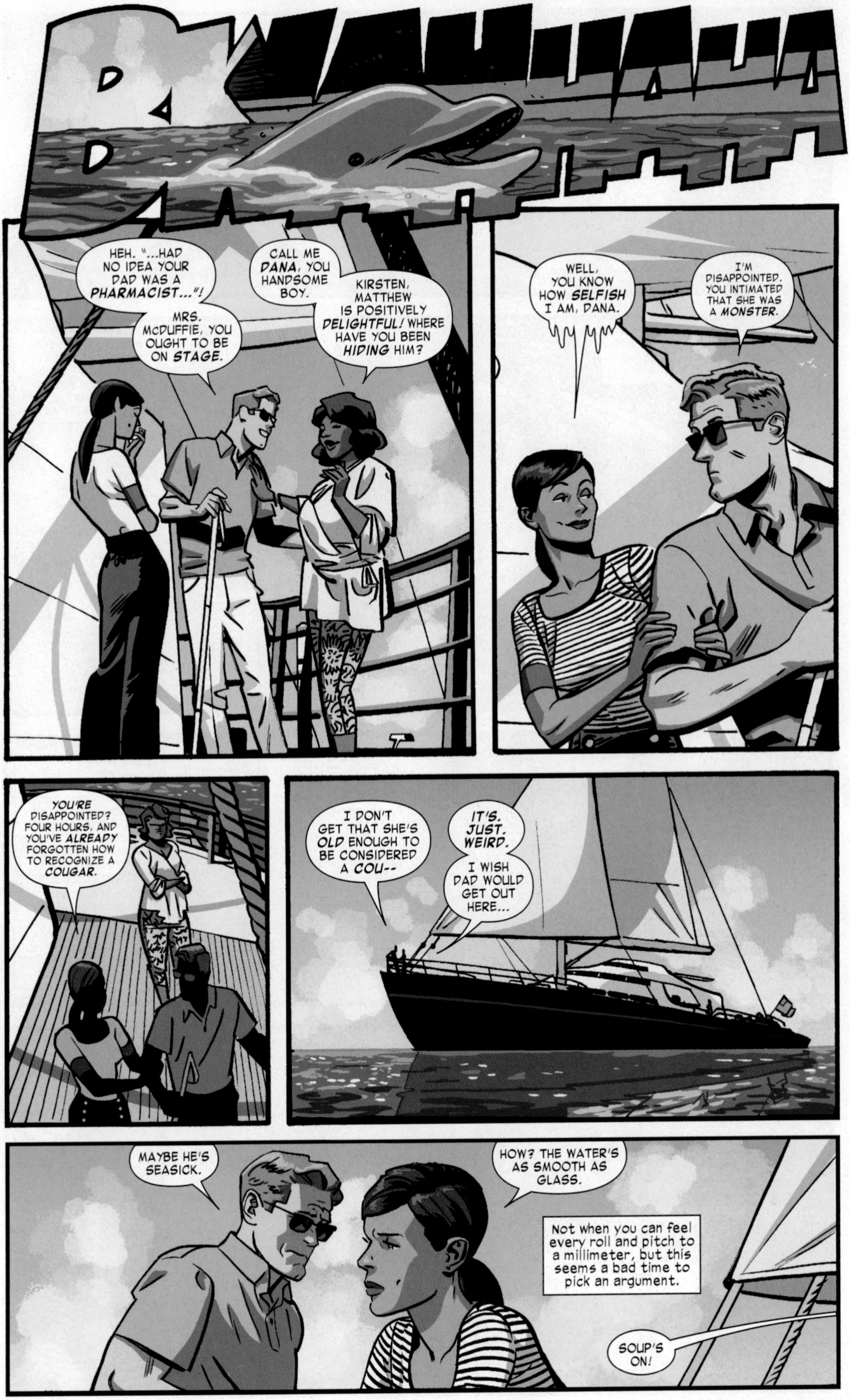

BWAHHAHA DADADA
HEH. "...HAD NO IDEA YOUR DAD WAS A PHARMACIST..."!
MRS. McDUFFIE, YOU OUGHT TO BE ON STAGE.
CALL ME DANA, YOU HANDSOME BOY.
KIRSTEN, MATTHEW IS POSITIVELY DELIGHTFUL! WHERE HAVE YOU BEEN HIDING HIM?
WELL, YOU KNOW HOW SELFISH I AM, DANA.
I'M DISAPPOINTED. YOU INTIMATED THAT SHE WAS A MONSTER.
YOU'RE DISAPPOINTED? FOUR HOURS, AND YOU'VE ALREADY FORGOTTEN HOW TO RECOGNIZE A COUGAR.
I DON'T GET THAT SHE'S OLD ENOUGH TO BE CONSIDERED A COU--
IT'S. JUST. WEIRD.
I WISH DAD WOULD GET OUT HERE...
MAYBE HE'S SEASICK.
HOW? THE WATER'S AS SMOOTH AS GLASS.
Not when you can feel every roll and pitch to a millimeter, but this seems a bad time to pick an argument.
SOUP'S ON!

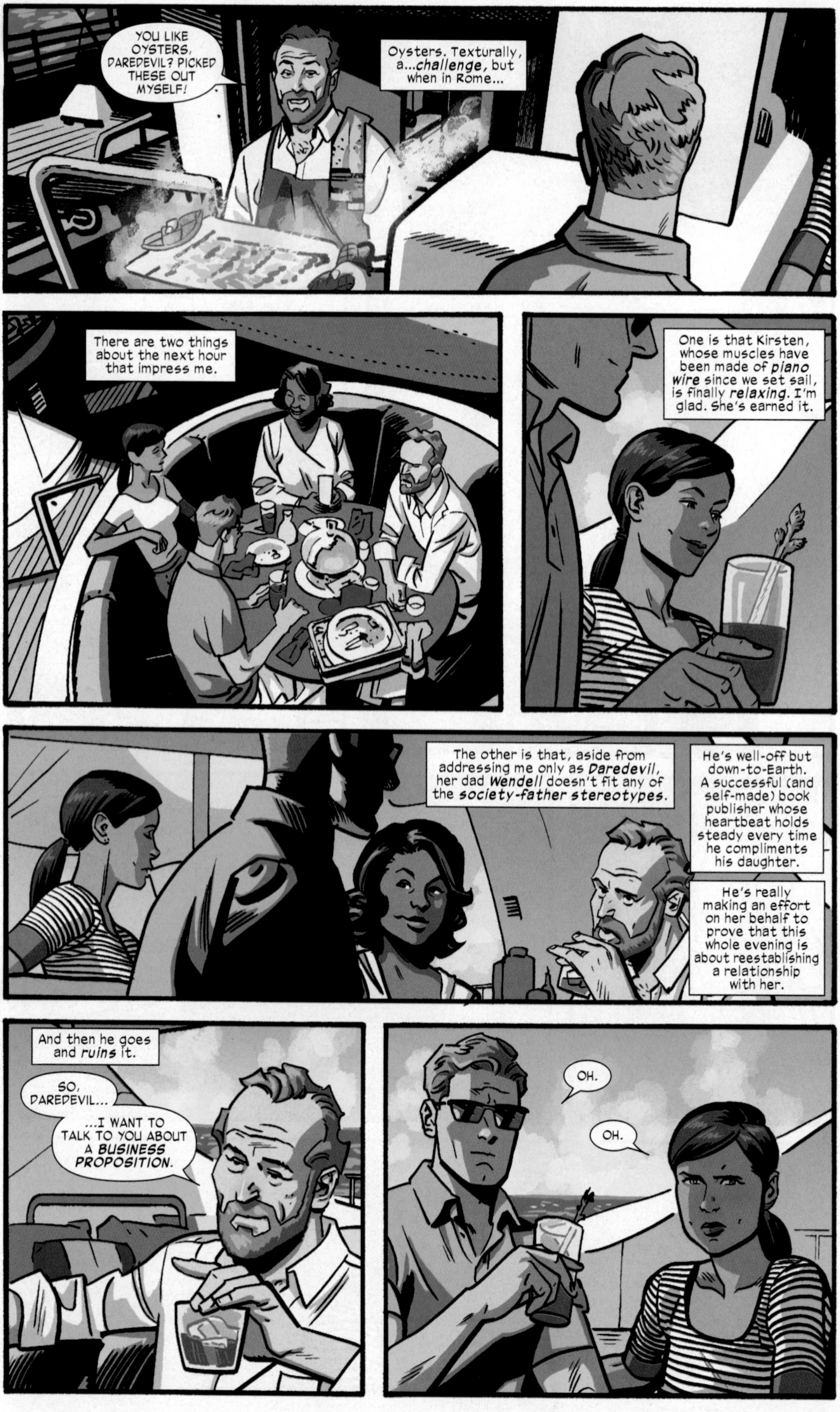

YOU LIKE OYSTERS, DAREDEVIL? PICKED THESE OUT MYSELF!
Oysters. Texturally, a...*challenge*, but when in Rome...
There are two things about the next hour that impress me.
One is that Kirsten, whose muscles have been made of *piano wire* since we set sail, is finally *relaxing*. I'm glad. She's earned it.
The other is that, aside from addressing me only as *Daredevil*, her dad *Wendell* doesn't fit any of the *society-father stereotypes*.
He's well-off but down-to-Earth. A successful (and self-made) book publisher whose heartbeat holds steady every time he compliments his daughter.
He's really making an effort on her behalf to prove that this whole evening is about reestablishing a relationship with her.
And then he goes and *ruins* it.
SO, DAREDEVIL...
...I WANT TO TALK TO YOU ABOUT A *BUSINESS PROPOSITION*.
OH.
OH.

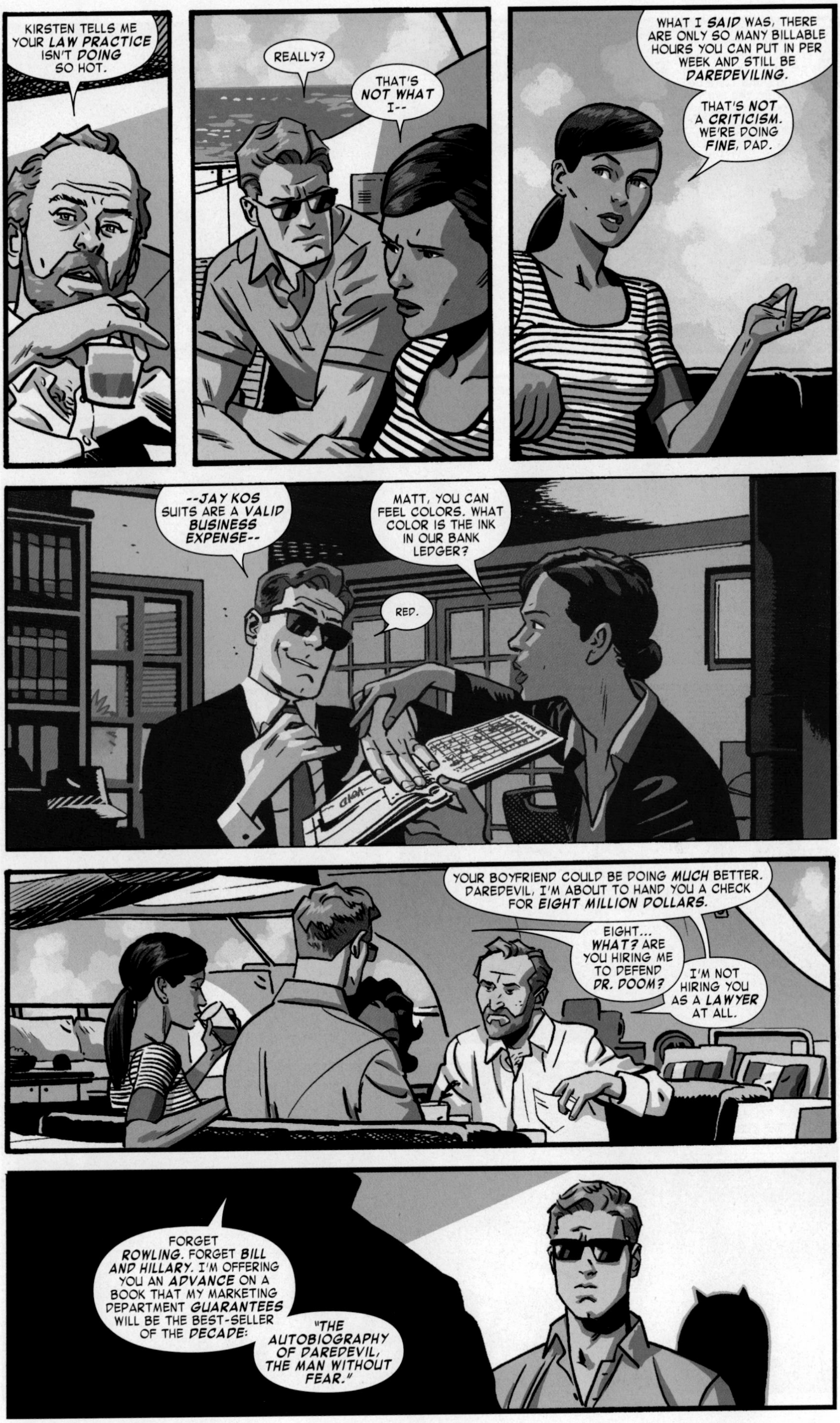
KIRSTEN TELLS ME YOUR LAW PRACTICE ISN'T DOING SO HOT.
REALLY?
THAT'S NOT WHAT I--
WHAT I SAID WAS, THERE ARE ONLY SO MANY BILLABLE HOURS YOU CAN PUT IN PER WEEK AND STILL BE DAREDEVILING.
THAT'S NOT A CRITICISM. WE'RE DOING FINE, DAD.
--JAY KOS SUITS ARE A VALID BUSINESS EXPENSE--
MATT, YOU CAN FEEL COLORS. WHAT COLOR IS THE INK IN OUR BANK LEDGER?
RED.
YOUR BOYFRIEND COULD BE DOING MUCH BETTER. DAREDEVIL, I'M ABOUT TO HAND YOU A CHECK FOR EIGHT MILLION DOLLARS.
EIGHT... WHAT? ARE YOU HIRING ME TO DEFEND DR. DOOM?
I'M NOT HIRING YOU AS A LAWYER AT ALL.
FORGET ROWLING. FORGET BILL AND HILLARY. I'M OFFERING YOU AN ADVANCE ON A BOOK THAT MY MARKETING DEPARTMENT GUARANTEES WILL BE THE BEST-SELLER OF THE DECADE:
"THE AUTOBIOGRAPHY OF DAREDEVIL, THE MAN WITHOUT FEAR."

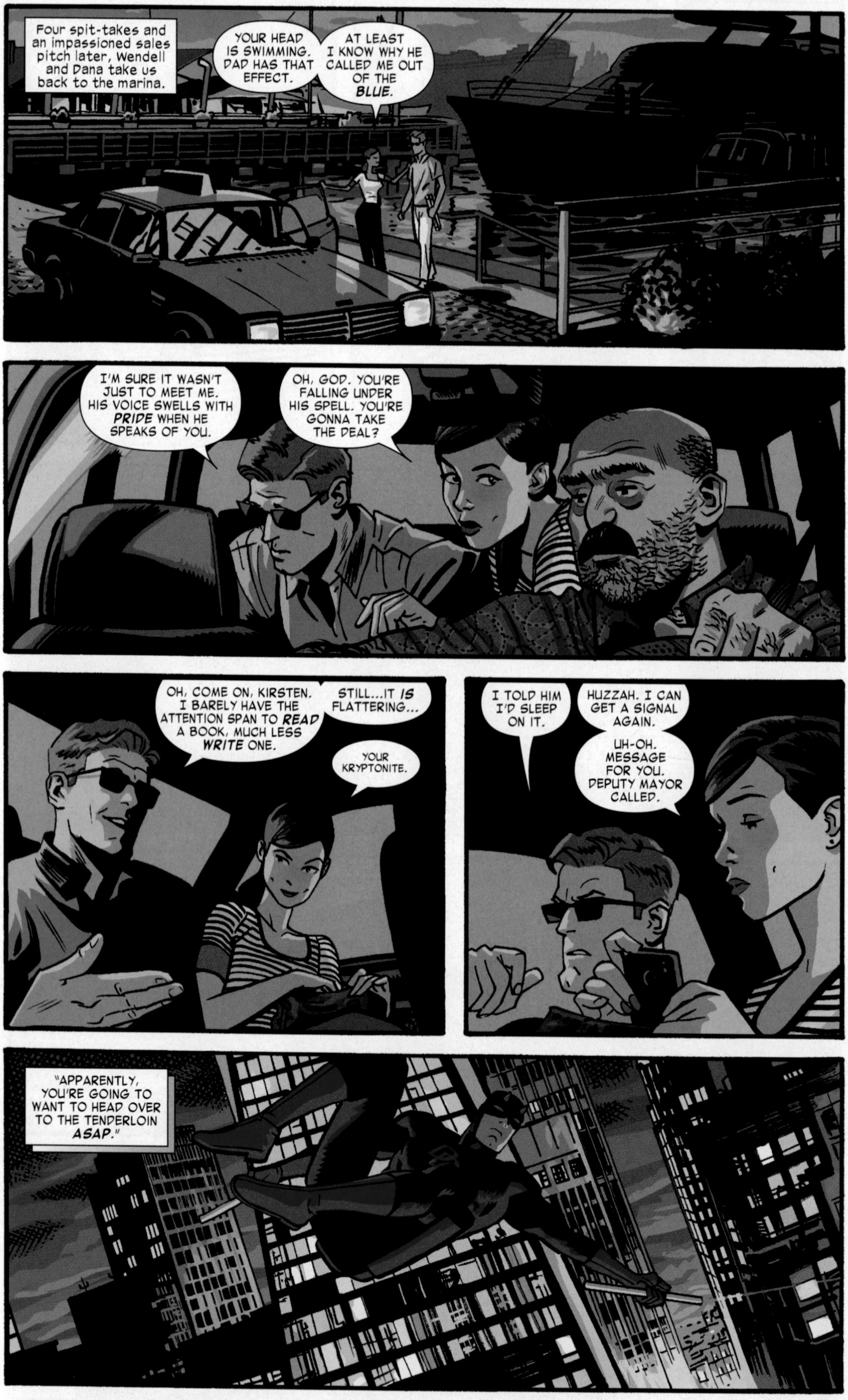

Four spit-takes and an impassioned sales pitch later, Wendell and Dana take us back to the marina.
YOUR HEAD IS SWIMMING. DAD HAS THAT EFFECT.
AT LEAST I KNOW WHY HE CALLED ME OUT OF THE BLUE.
I'M SURE IT WASN'T JUST TO MEET ME. HIS VOICE SWELLS WITH PRIDE WHEN HE SPEAKS OF YOU.
OH, GOD. YOU'RE FALLING UNDER HIS SPELL. YOU'RE GONNA TAKE THE DEAL?
OH, COME ON, KIRSTEN. I BARELY HAVE THE ATTENTION SPAN TO READ A BOOK, MUCH LESS WRITE ONE.
STILL...IT IS FLATTERING...
YOUR KRYPTONITE.
I TOLD HIM I'D SLEEP ON IT.
HUZZAH. I CAN GET A SIGNAL AGAIN.
UH-OH. MESSAGE FOR YOU. DEPUTY MAYOR CALLED.
"APPARENTLY, YOU'RE GOING TO WANT TO HEAD OVER TO THE TENDERLOIN ASAP."

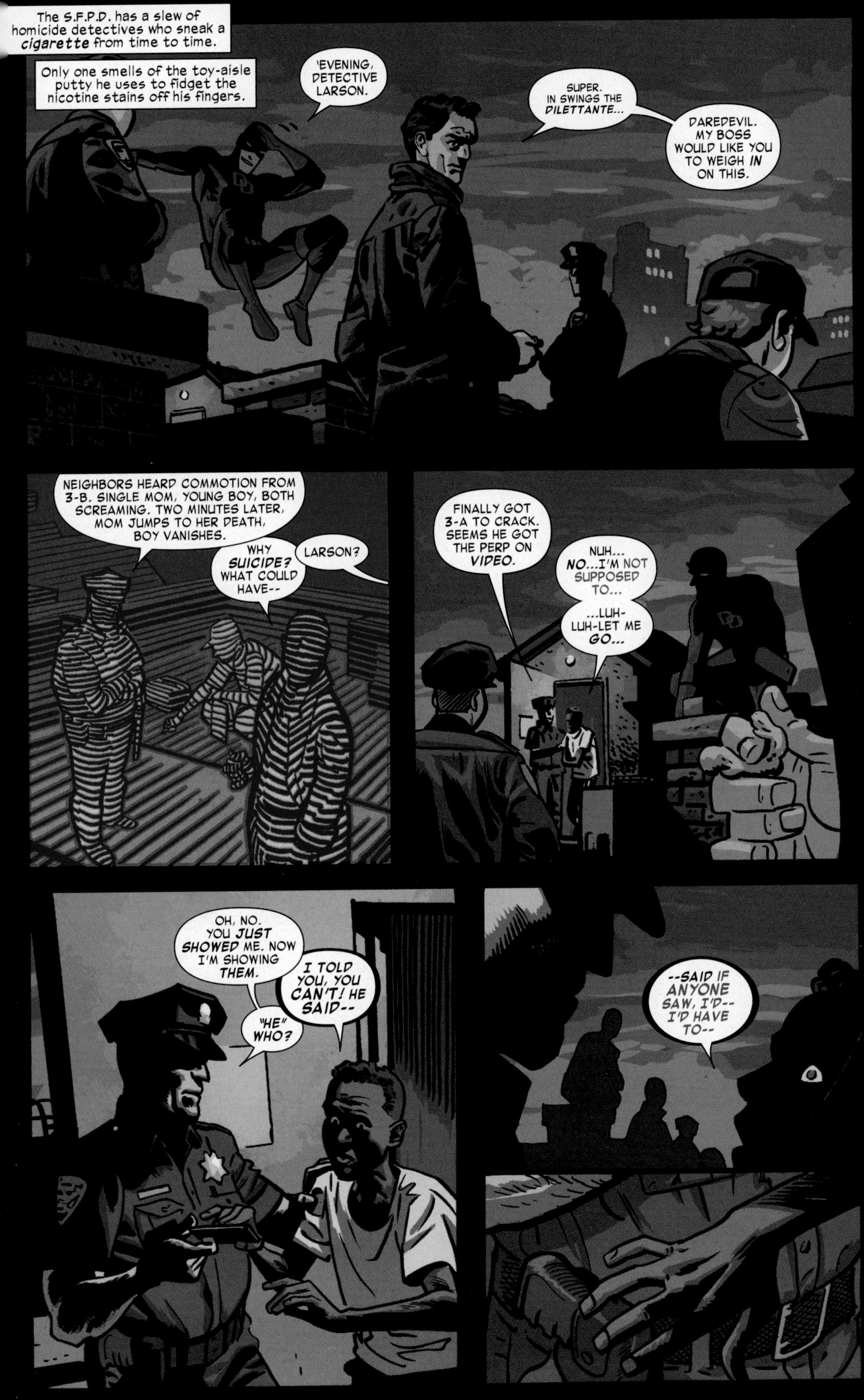
The S.F.P.D. has a slew of homicide detectives who sneak a *cigarette* from time to time.
Only one smells of the toy-aisle putty he uses to fidget the nicotine stains off his fingers.
'EVENING, DETECTIVE LARSON.
SUPER. IN SWINGS THE *DILETTANTE*...
DAREDEVIL. MY BOSS WOULD LIKE YOU TO WEIGH *IN* ON THIS.
NEIGHBORS HEARD COMMOTION FROM 3-B. SINGLE MOM, YOUNG BOY, BOTH SCREAMING. TWO MINUTES LATER, MOM JUMPS TO HER DEATH, BOY VANISHES.
WHY *SUICIDE?* WHAT COULD HAVE--
LARSON?
FINALLY GOT 3-A TO CRACK. SEEMS HE GOT THE PERP ON *VIDEO.*
NUH... *NO*...I'M NOT SUPPOSED TO...
...LUH-LUH-LET ME *GO*...
OH, NO. YOU *JUST SHOWED* ME. NOW I'M SHOWING *THEM.*
I TOLD YOU, YOU *CAN'T!* HE *SAID*--
"HE" WHO?
--*SAID* IF *ANYONE* SAW, I'D--I'D HAVE TO--

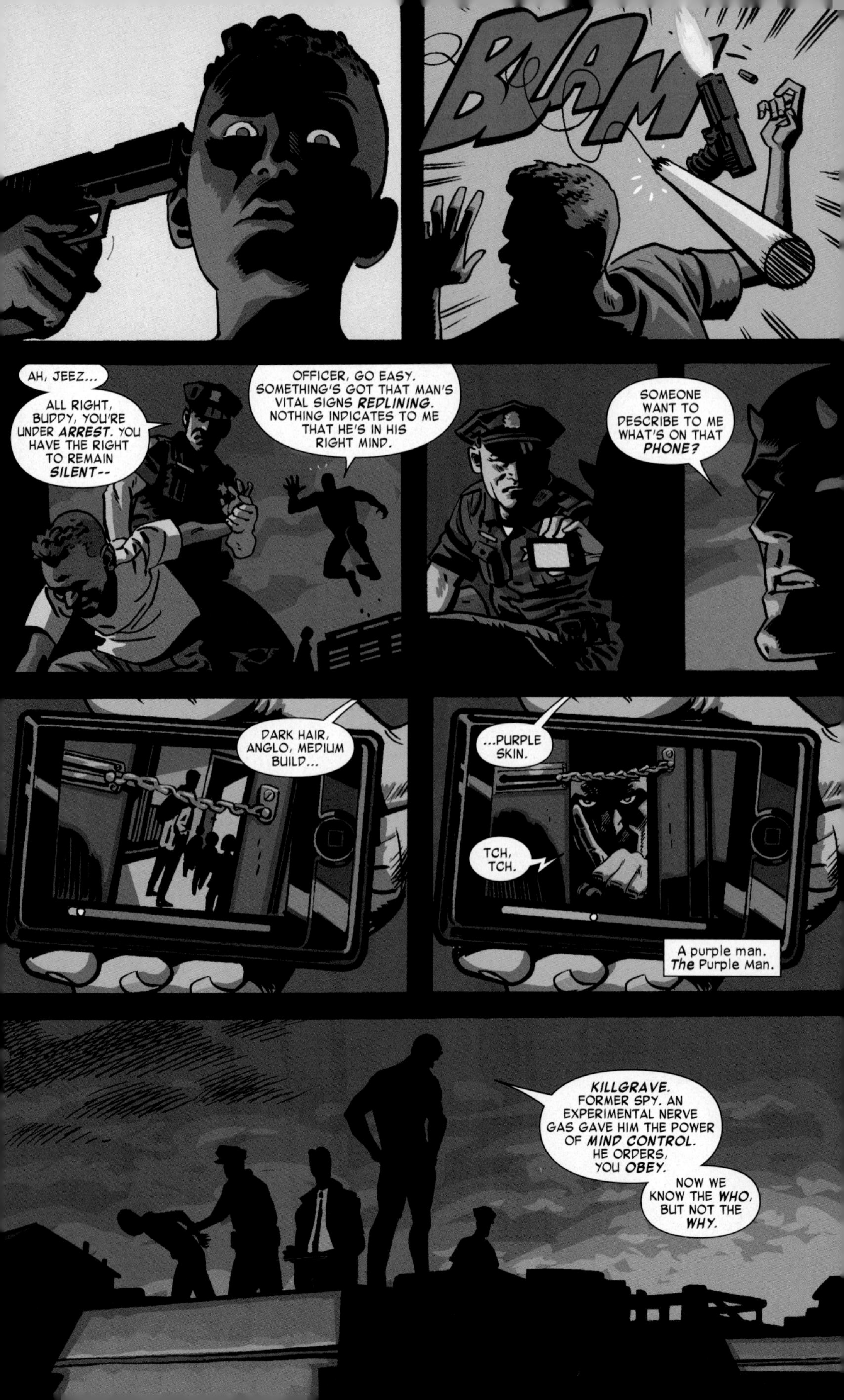
BLAM
AH, JEEZ...
ALL RIGHT, BUDDY, YOU'RE UNDER ARREST. YOU HAVE THE RIGHT TO REMAIN SILENT--
OFFICER, GO EASY. SOMETHING'S GOT THAT MAN'S VITAL SIGNS REDLINING. NOTHING INDICATES TO ME THAT HE'S IN HIS RIGHT MIND.
SOMEONE WANT TO DESCRIBE TO ME WHAT'S ON THAT PHONE?
DARK HAIR, ANGLO, MEDIUM BUILD...
...PURPLE SKIN.
TCH, TCH.
A purple man. The Purple Man.
KILLGRAVE. FORMER SPY. AN EXPERIMENTAL NERVE GAS GAVE HIM THE POWER OF MIND CONTROL. HE ORDERS, YOU OBEY.
NOW WE KNOW THE WHO, BUT NOT THE WHY.

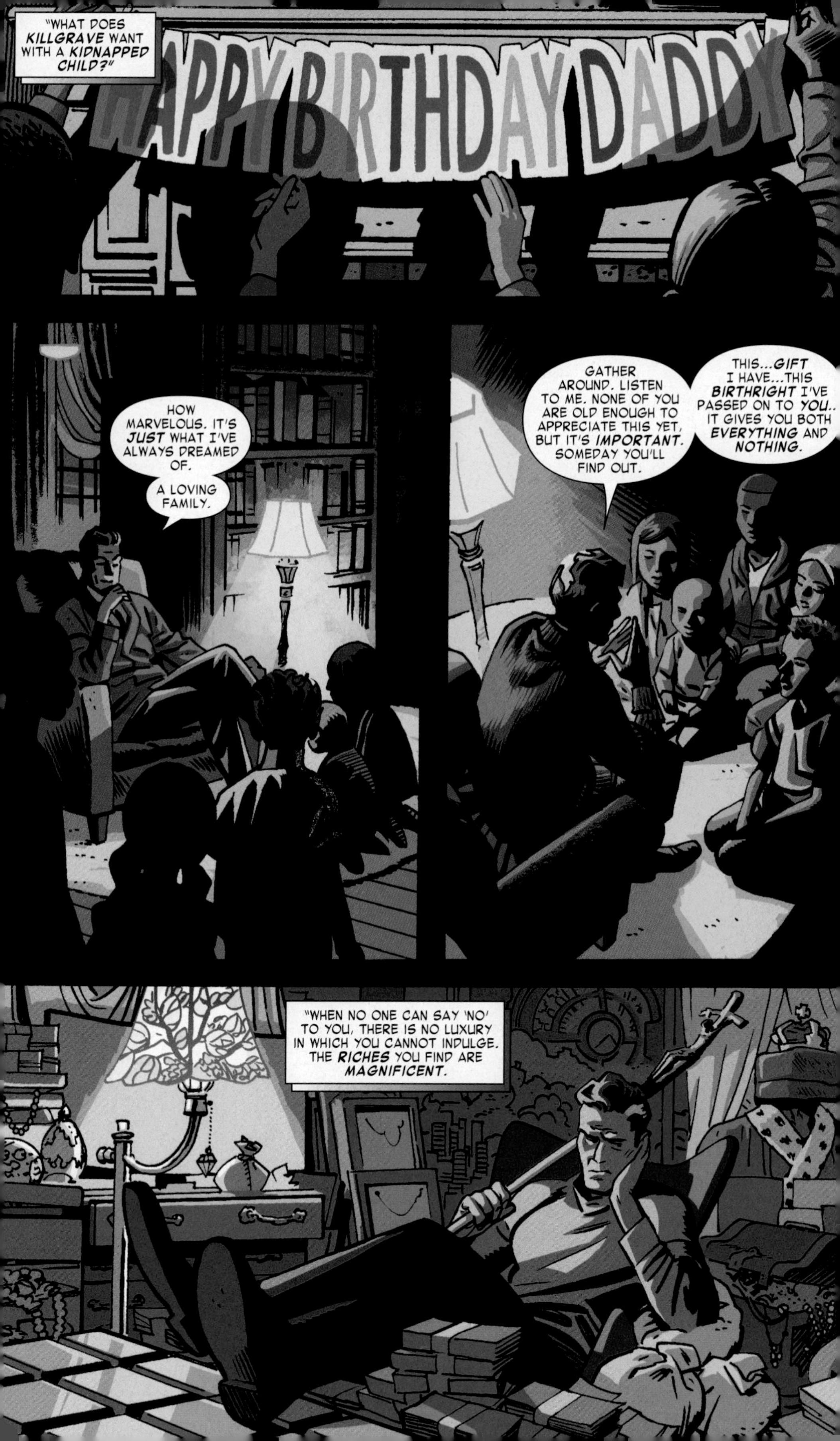
"WHAT DOES KILLGRAVE WANT WITH A KIDNAPPED CHILD?"
HAPPY BIRTHDAY DADDY
HOW MARVELOUS. IT'S JUST WHAT I'VE ALWAYS DREAMED OF.
A LOVING FAMILY.
GATHER AROUND. LISTEN TO ME. NONE OF YOU ARE OLD ENOUGH TO APPRECIATE THIS YET, BUT IT'S IMPORTANT. SOMEDAY YOU'LL FIND OUT.
THIS...GIFT I HAVE...THIS BIRTHRIGHT I'VE PASSED ON TO YOU.. IT GIVES YOU BOTH EVERYTHING AND NOTHING.
"WHEN NO ONE CAN SAY 'NO' TO YOU, THERE IS NO LUXURY IN WHICH YOU CANNOT INDULGE. THE RICHES YOU FIND ARE MAGNIFICENT.

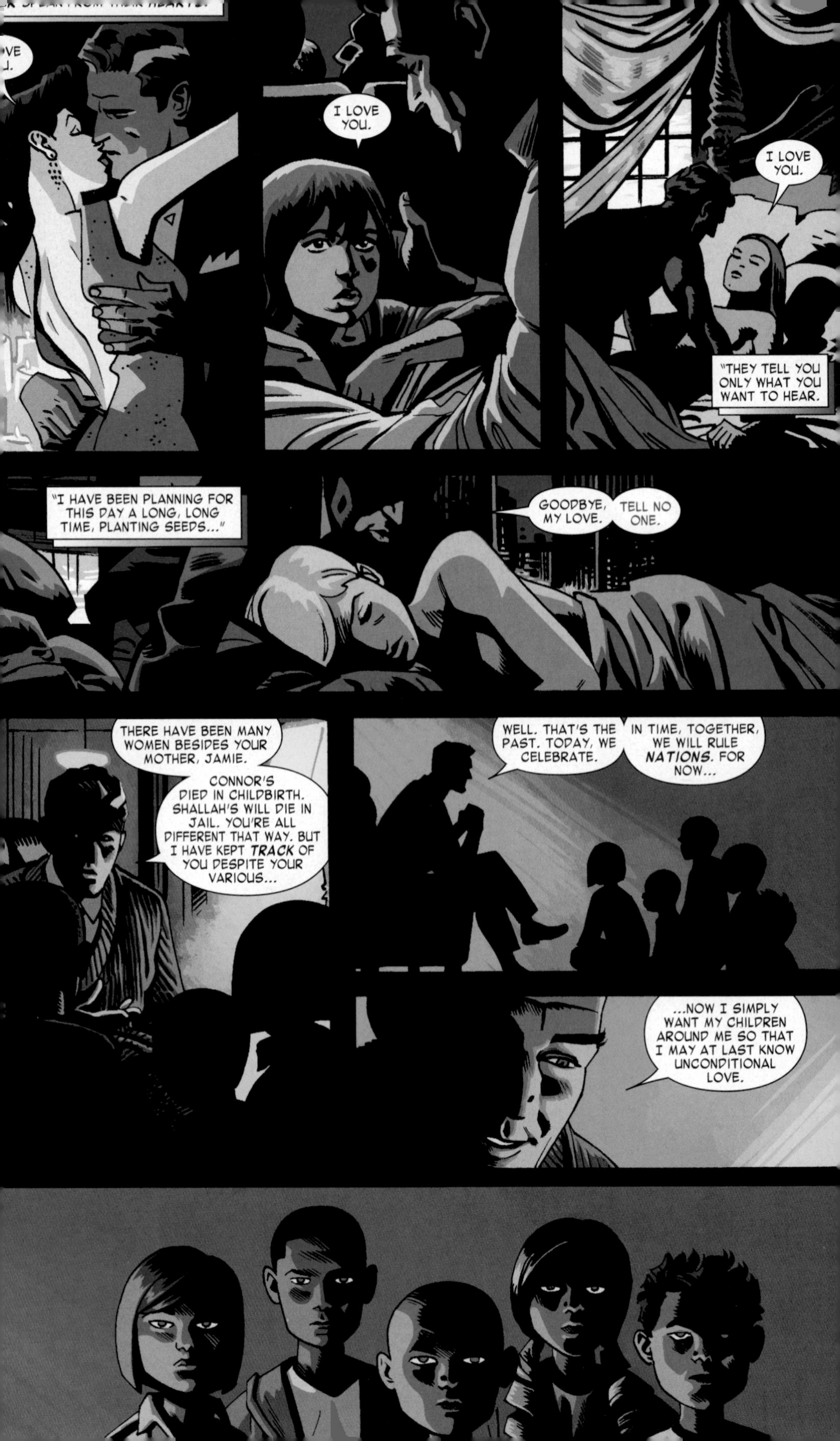
I LOVE YOU.
I LOVE YOU.
"THEY TELL YOU ONLY WHAT YOU WANT TO HEAR.
"I HAVE BEEN PLANNING FOR THIS DAY A LONG, LONG TIME, PLANTING SEEDS..."
GOODBYE, MY LOVE.
TELL NO ONE.
THERE HAVE BEEN MANY WOMEN BESIDES YOUR MOTHER, JAMIE.
CONNOR'S DIED IN CHILDBIRTH. SHALLAH'S WILL DIE IN JAIL. YOU'RE ALL DIFFERENT THAT WAY. BUT I HAVE KEPT TRACK OF YOU DESPITE YOUR VARIOUS...
WELL. THAT'S THE PAST. TODAY, WE CELEBRATE.
IN TIME, TOGETHER, WE WILL RULE NATIONS. FOR NOW...
...NOW I SIMPLY WANT MY CHILDREN AROUND ME SO THAT I MAY AT LAST KNOW UNCONDITIONAL LOVE.

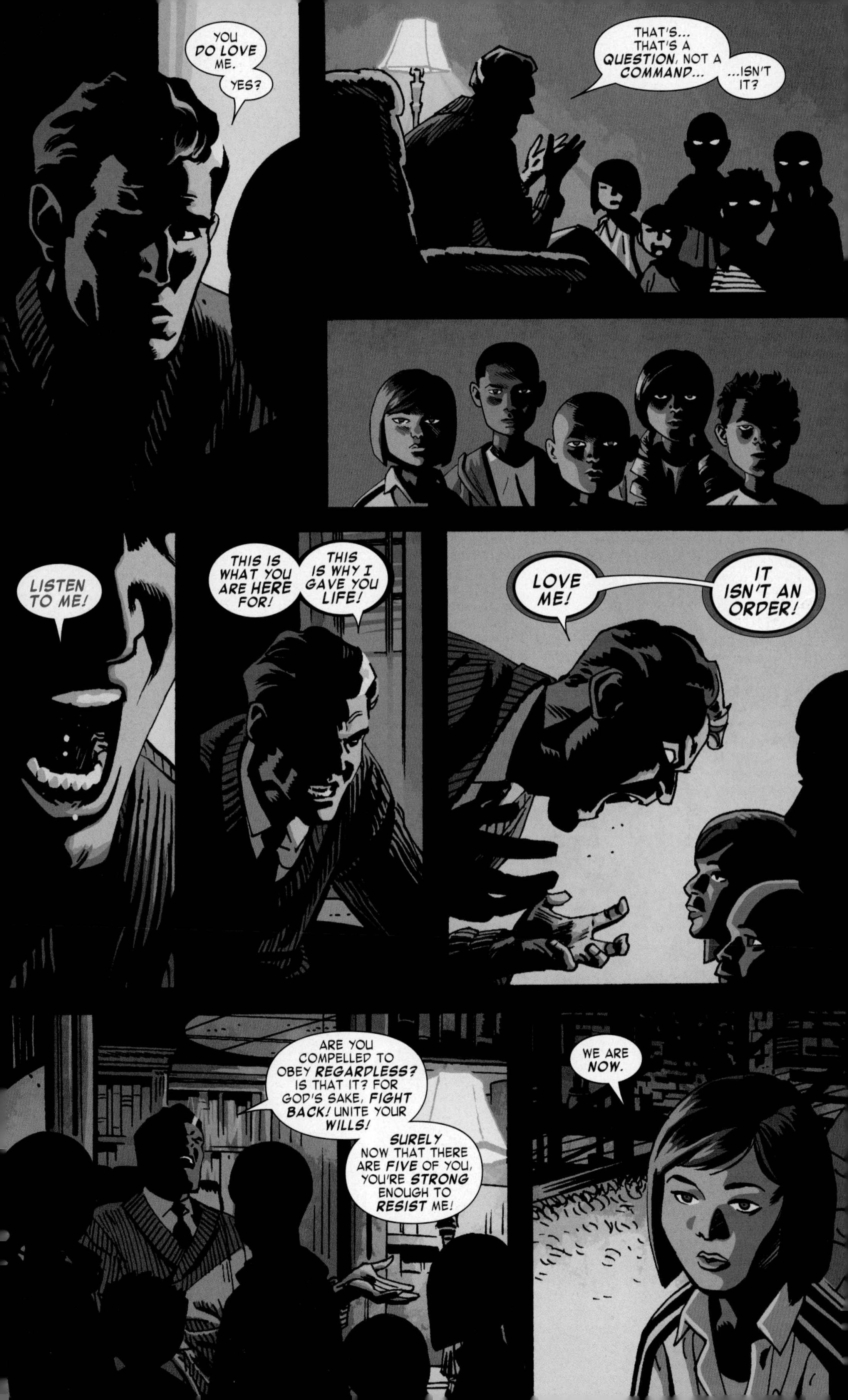
YOU DO LOVE ME.
YES?
THAT'S... THAT'S A QUESTION, NOT A COMMAND...
...ISN'T IT?
LISTEN TO ME!
THIS IS WHAT YOU ARE HERE FOR!
THIS IS WHY I GAVE YOU LIFE!
LOVE ME!
IT ISN'T AN ORDER!
ARE YOU COMPELLED TO OBEY REGARDLESS? IS THAT IT? FOR GOD'S SAKE, FIGHT BACK! UNITE YOUR WILLS!
SURELY NOW THAT THERE ARE FIVE OF YOU, YOU'RE STRONG ENOUGH TO RESIST ME!
WE ARE NOW.

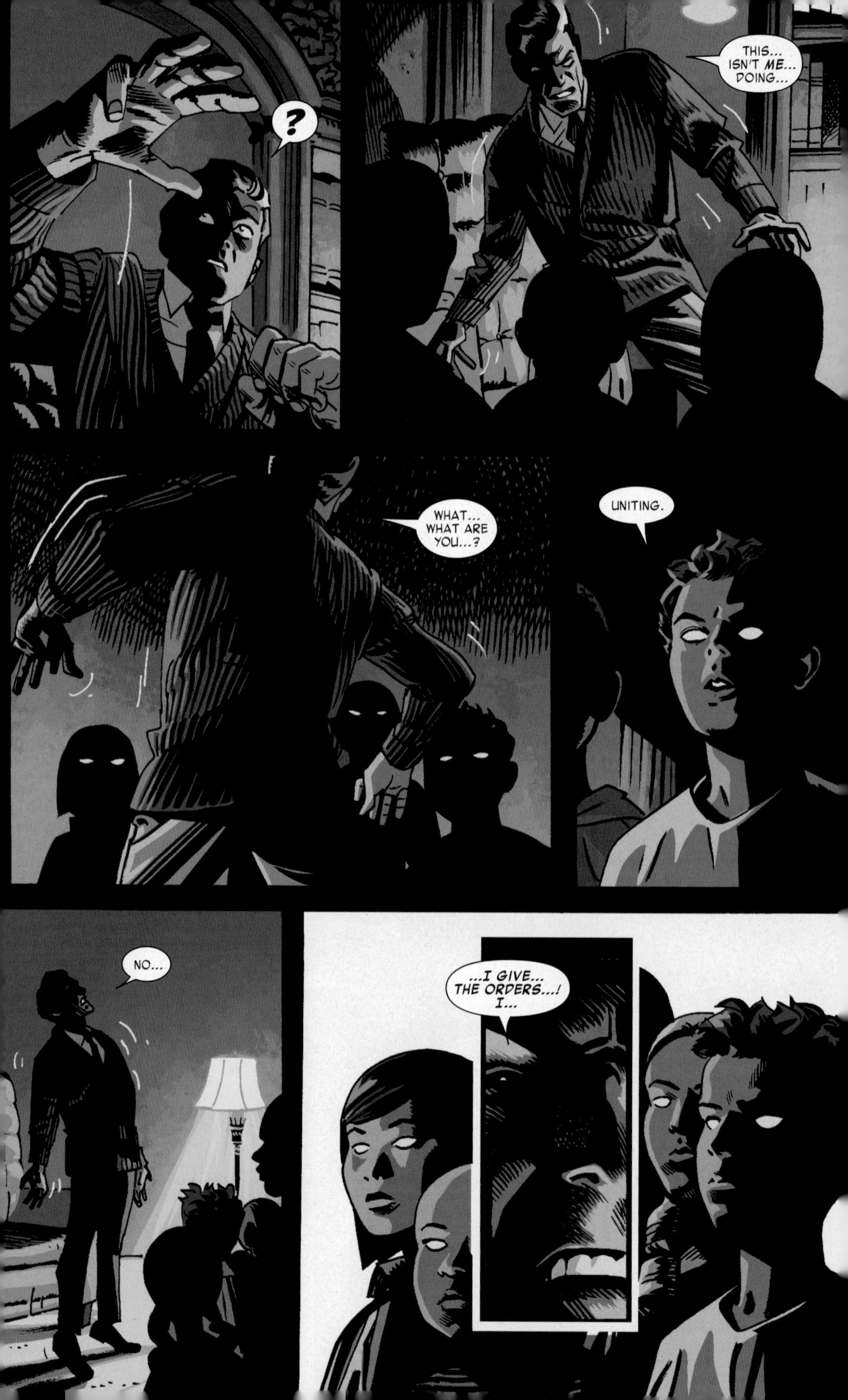
?
THIS... ISN'T ME... DOING...
WHAT... WHAT ARE YOU...?
UNITING.
NO...
...I GIVE... THE ORDERS...! I...

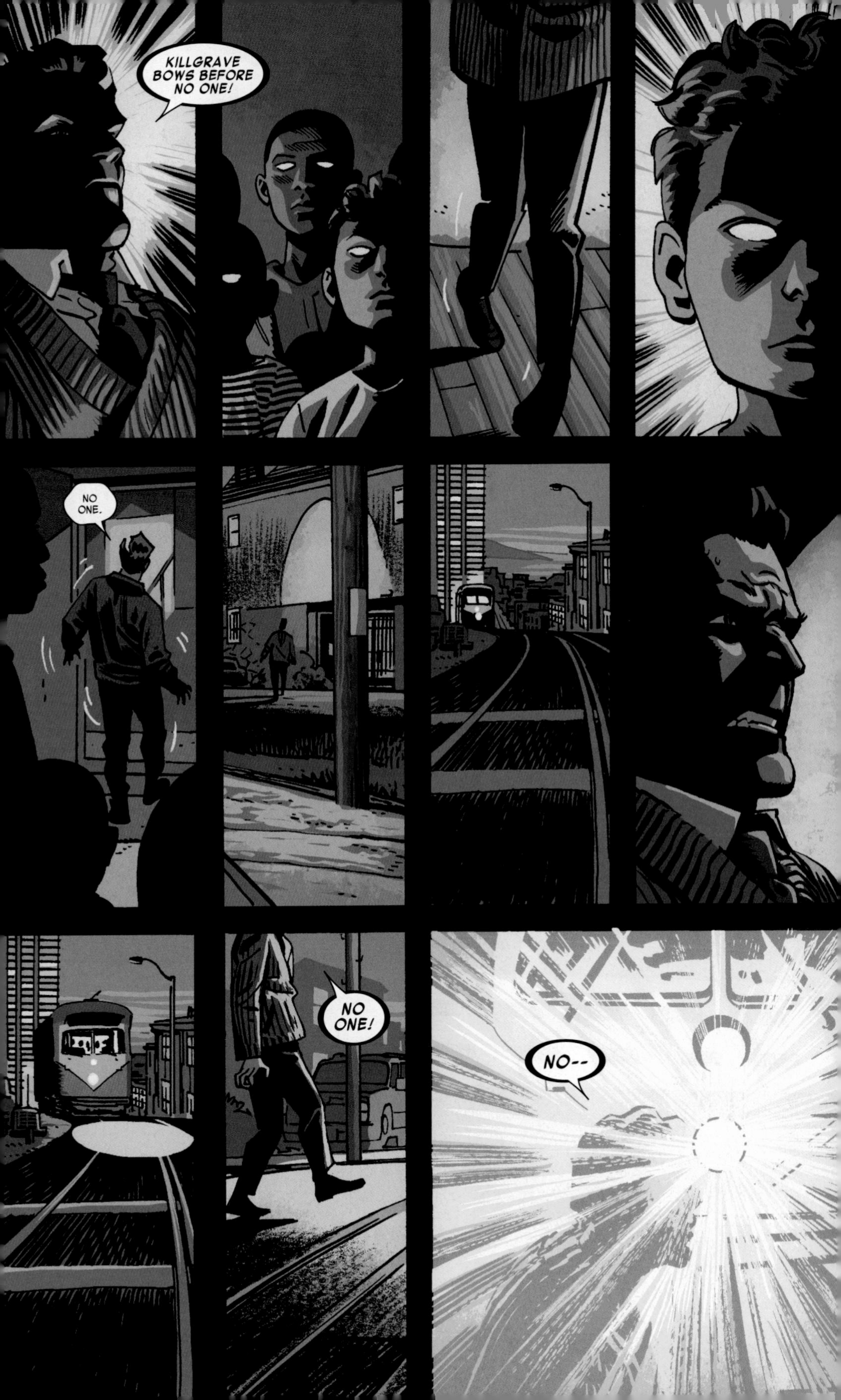
KILLGRAVE BOWS BEFORE NO ONE!
NO ONE.
NO ONE!
NO--

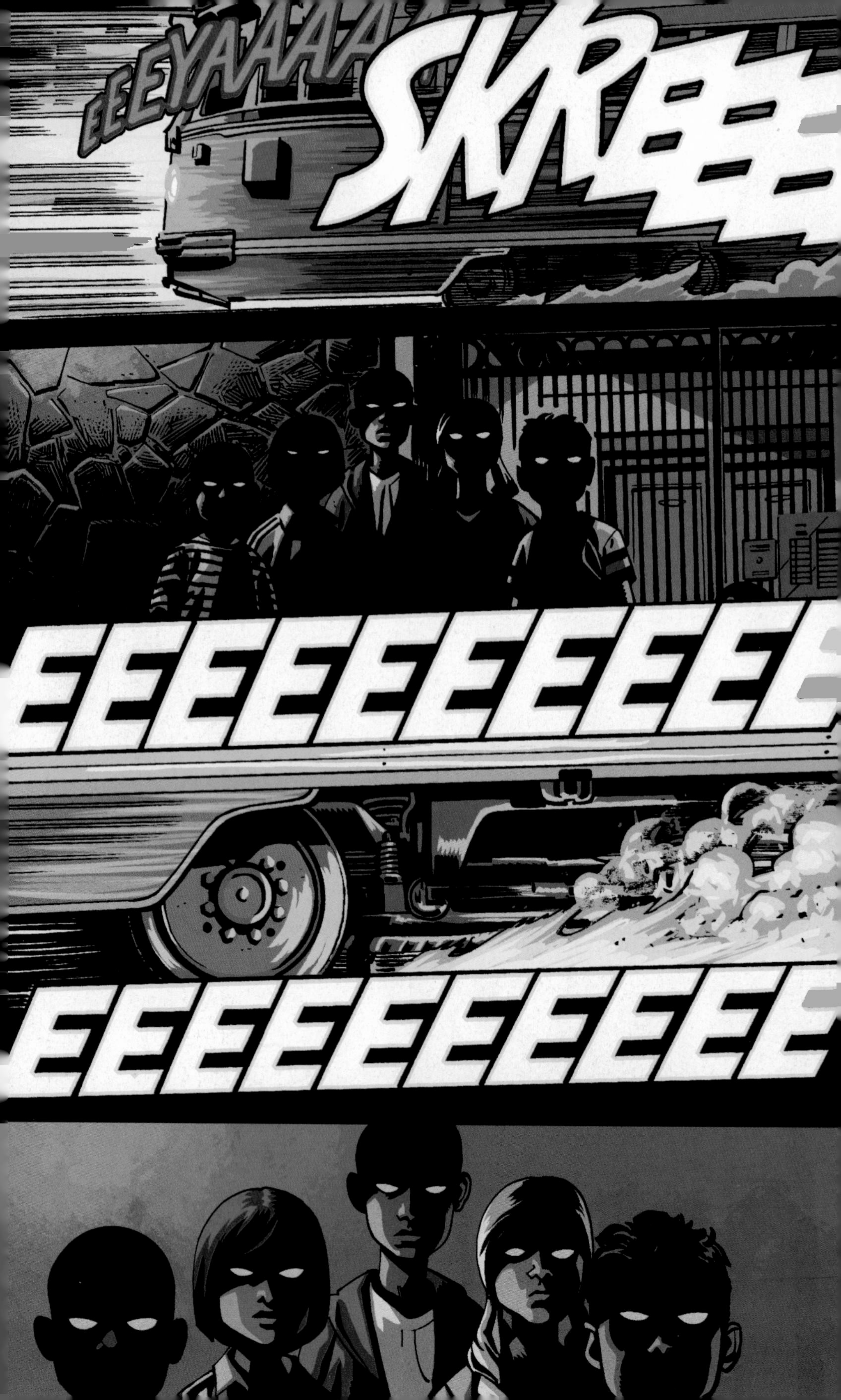
EEEYAAAA
SKREEE
EEEEEEEEEEE
EEEEEEEEEEE

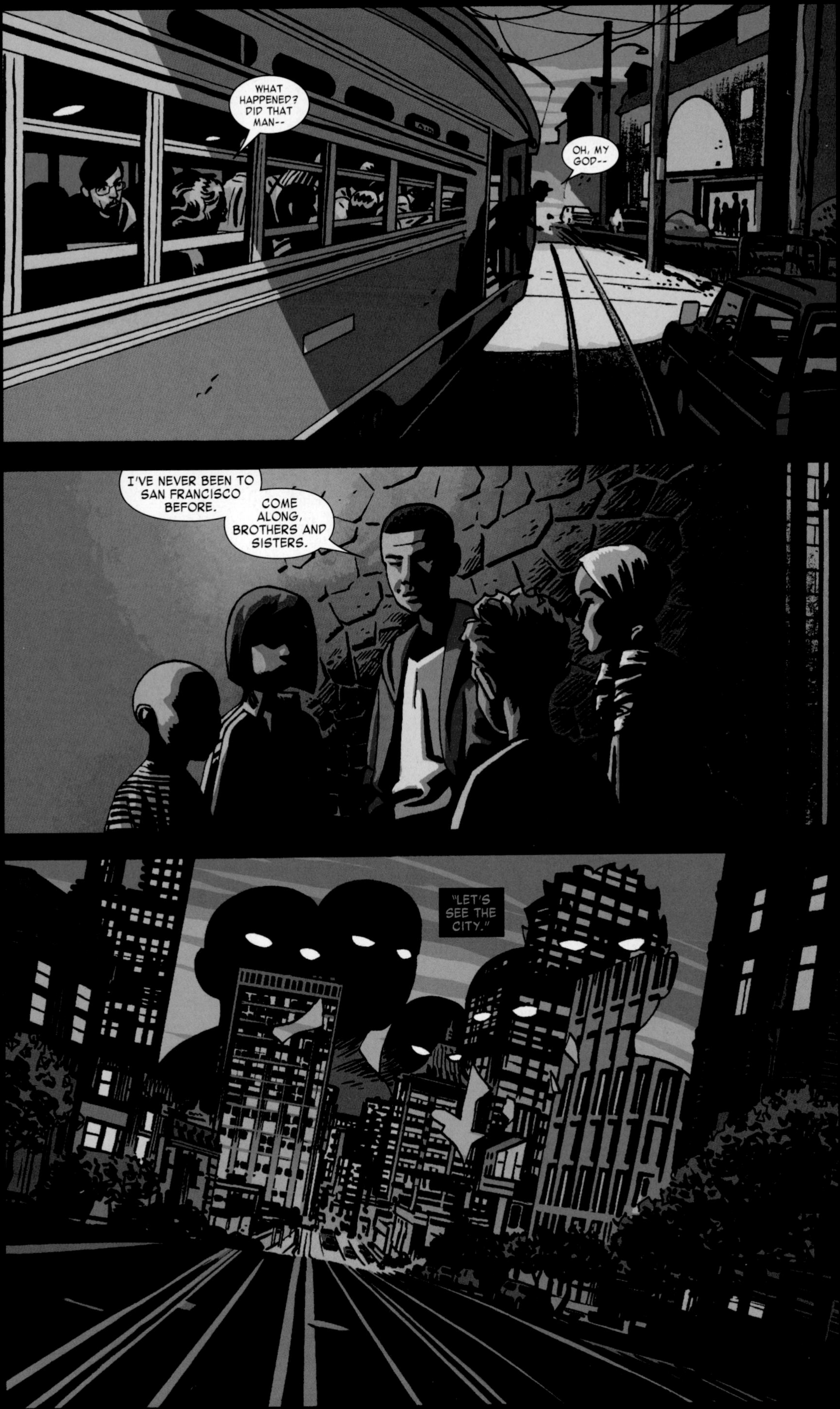
WHAT HAPPENED? DID THAT MAN--
OH, MY GOD--
I'VE NEVER BEEN TO SAN FRANCISCO BEFORE.
COME ALONG, BROTHERS AND SISTERS.
"LET'S SEE THE CITY."

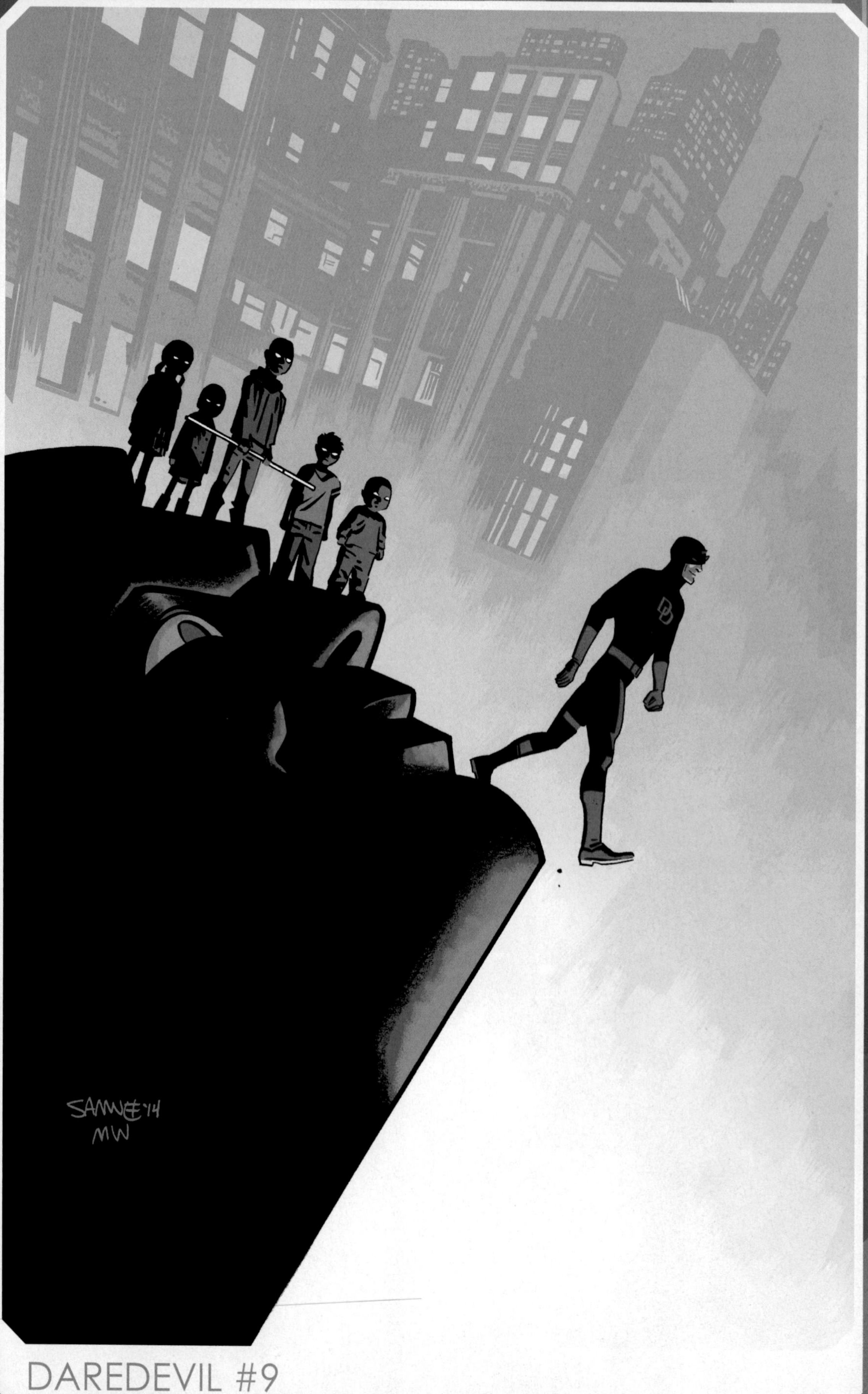

DAREDEVIL #9

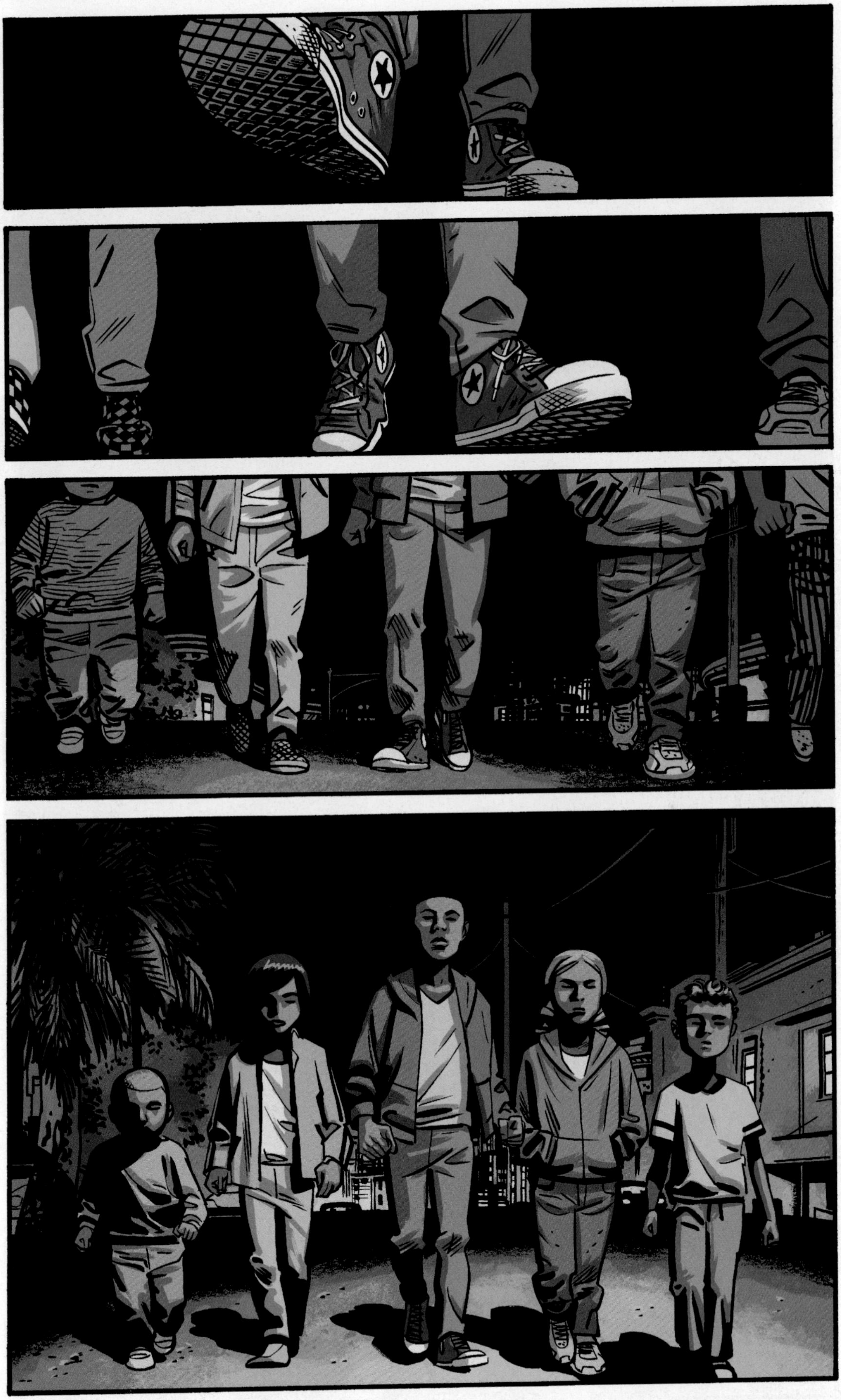

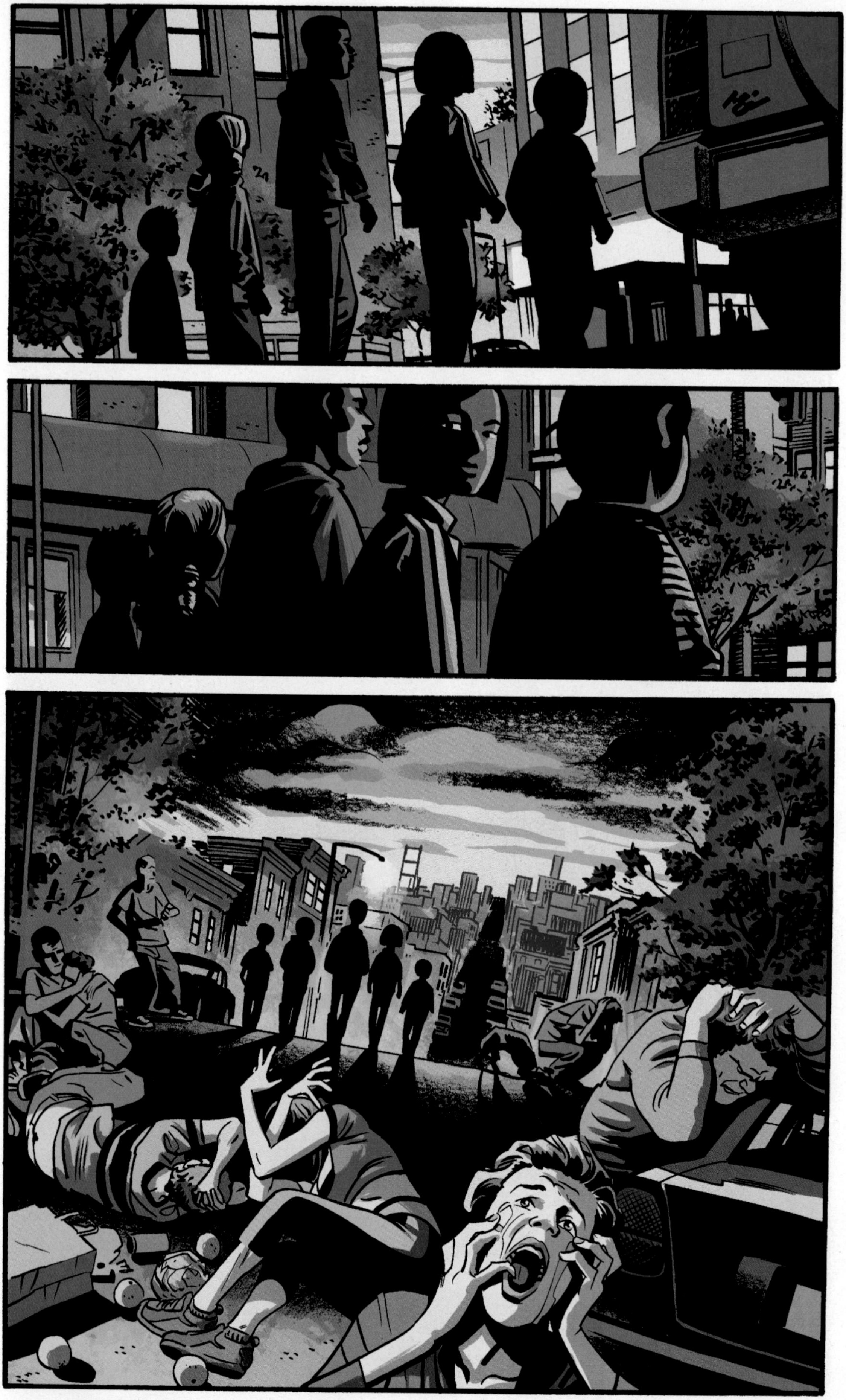

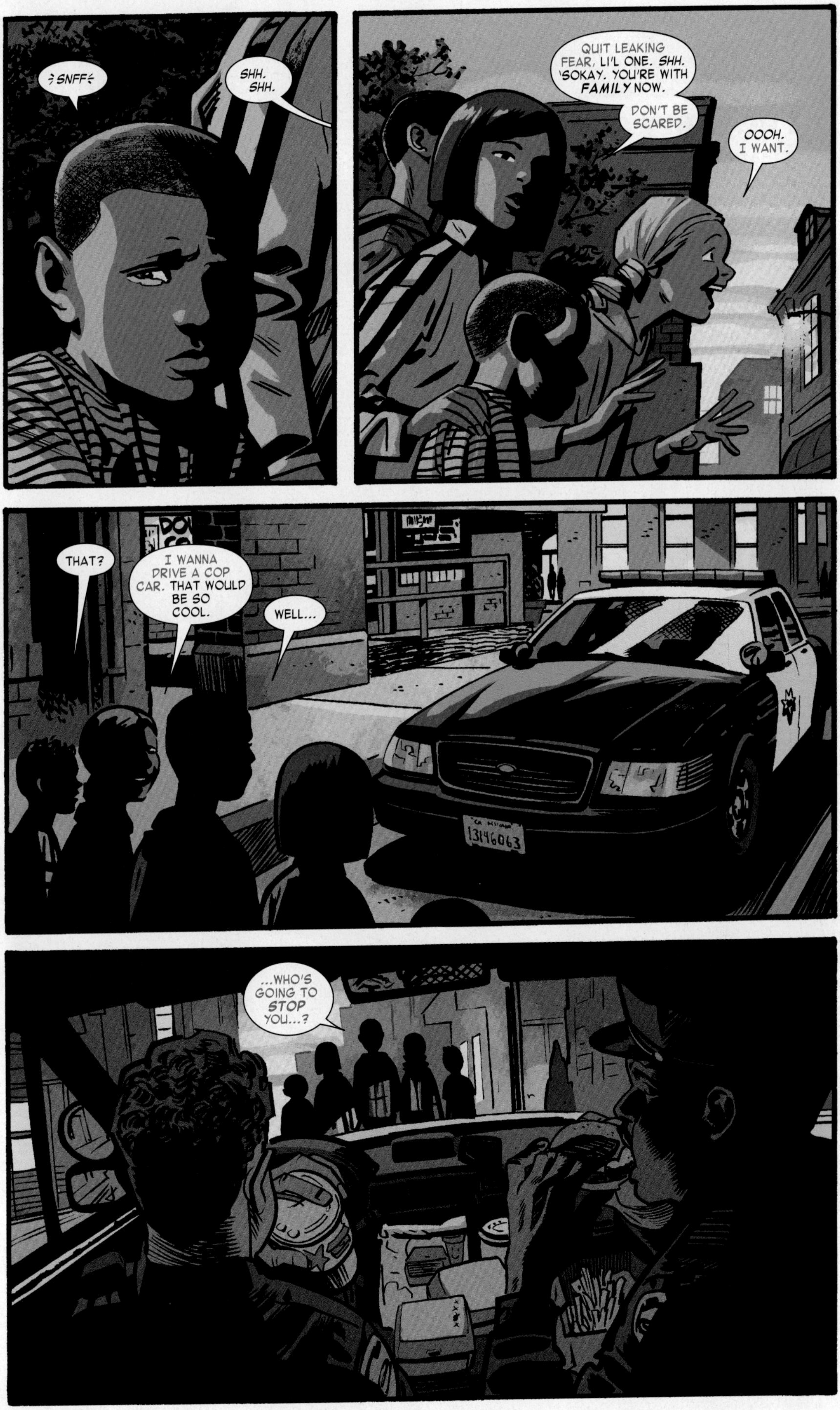

SNFF
SHH. SHH.
QUIT LEAKING FEAR, LI'L ONE. SHH. 'SOKAY. YOU'RE WITH FAMILY NOW.
DON'T BE SCARED.
OOOH. I WANT.
THAT?
I WANNA DRIVE A COP CAR. THAT WOULD BE SO COOL.
WELL...
...WHO'S GOING TO STOP YOU...?

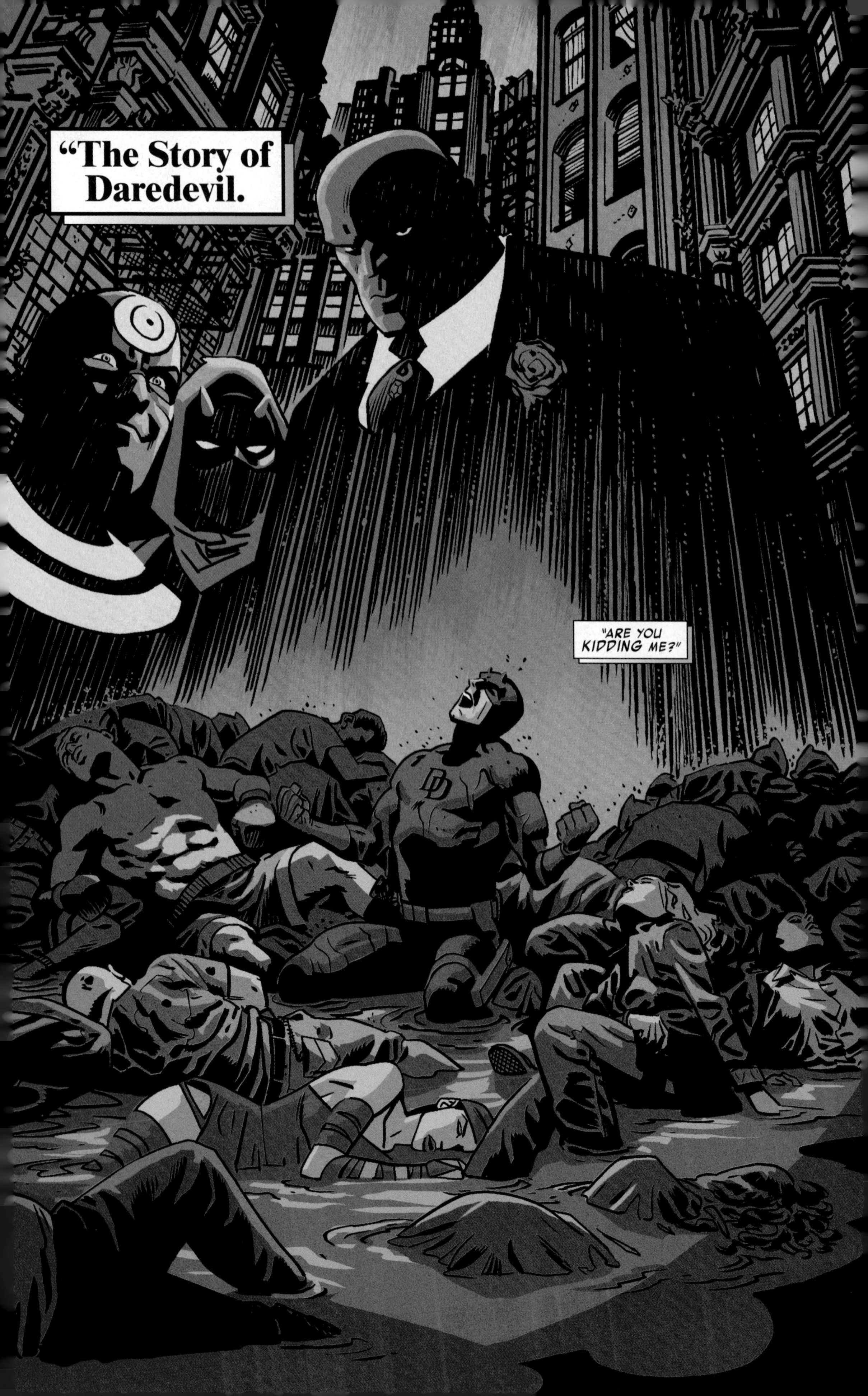
"The Story of Daredevil.
"ARE YOU KIDDING ME?"

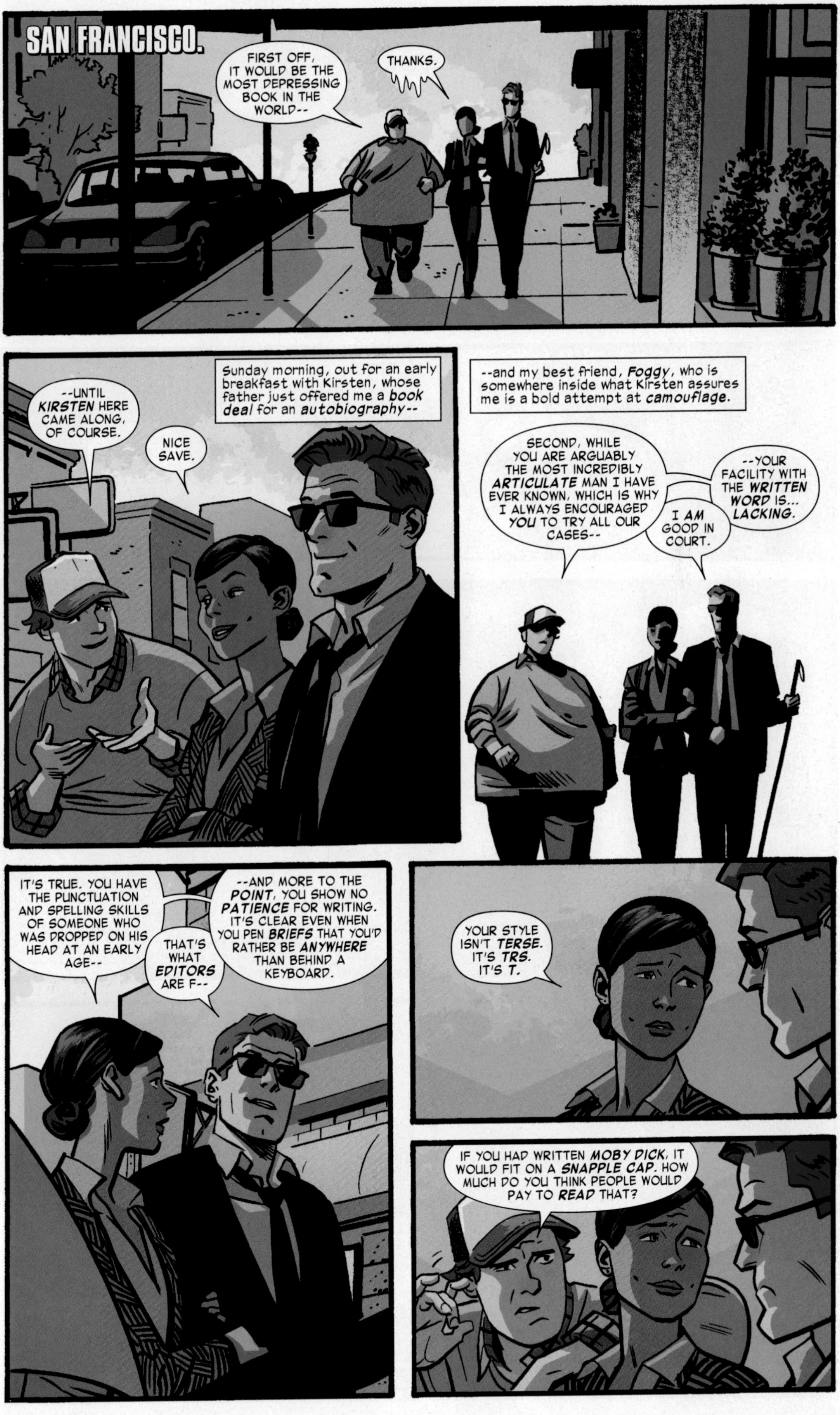

SAN FRANCISCO.
FIRST OFF, IT WOULD BE THE MOST DEPRESSING BOOK IN THE WORLD--
THANKS.
--UNTIL KIRSTEN HERE CAME ALONG, OF COURSE.
NICE SAVE.
Sunday morning, out for an early breakfast with Kirsten, whose father just offered me a book deal for an autobiography--
--and my best friend, Foggy, who is somewhere inside what Kirsten assures me is a bold attempt at camouflage.
SECOND, WHILE YOU ARE ARGUABLY THE MOST INCREDIBLY ARTICULATE MAN I HAVE EVER KNOWN, WHICH IS WHY I ALWAYS ENCOURAGED YOU TO TRY ALL OUR CASES--
--YOUR FACILITY WITH THE WRITTEN WORD IS... LACKING.
I AM GOOD IN COURT.
IT'S TRUE. YOU HAVE THE PUNCTUATION AND SPELLING SKILLS OF SOMEONE WHO WAS DROPPED ON HIS HEAD AT AN EARLY AGE--
THAT'S WHAT EDITORS ARE F--
--AND MORE TO THE POINT, YOU SHOW NO PATIENCE FOR WRITING. IT'S CLEAR EVEN WHEN YOU PEN BRIEFS THAT YOU'D RATHER BE ANYWHERE THAN BEHIND A KEYBOARD.
YOUR STYLE ISN'T TERSE. IT'S TRS. IT'S T.
IF YOU HAD WRITTEN MOBY DICK, IT WOULD FIT ON A SNAPPLE CAP. HOW MUCH DO YOU THINK PEOPLE WOULD PAY TO READ THAT?

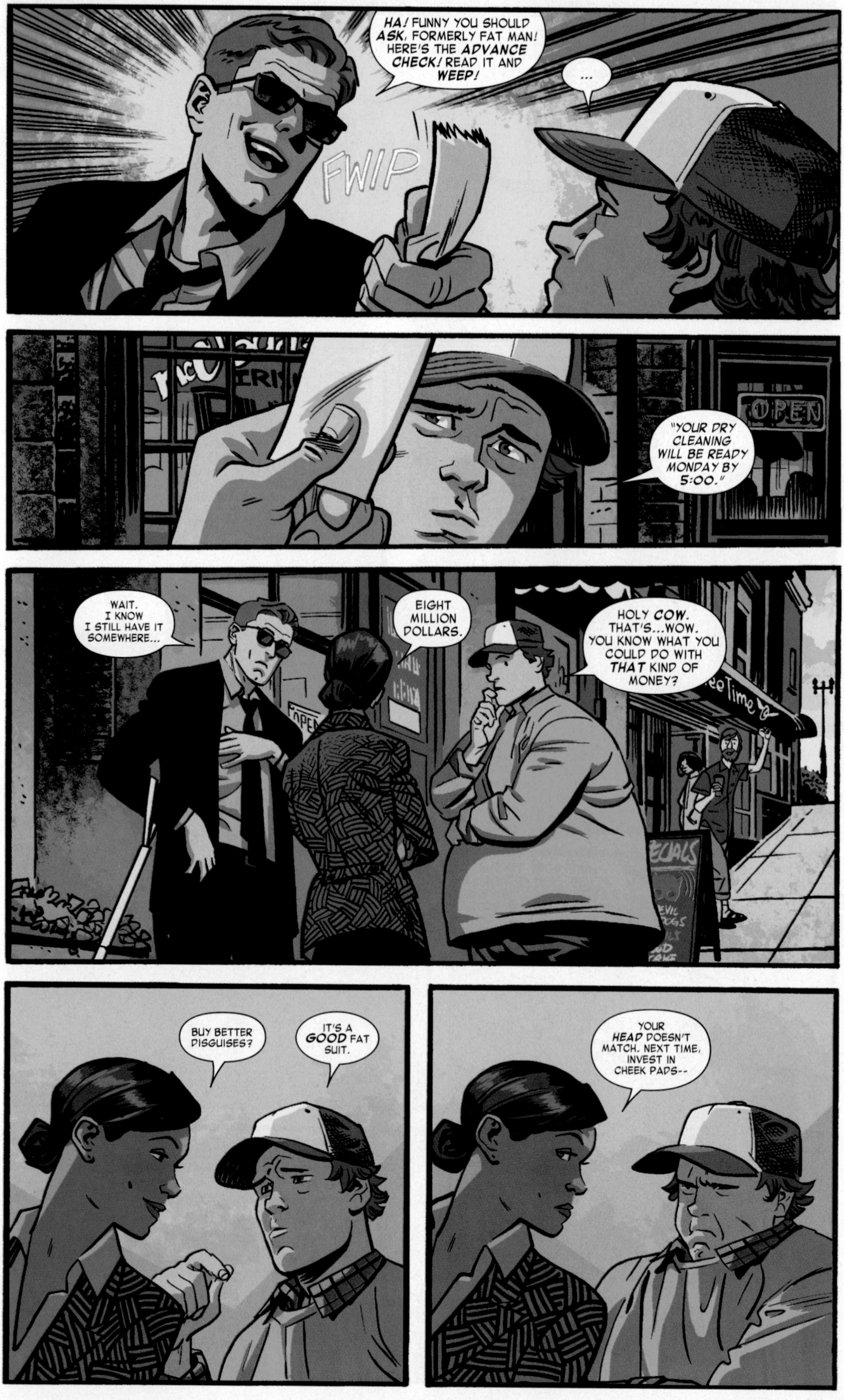
HA! FUNNY YOU SHOULD ASK, FORMERLY FAT MAN! HERE'S THE ADVANCE CHECK! READ IT AND WEEP!
...
FWIP
OPEN
"YOUR DRY CLEANING WILL BE READY MONDAY BY 5:00."
WAIT. I KNOW I STILL HAVE IT SOMEWHERE...
EIGHT MILLION DOLLARS.
HOLY COW. THAT'S...WOW. YOU KNOW WHAT YOU COULD DO WITH THAT KIND OF MONEY?
BUY BETTER DISGUISES?
IT'S A GOOD FAT SUIT.
YOUR HEAD DOESN'T MATCH. NEXT TIME, INVEST IN CHEEK PADS--

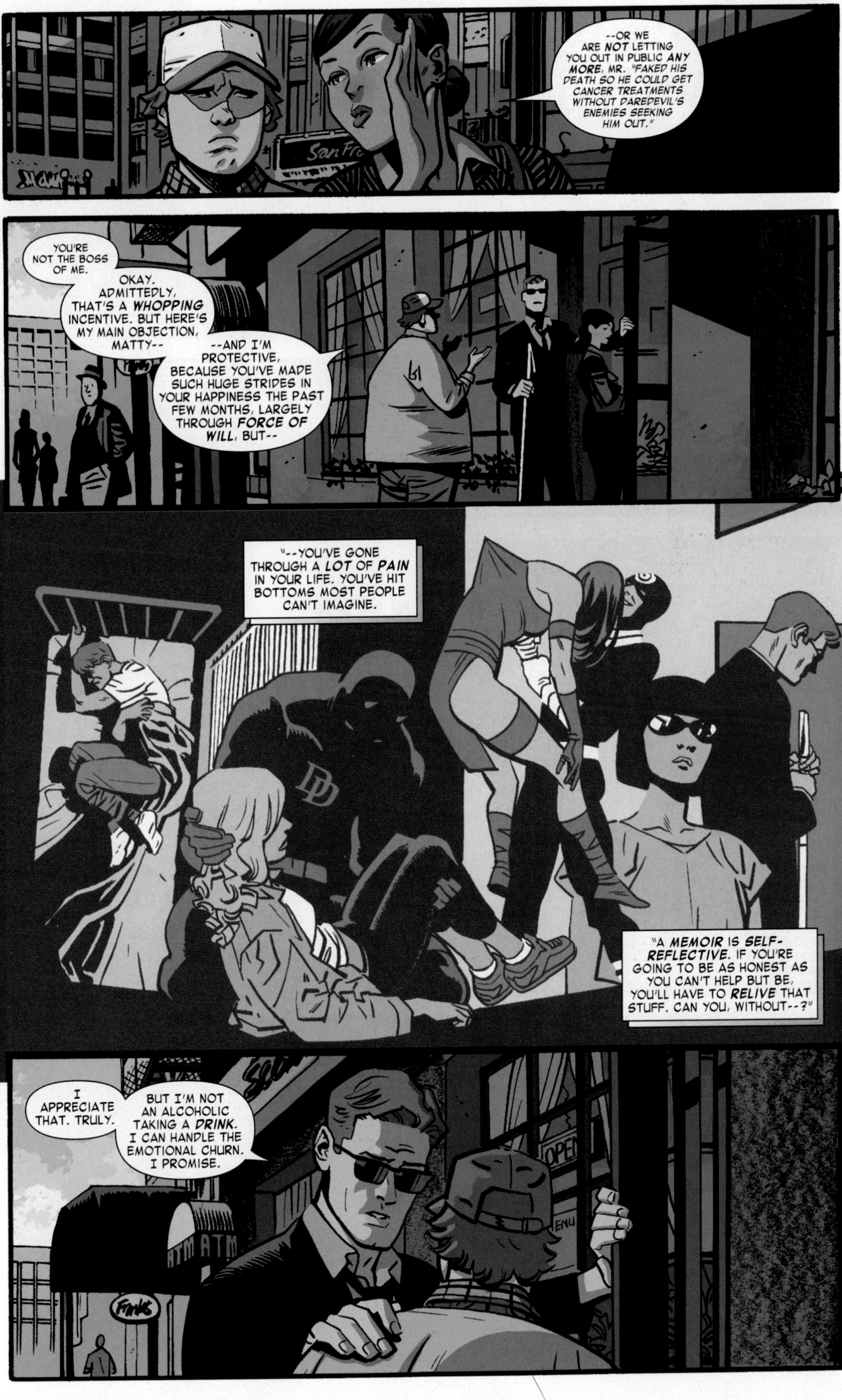

--OR WE ARE NOT LETTING YOU OUT IN PUBLIC ANY MORE, MR. "FAKED HIS DEATH SO HE COULD GET CANCER TREATMENTS WITHOUT DAREDEVIL'S ENEMIES SEEKING HIM OUT."
YOU'RE NOT THE BOSS OF ME.
OKAY. ADMITTEDLY, THAT'S A WHOPPING INCENTIVE. BUT HERE'S MY MAIN OBJECTION, MATTY--
--AND I'M PROTECTIVE, BECAUSE YOU'VE MADE SUCH HUGE STRIDES IN YOUR HAPPINESS THE PAST FEW MONTHS, LARGELY THROUGH FORCE OF WILL, BUT--
"--YOU'VE GONE THROUGH A LOT OF PAIN IN YOUR LIFE. YOU'VE HIT BOTTOMS MOST PEOPLE CAN'T IMAGINE.
"A MEMOIR IS SELF-REFLECTIVE. IF YOU'RE GOING TO BE AS HONEST AS YOU CAN'T HELP BUT BE, YOU'LL HAVE TO RELIVE THAT STUFF. CAN YOU, WITHOUT--?"
I APPRECIATE THAT. TRULY.
BUT I'M NOT AN ALCOHOLIC TAKING A DRINK. I CAN HANDLE THE EMOTIONAL CHURN. I PROMISE.
OPEN
ATM

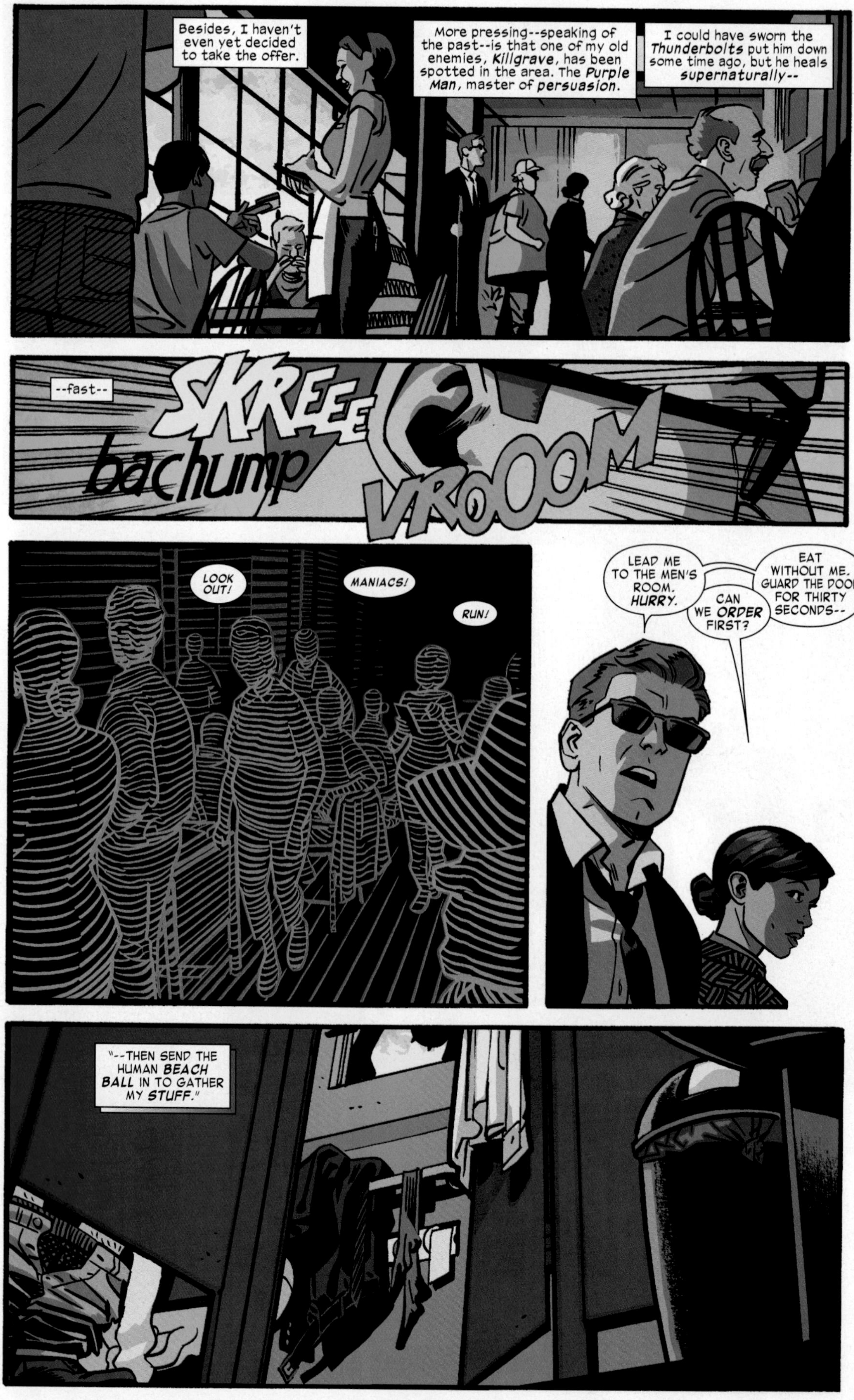
Besides, I haven't even yet decided to take the offer.
More pressing--speaking of the past--is that one of my old enemies, Killgrave, has been spotted in the area. The Purple Man, master of persuasion.
I could have sworn the Thunderbolts put him down some time ago, but he heals supernaturally--
--fast--
SKREEE
bachump
VROOOM
LOOK OUT!
MANIACS!
RUN!
LEAD ME TO THE MEN'S ROOM. HURRY.
CAN WE ORDER FIRST?
EAT WITHOUT ME. GUARD THE DOOR FOR THIRTY SECONDS--
"--THEN SEND THE HUMAN BEACH BALL IN TO GATHER MY STUFF."

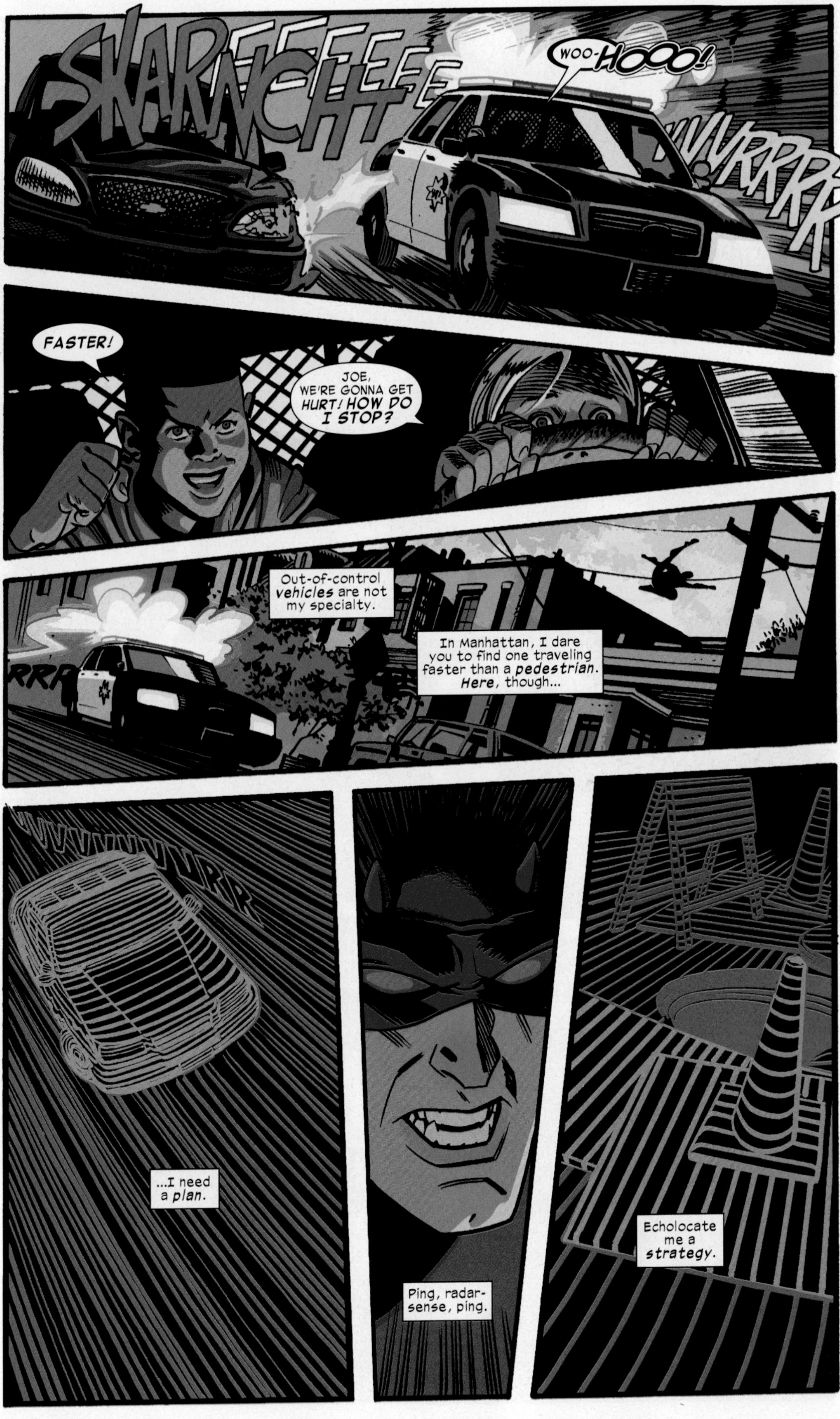
SKARNCHT
EEEEEE
WOO-HOOOO!
VVVURRRRR
FASTER!
JOE, WE'RE GONNA GET HURT! HOW DO I STOP?
Out-of-control vehicles are not my specialty.
In Manhattan, I dare you to find one traveling faster than a pedestrian. Here, though...
RRR
VVVVVVVVURRR
...I need a plan.
Ping, radar-sense, ping.
Echolocate me a strategy.

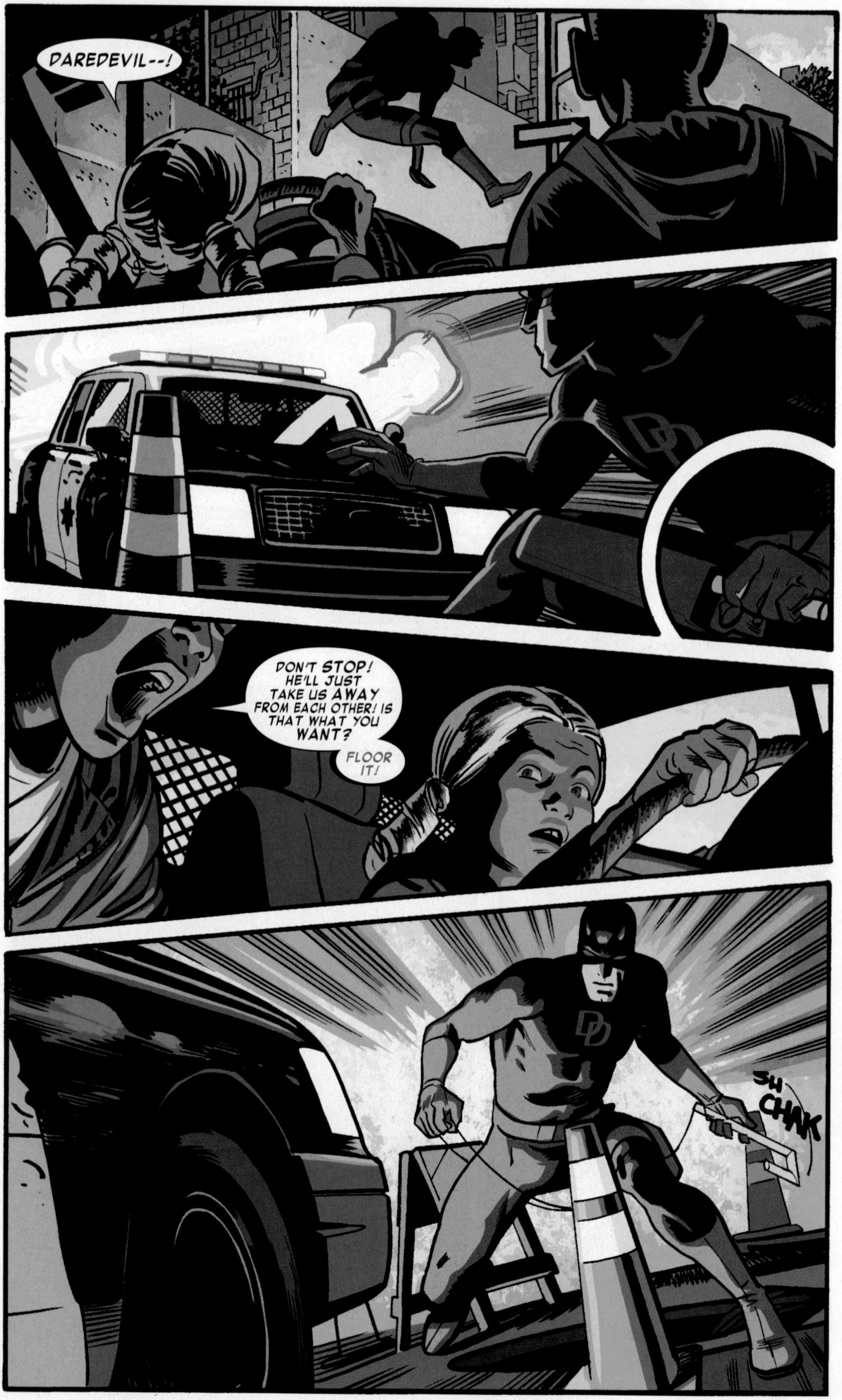
DAREDEVIL--!
DON'T STOP! HE'LL JUST TAKE US AWAY FROM EACH OTHER! IS THAT WHAT YOU WANT?
FLOOR IT!
SH CHAK

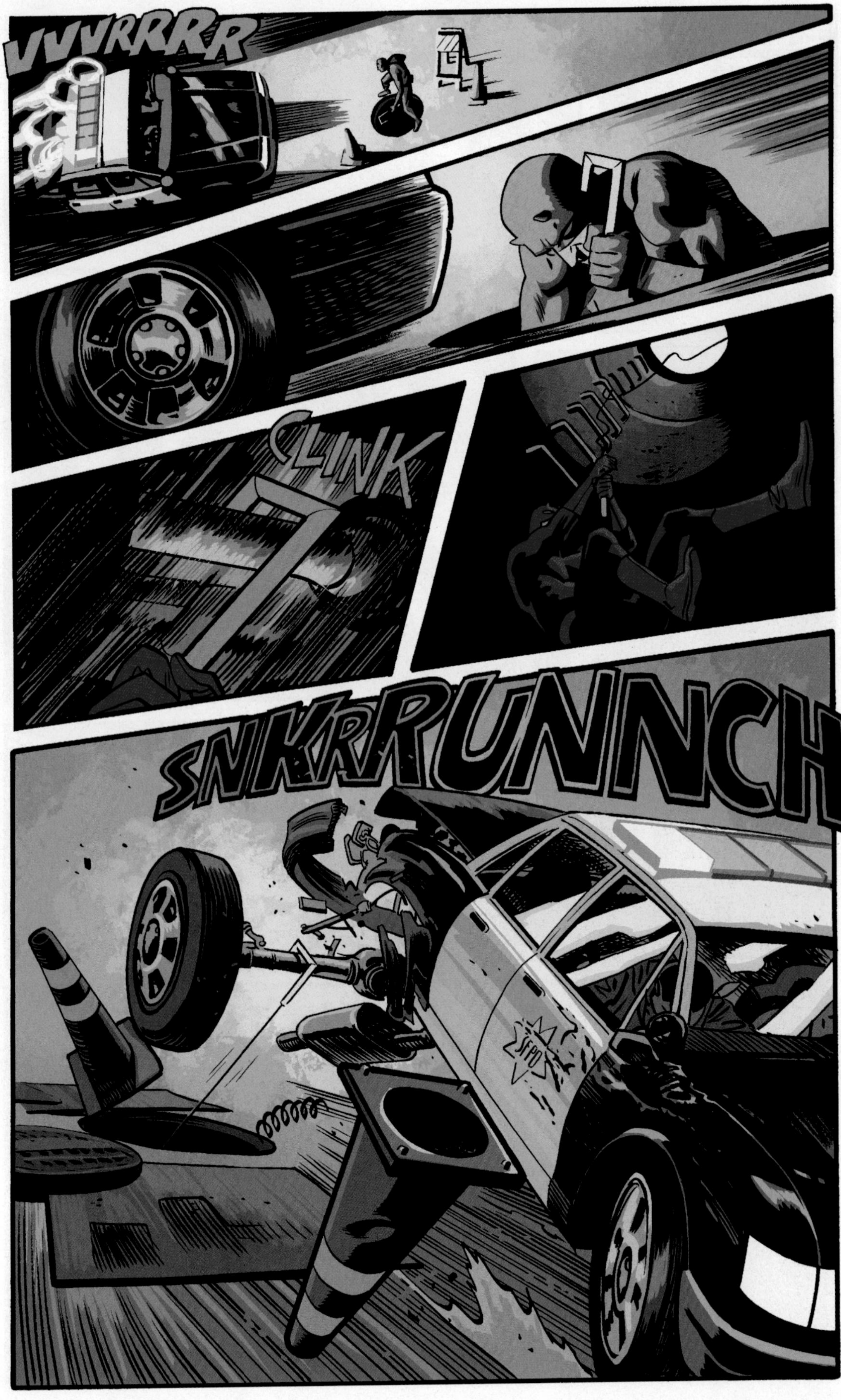
VVVRRRR
CLINK
SNKRRUNNCH
SFPD

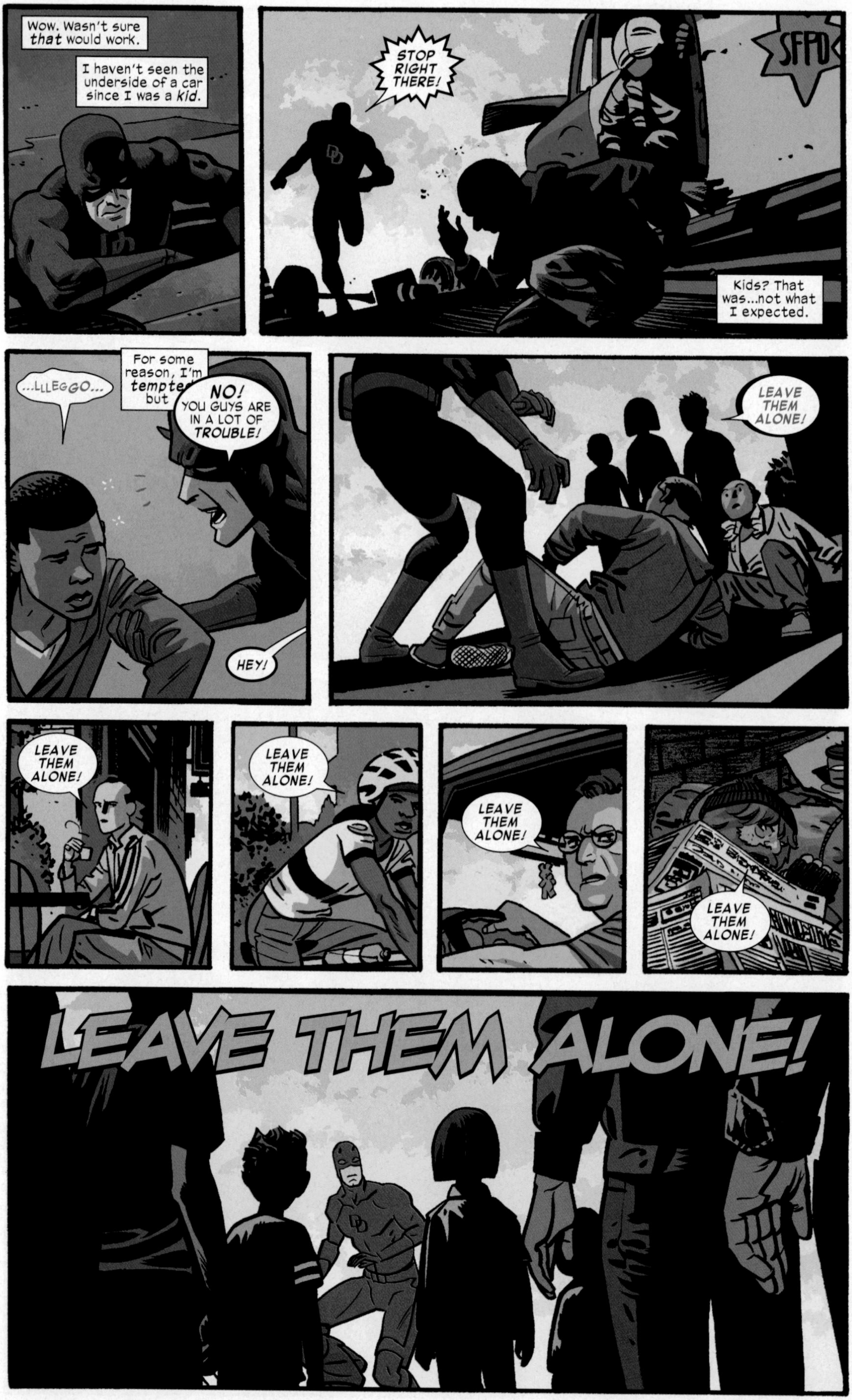

Wow. Wasn't sure *that* would work.
I haven't seen the underside of a car since I was a *kid*.
STOP RIGHT THERE!
SFPD
Kids? That was...not what I expected.
...LLLEGGO...
For some reason, I'm tempte... but
NO! YOU GUYS ARE IN A LOT OF TROUBLE!
HEY!
LEAVE THEM ALONE!
LEAVE THEM ALONE!
LEAVE THEM ALONE!
LEAVE THEM ALONE!
LEAVE THEM ALONE!
LEAVE THEM ALONE!

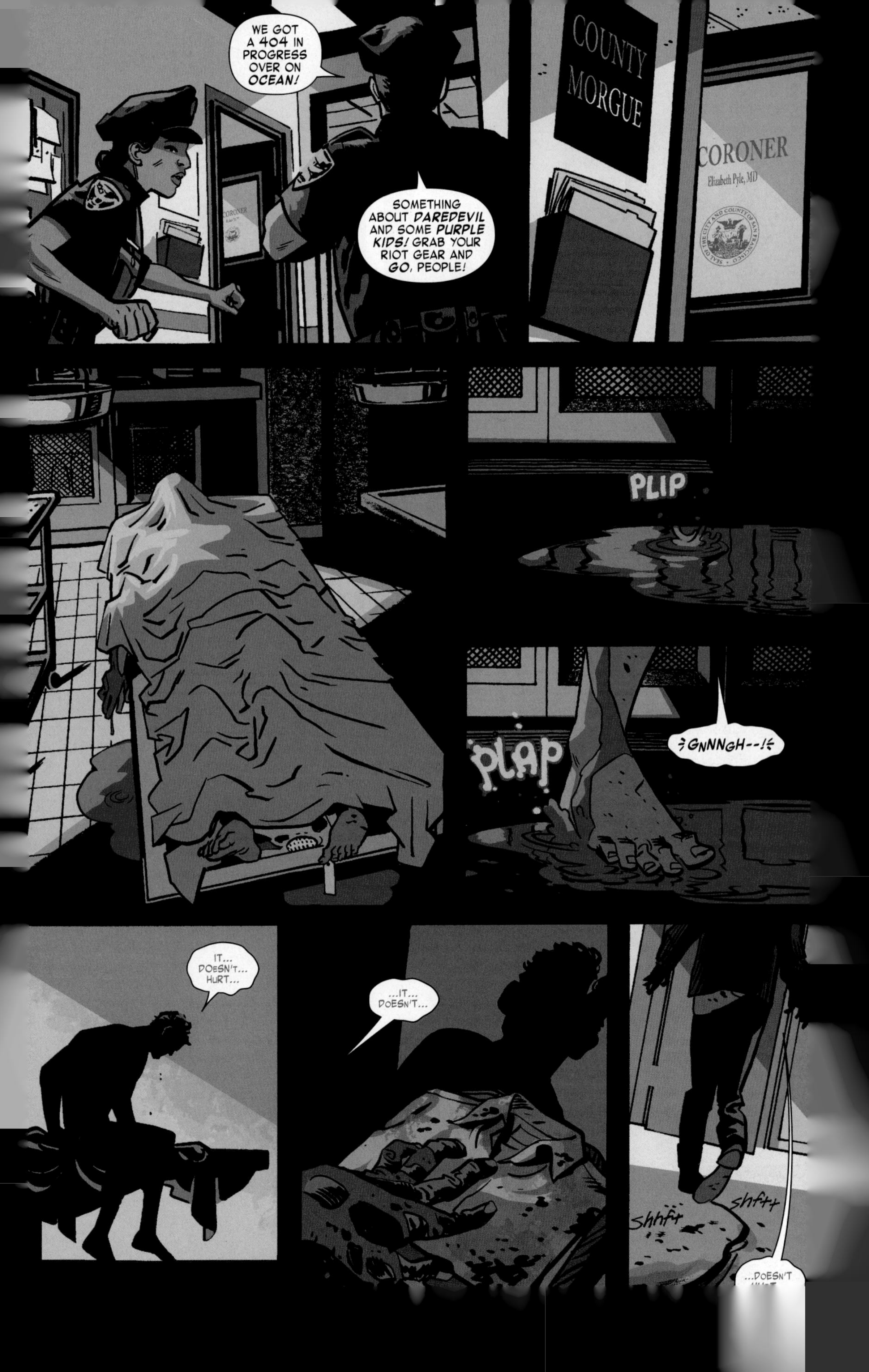
WE GOT A 404 IN PROGRESS OVER ON OCEAN!
COUNTY MORGUE
CORONER
Elizabeth Pyle, MD
SOMETHING ABOUT DAREDEVIL AND SOME PURPLE KIDS! GRAB YOUR RIOT GEAR AND GO, PEOPLE!
PLIP
PLAP
GNNNGH--!
IT... DOESN'T... HURT...
...IT... DOESN'T...
shhftt
shftt
...DOESN'T

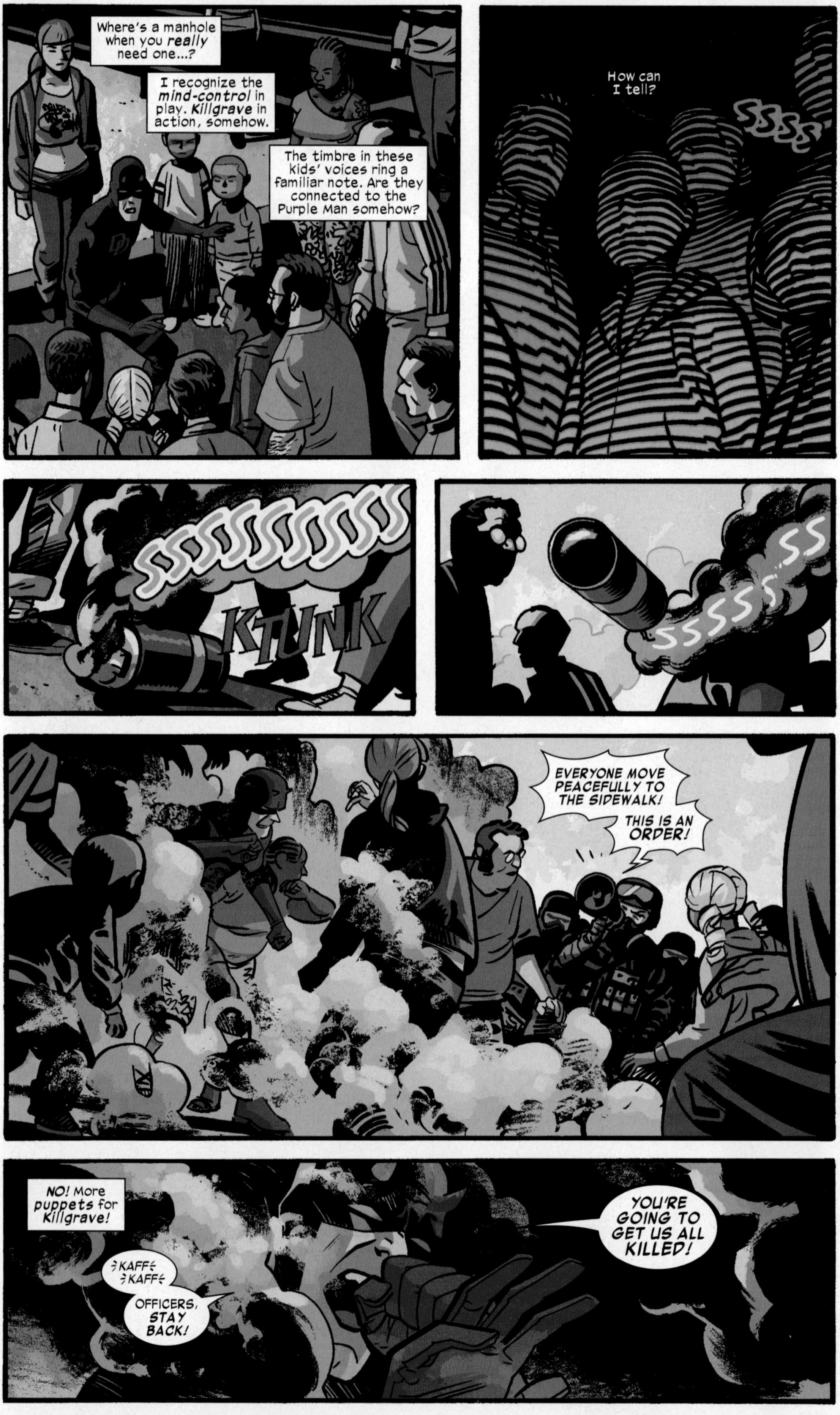

Where's a manhole when you *really* need one...?
I recognize the *mind-control* in play. *Killgrave* in action, somehow.
The timbre in these kids' voices ring a familiar note. Are they connected to the Purple Man somehow?
How can I tell?
SSSS
SSSSSSSSSSSS
KTUNK
SSSSSS...SS
EVERYONE MOVE PEACEFULLY TO THE SIDEWALK!
THIS IS AN ORDER!
NO! More *puppets* for *Killgrave!*
YOU'RE GOING TO GET US ALL KILLED!
KAFF KAFF
OFFICERS, STAY BACK!

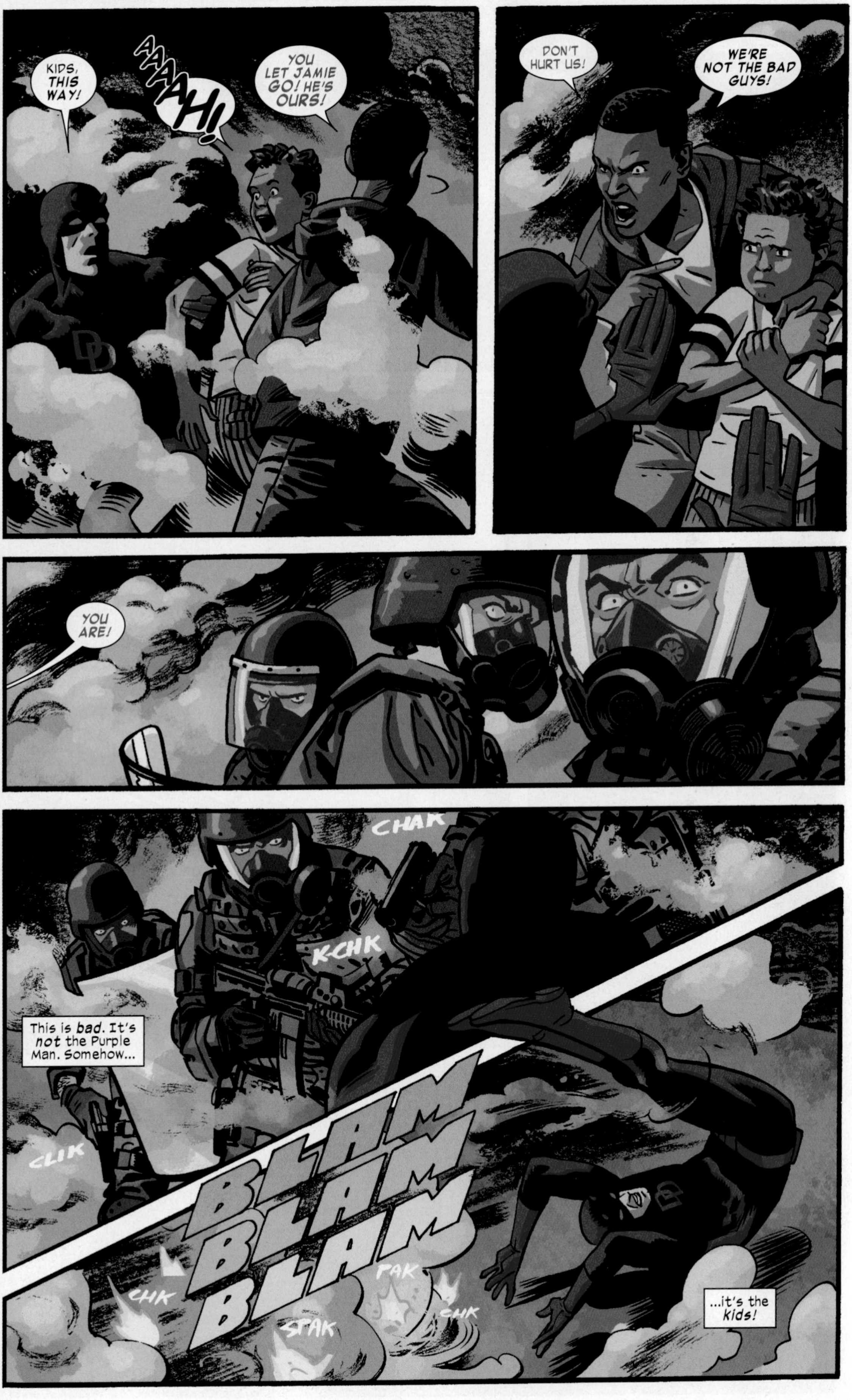
KIDS, THIS WAY!
AAAAAH!
YOU LET JAMIE GO! HE'S OURS!
DON'T HURT US!
WE'RE NOT THE BAD GUYS!
YOU ARE!
CHAK
K-CHK
This is bad. It's not the Purple Man. Somehow...
CLIK
BLAM BLAM BLAM
CHK
PAK
SPAK
CHK
...it's the kids!

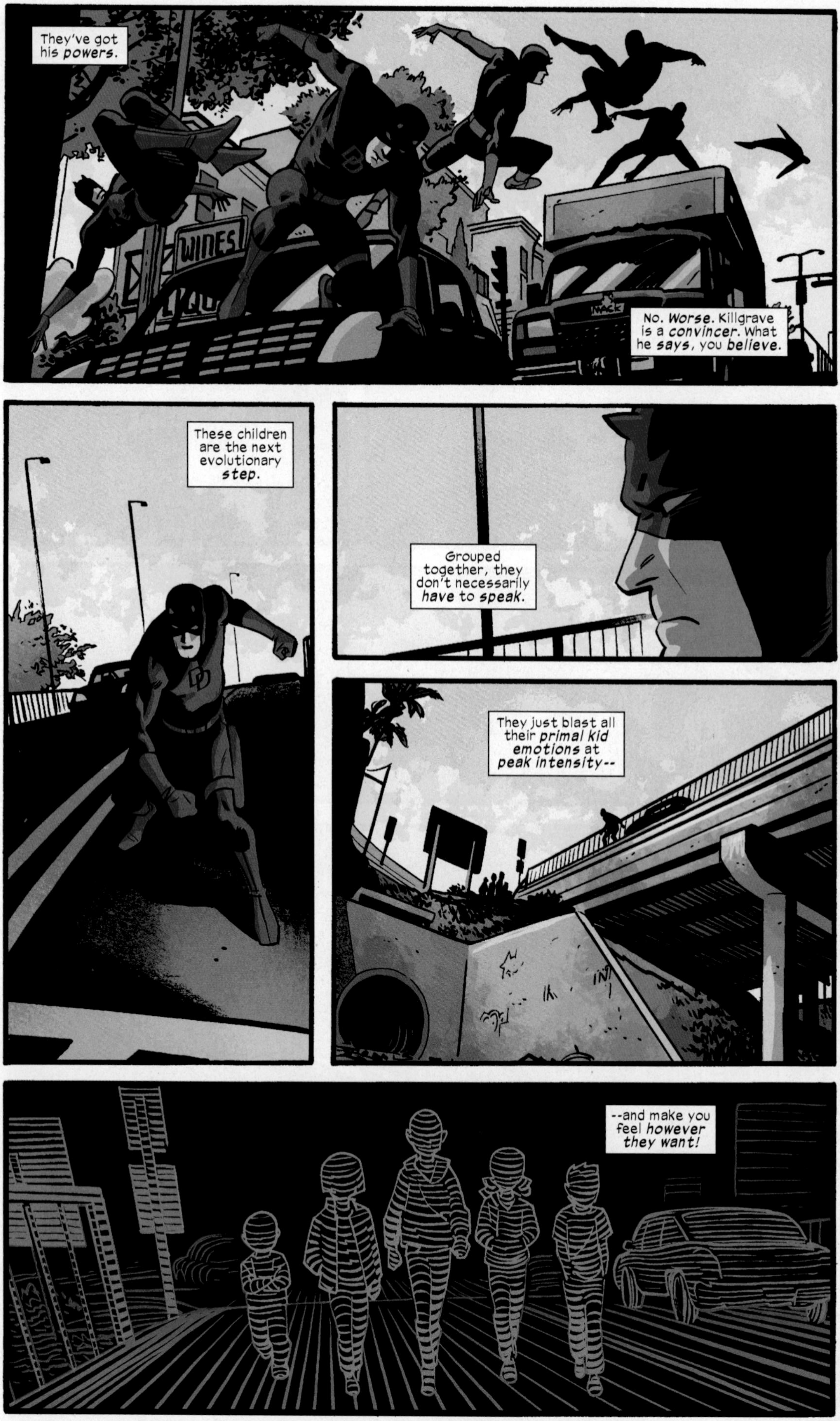
They've got his powers.
WINES
LIQU
MACK
No. Worse. Killgrave is a convincer. What he says, you believe.
These children are the next evolutionary step.
Grouped together, they don't necessarily have to speak.
They just blast all their primal kid emotions at peak intensity--
--and make you feel however they want!

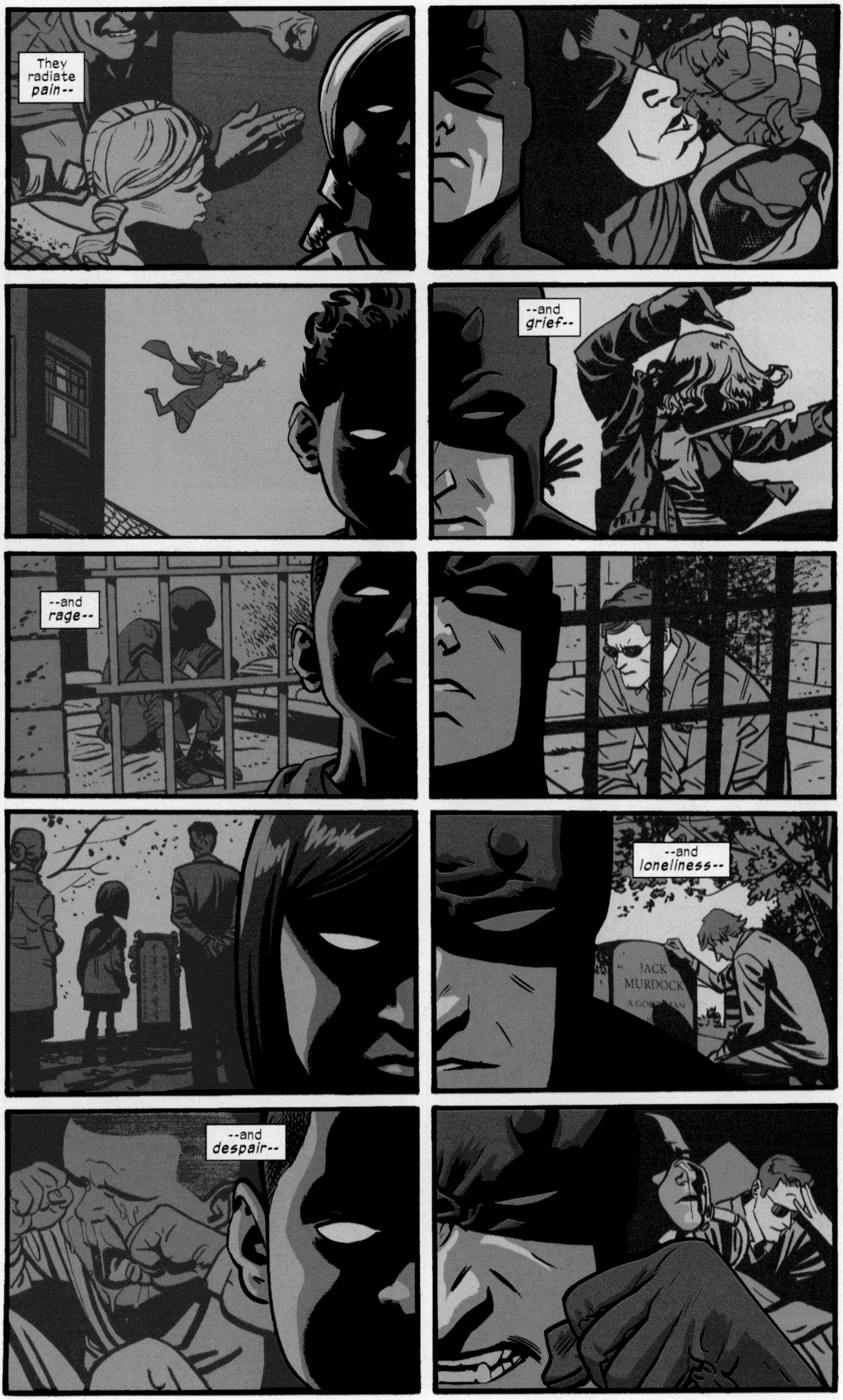
They radiate *pain*--
--and *grief*--
--and *rage*--
--and *loneliness*--
JACK
MURDOCK
--and *despair*--

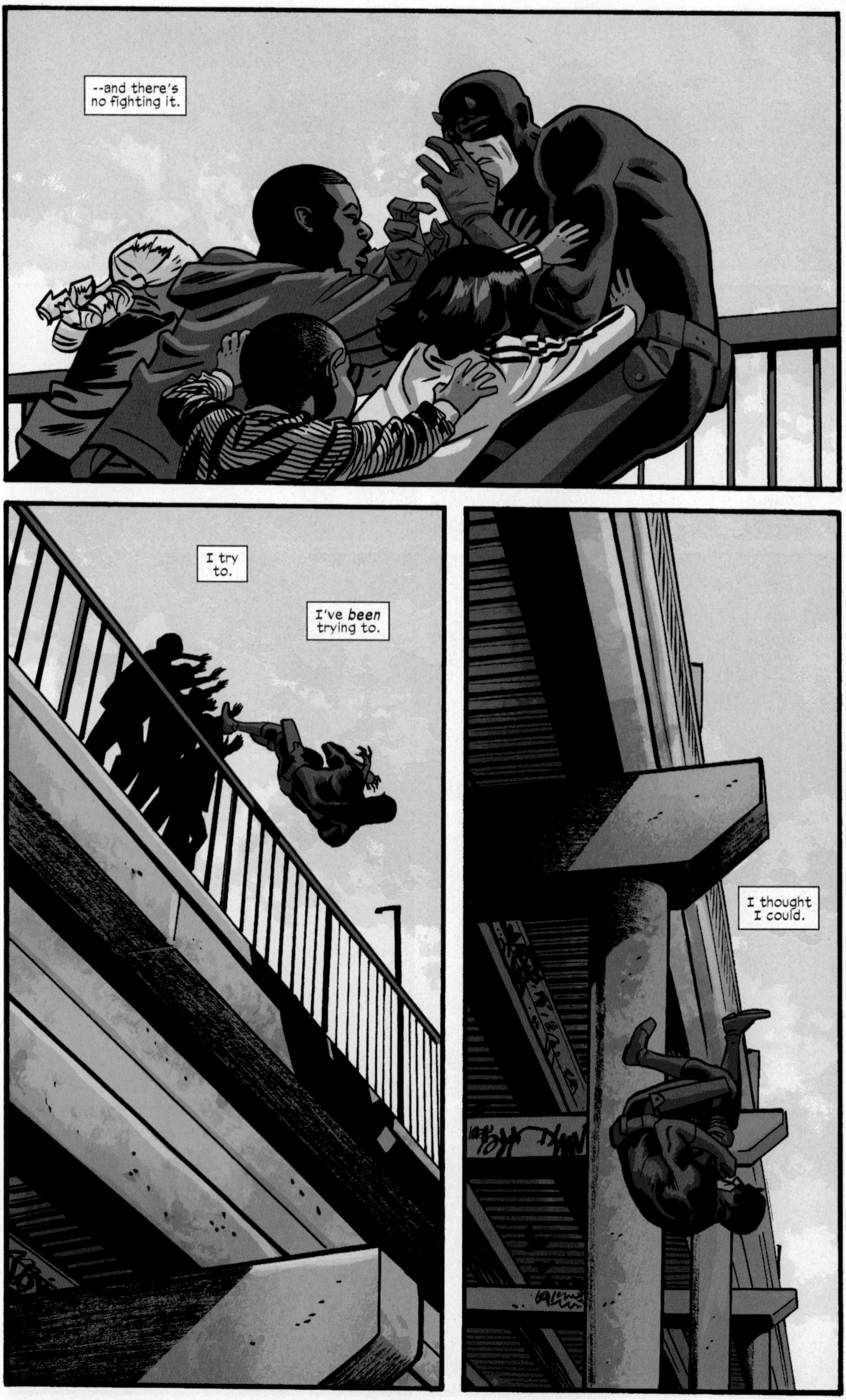
--and there's no fighting it.
I try to.
I've *been* trying to.
I thought I could.

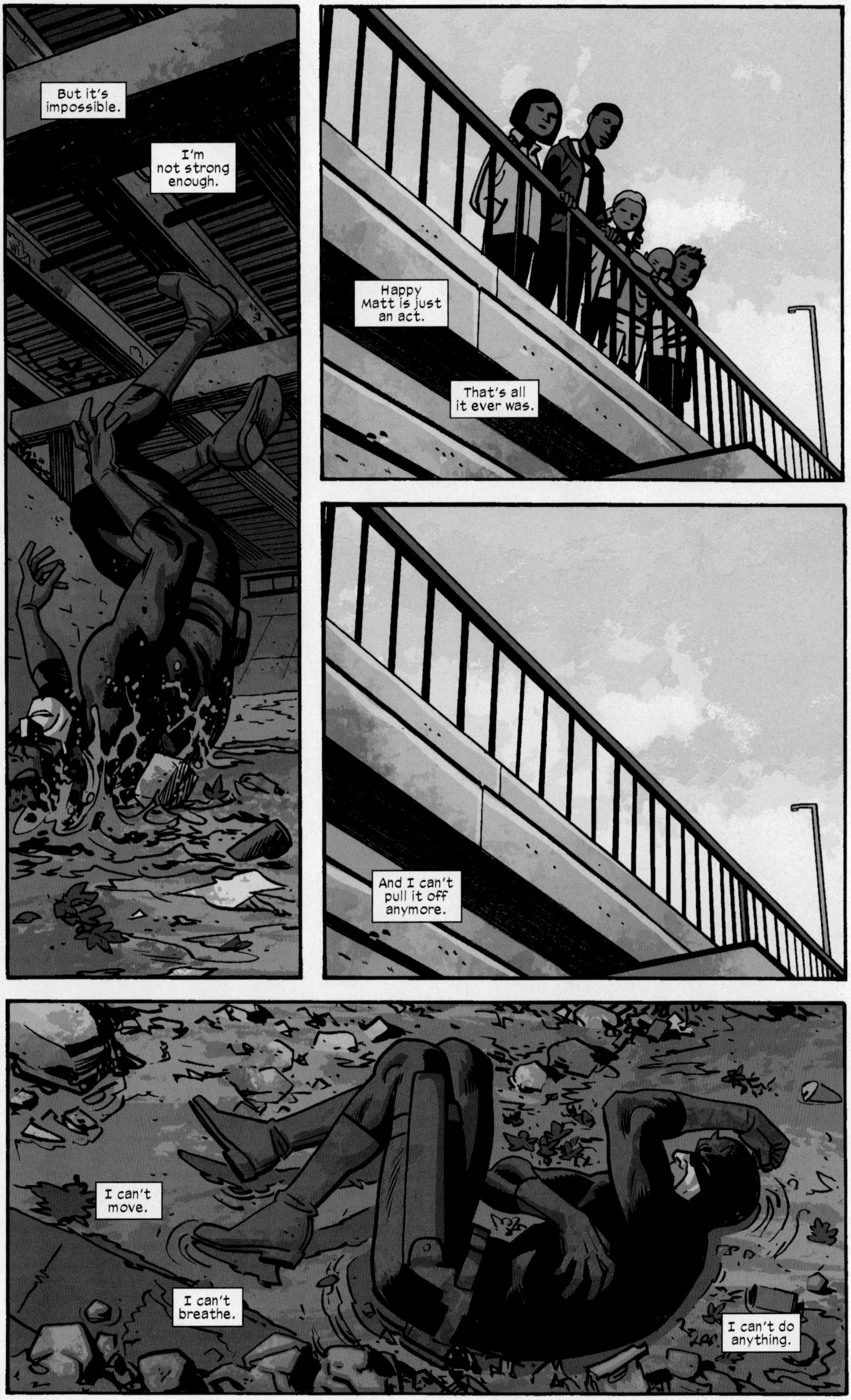

But it's impossible.
I'm not strong enough.
Happy Matt is just an act.
That's all it ever was.
And I can't pull it off anymore.
I can't move.
I can't breathe.
I can't do anything.

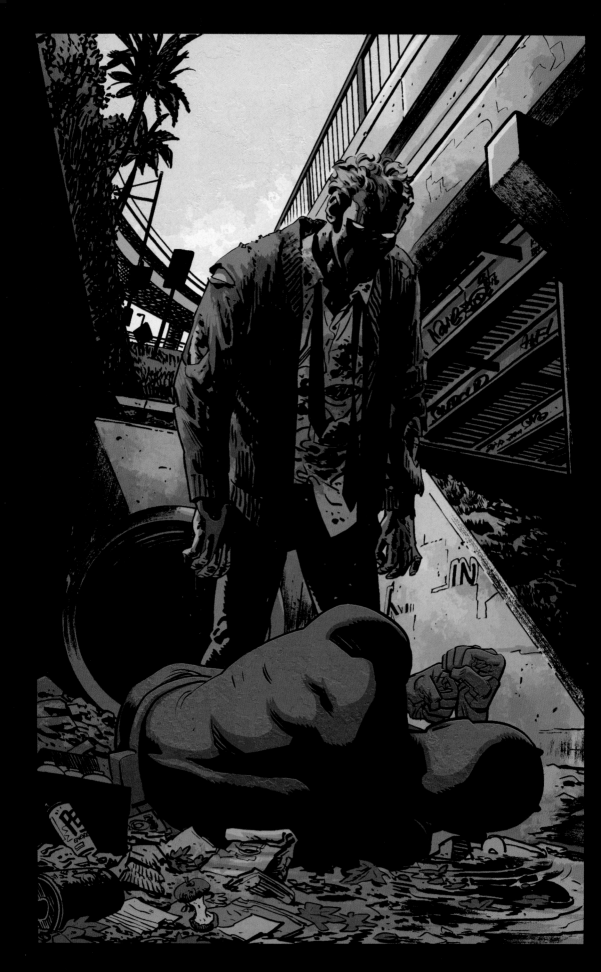

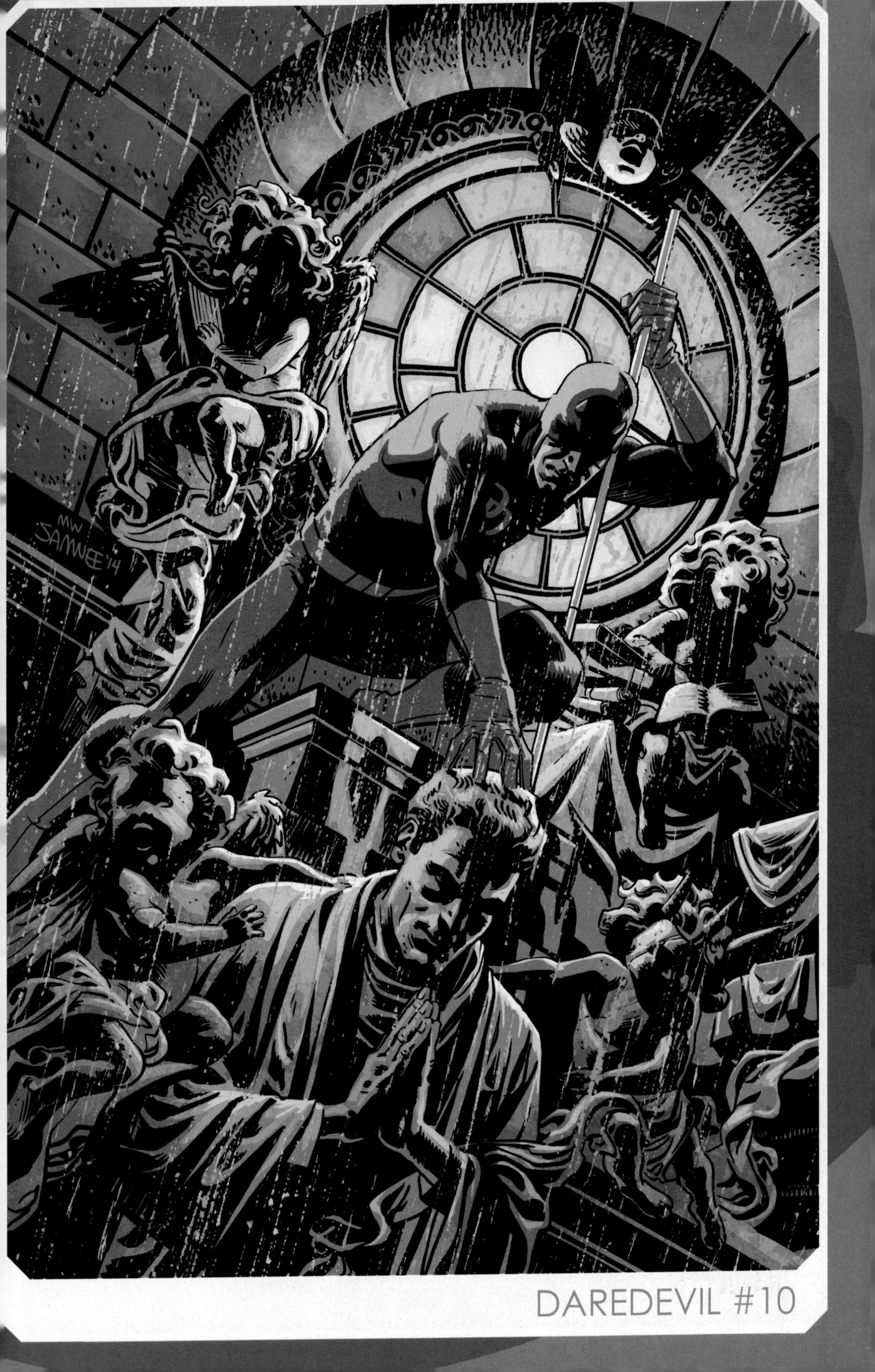
MW
SAMNEE '14

DAREDEVIL #10

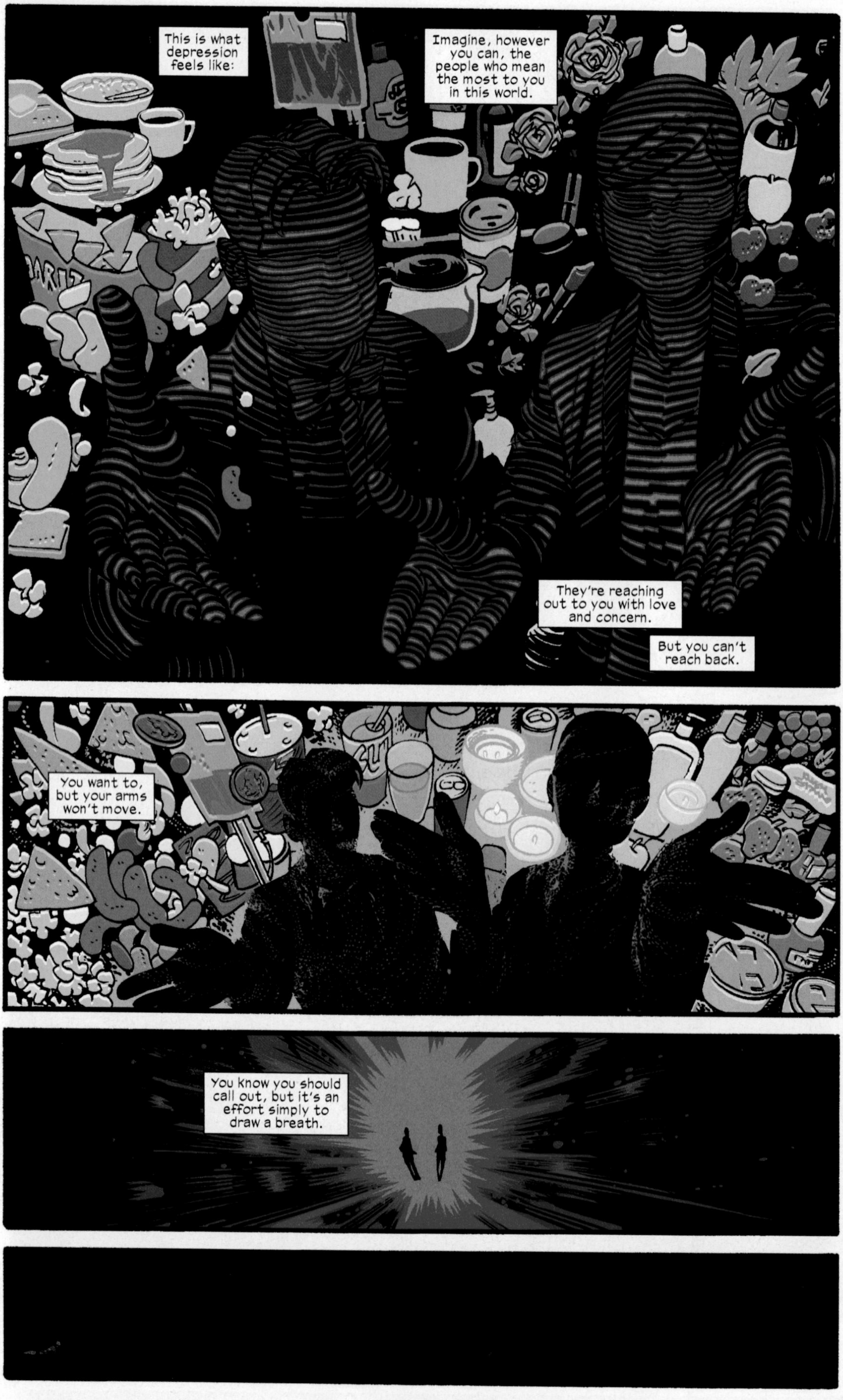
This is what depression feels like:
Imagine, however you can, the people who mean the most to you in this world.
They're reaching out to you with love and concern.
But you can't reach back.
You want to, but your arms won't move.
You know you should call out, but it's an effort simply to draw a breath.

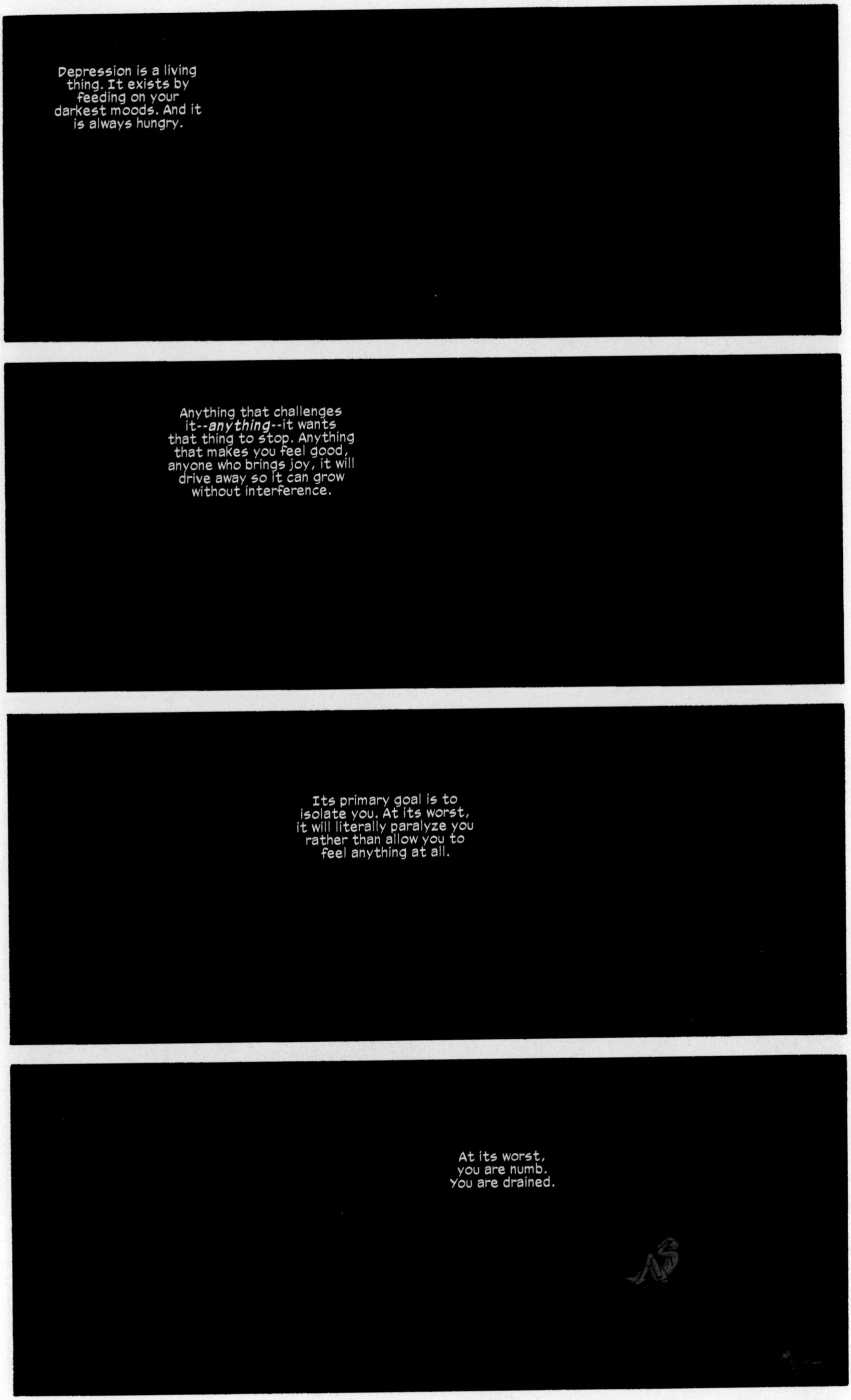
Depression is a living thing. It exists by feeding on your darkest moods. And it is always hungry.
Anything that challenges it--*anything*--it wants that thing to stop. Anything that makes you feel good, anyone who brings joy, it will drive away so it can grow without interference.
Its primary goal is to isolate you. At its worst, it will literally paralyze you rather than allow you to feel anything at all.
At its worst, you are numb. You are drained.

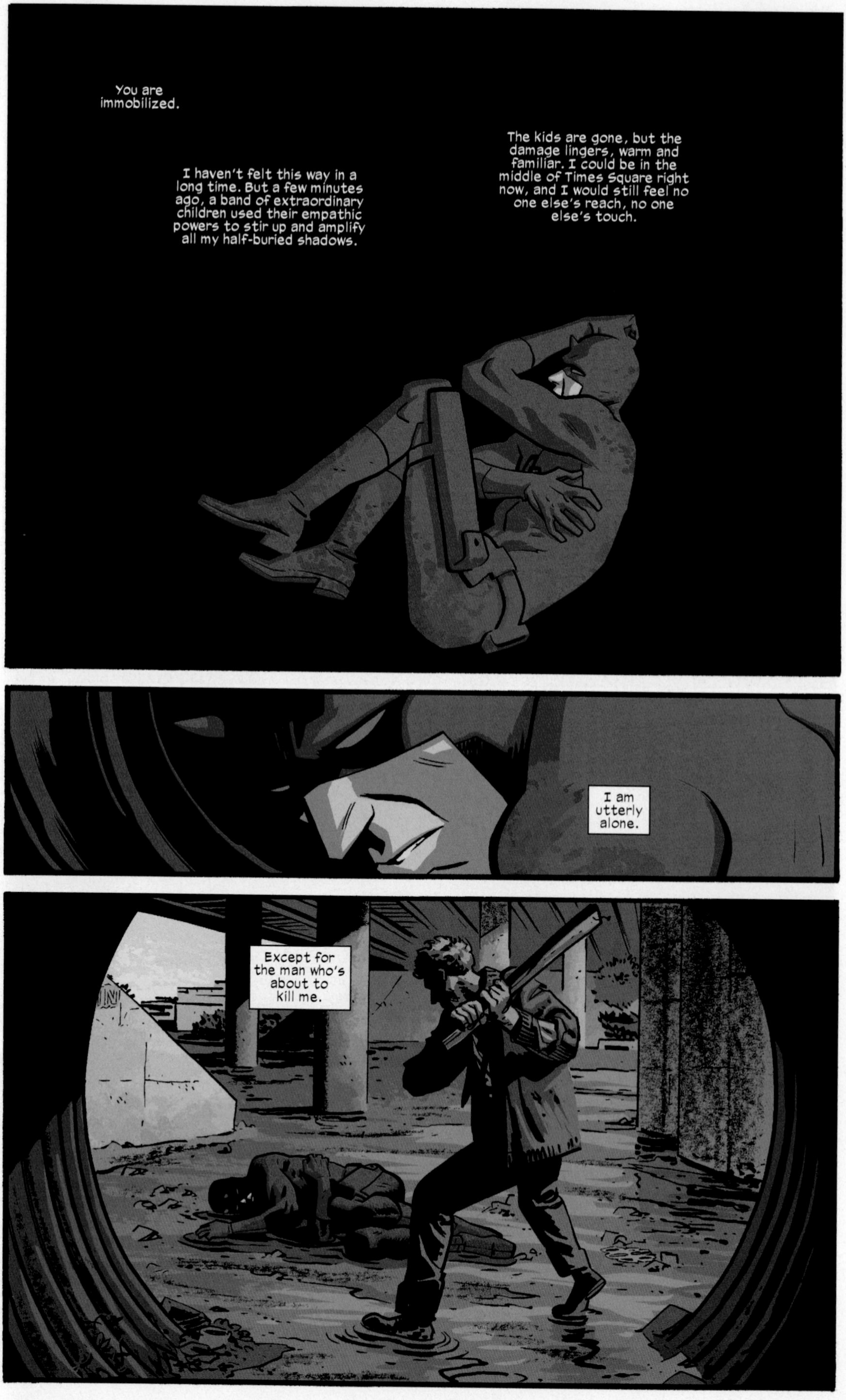
You are immobilized.
I haven't felt this way in a long time. But a few minutes ago, a band of extraordinary children used their empathic powers to stir up and amplify all my half-buried shadows.
The kids are gone, but the damage lingers, warm and familiar. I could be in the middle of Times Square right now, and I would still feel no one else's reach, no one else's touch.
I am utterly alone.
Except for the man who's about to kill me.

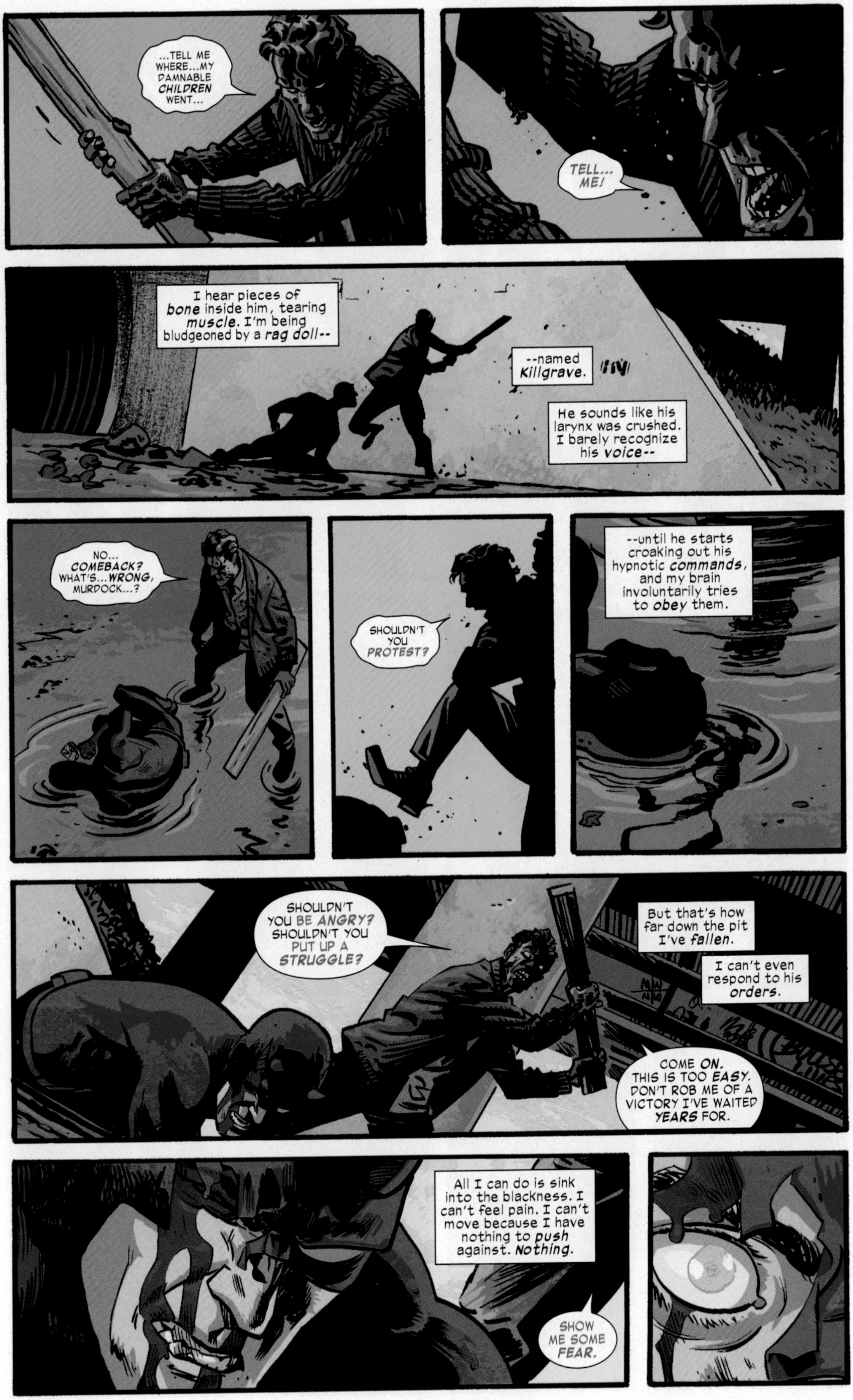
...TELL ME WHERE...MY DAMNABLE CHILDREN WENT...
TELL... ME!
I hear pieces of bone inside him, tearing muscle. I'm being bludgeoned by a rag doll--
--named Killgrave.
He sounds like his larynx was crushed. I barely recognize his voice--
NO... COMEBACK? WHAT'S...WRONG, MURDOCK...?
SHOULDN'T YOU PROTEST?
--until he starts croaking out his hypnotic commands, and my brain involuntarily tries to obey them.
SHOULDN'T YOU BE ANGRY? SHOULDN'T YOU PUT UP A STRUGGLE?
But that's how far down the pit I've fallen.
I can't even respond to his orders.
COME ON. THIS IS TOO EASY. DON'T ROB ME OF A VICTORY I'VE WAITED YEARS FOR.
All I can do is sink into the blackness. I can't feel pain. I can't move because I have nothing to push against. Nothing.
SHOW ME SOME FEAR.

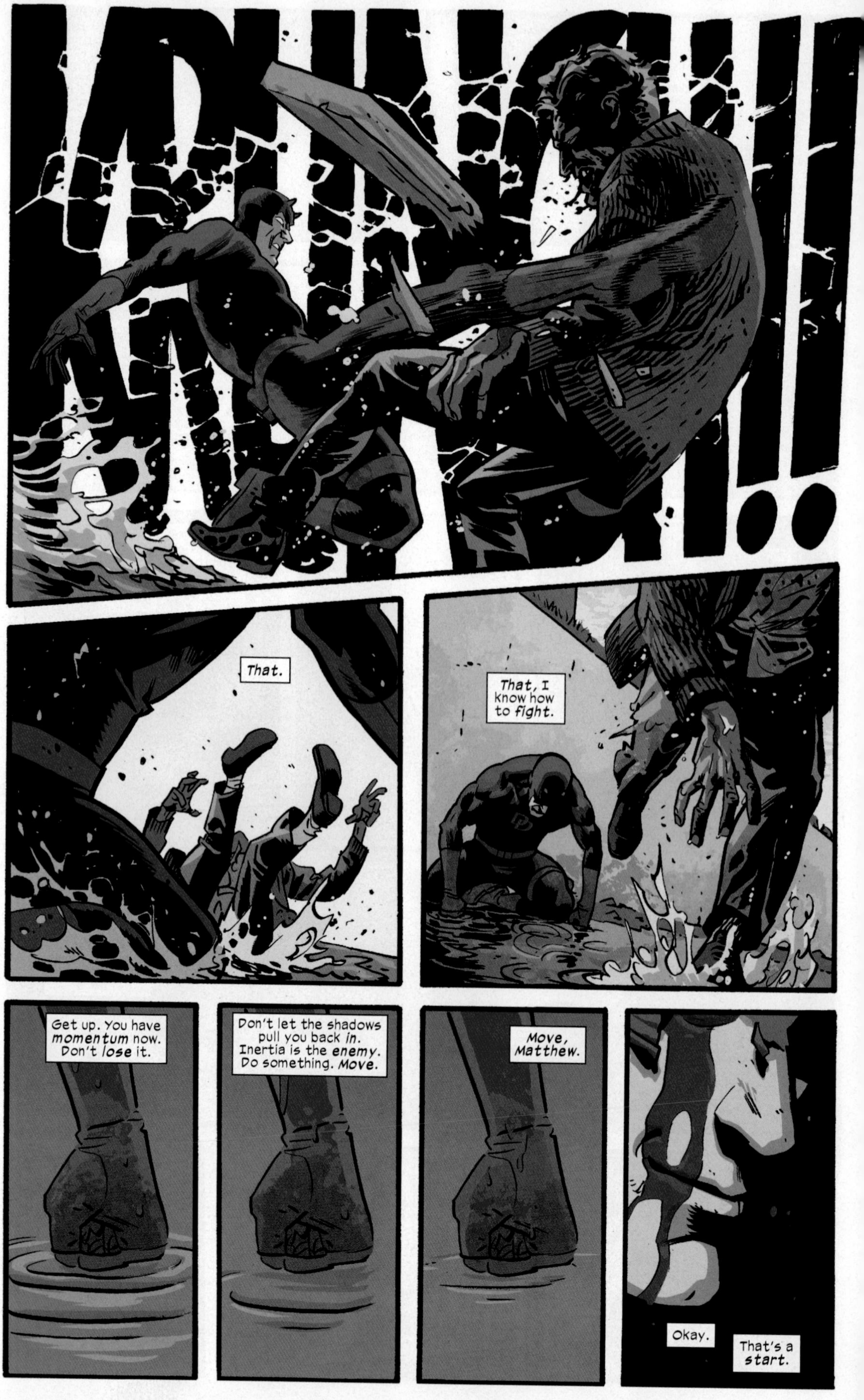
That.
That, I know how to fight.
Get up. You have momentum now. Don't lose it.
Don't let the shadows pull you back in. Inertia is the enemy. Do something. Move.
Move, Matthew.
Okay.
That's a start.

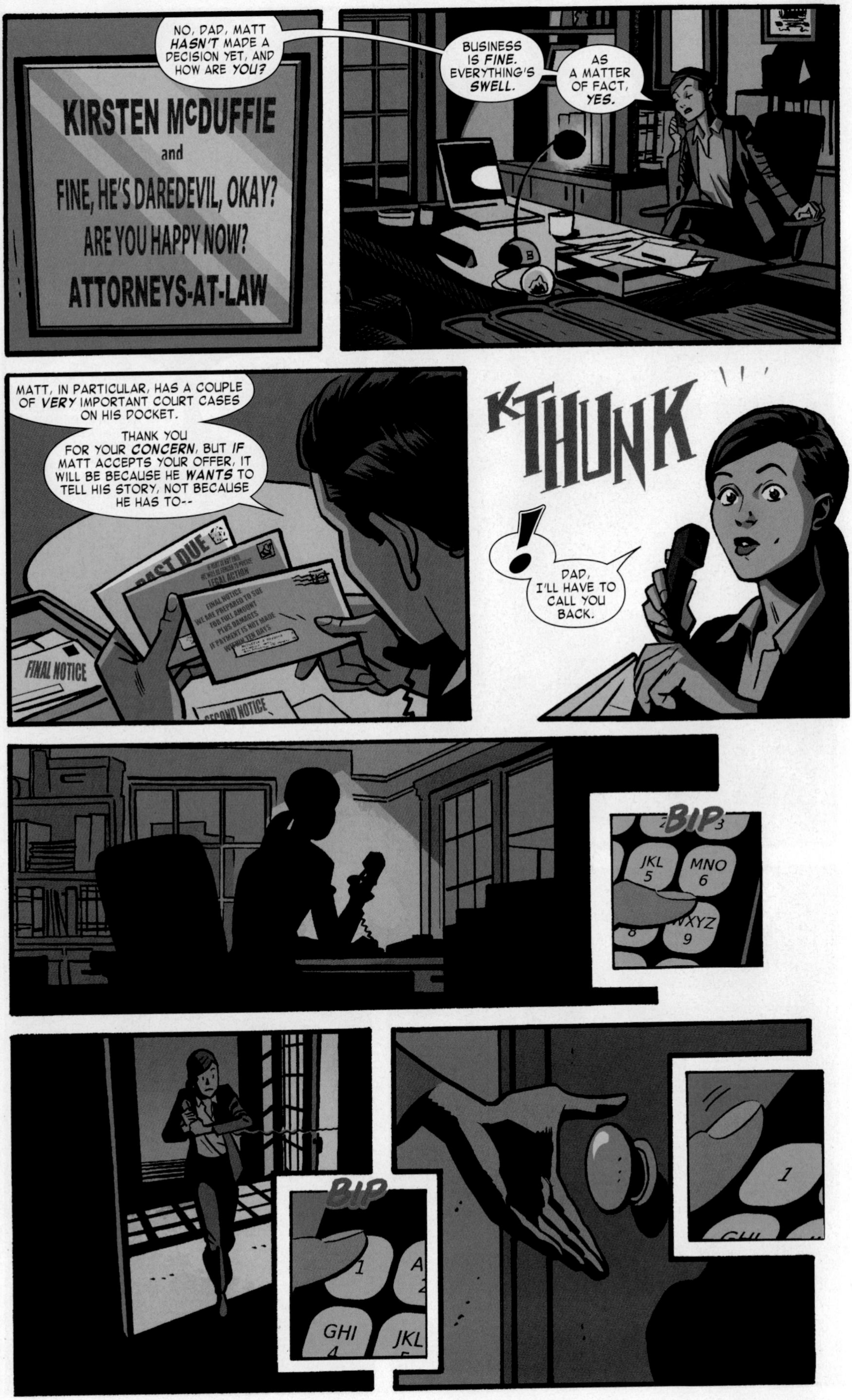

NO, DAD, MATT HASN'T MADE A DECISION YET, AND HOW ARE YOU?
KIRSTEN McDUFFIE
and
FINE, HE'S DAREDEVIL, OKAY? ARE YOU HAPPY NOW?
ATTORNEYS-AT-LAW
BUSINESS IS FINE. EVERYTHING'S SWELL.
AS A MATTER OF FACT, YES.
MATT, IN PARTICULAR, HAS A COUPLE OF VERY IMPORTANT COURT CASES ON HIS DOCKET.
THANK YOU FOR YOUR CONCERN, BUT IF MATT ACCEPTS YOUR OFFER, IT WILL BE BECAUSE HE WANTS TO TELL HIS STORY, NOT BECAUSE HE HAS TO--
LEGAL ACTION
FINAL NOTICE
WE ARE PREPARED TO SUE
FOR FULL AMOUNT
PLUS DAMAGES
IF PAYMENT IS NOT MADE
WITHIN TEN DAYS
FINAL NOTICE
SECOND NOTICE
KTHUNK
!
DAD, I'LL HAVE TO CALL YOU BACK.
BIP
JKL 5
MNO 6
BIP
1
GHI

FWAM

HEY.

YOW. I HEARD ABOUT THE RIOT ON *OCEAN.* I THOUGHT YOUR PUBLIC WAS *ADORING.*

NOT WHEN IT'S BEING MIND-CONTROLLED BY FIVE LITTLE BOYS AND GIRLS WHO ARE, APPARENTLY, THE CHILDREN OF *ZEBEDIAH KILLGRAVE.*

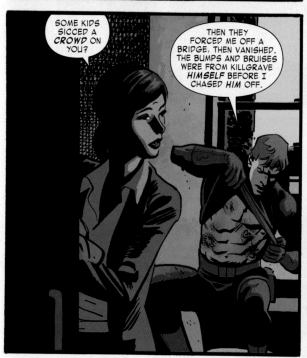

SOME KIDS SICCED A *CROWD* ON YOU?

THEN THEY FORCED ME OFF A BRIDGE, THEN VANISHED. THE BUMPS AND BRUISES WERE FROM KILLGRAVE *HIMSELF* BEFORE I CHASED *HIM* OFF.

TO WHERE?

I HAVE NO IDEA WHERE *ANYONE* IS.

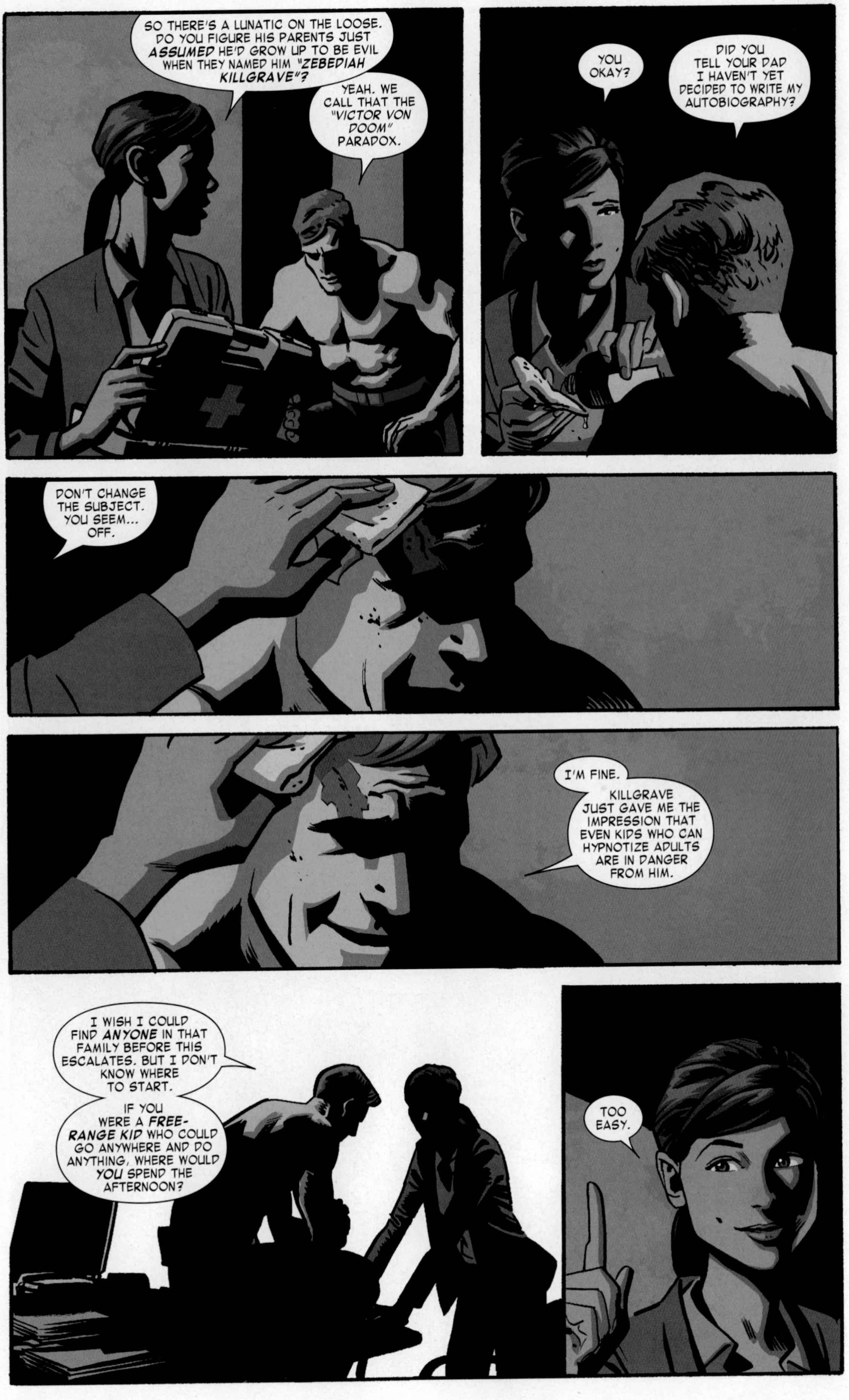
SO THERE'S A LUNATIC ON THE LOOSE. DO YOU FIGURE HIS PARENTS JUST ASSUMED HE'D GROW UP TO BE EVIL WHEN THEY NAMED HIM "ZEBEDIAH KILLGRAVE"?
YEAH. WE CALL THAT THE "VICTOR VON DOOM" PARADOX.
YOU OKAY?
DID YOU TELL YOUR DAD I HAVEN'T YET DECIDED TO WRITE MY AUTOBIOGRAPHY?
DON'T CHANGE THE SUBJECT. YOU SEEM... OFF.
I'M FINE.
KILLGRAVE JUST GAVE ME THE IMPRESSION THAT EVEN KIDS WHO CAN HYPNOTIZE ADULTS ARE IN DANGER FROM HIM.
I WISH I COULD FIND ANYONE IN THAT FAMILY BEFORE THIS ESCALATES. BUT I DON'T KNOW WHERE TO START.
IF YOU WERE A FREE-RANGE KID WHO COULD GO ANYWHERE AND DO ANYTHING, WHERE WOULD YOU SPEND THE AFTERNOON?
TOO EASY.

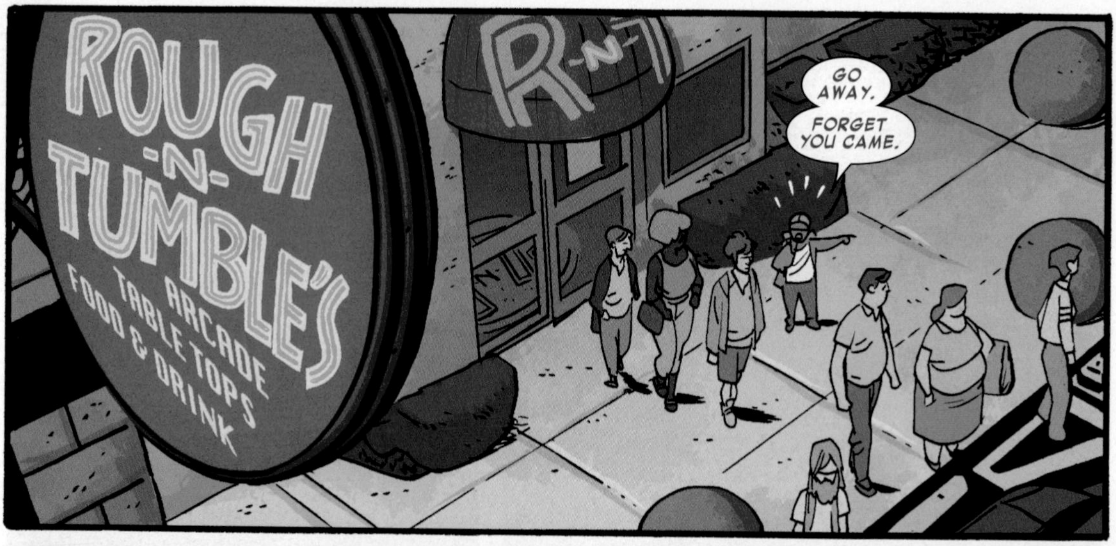
ROUGH -N- TUMBLE'S
ARCADE
TABLE TOPS
FOOD & DRINK
R-N-T
GO AWAY.
FORGET YOU CAME.

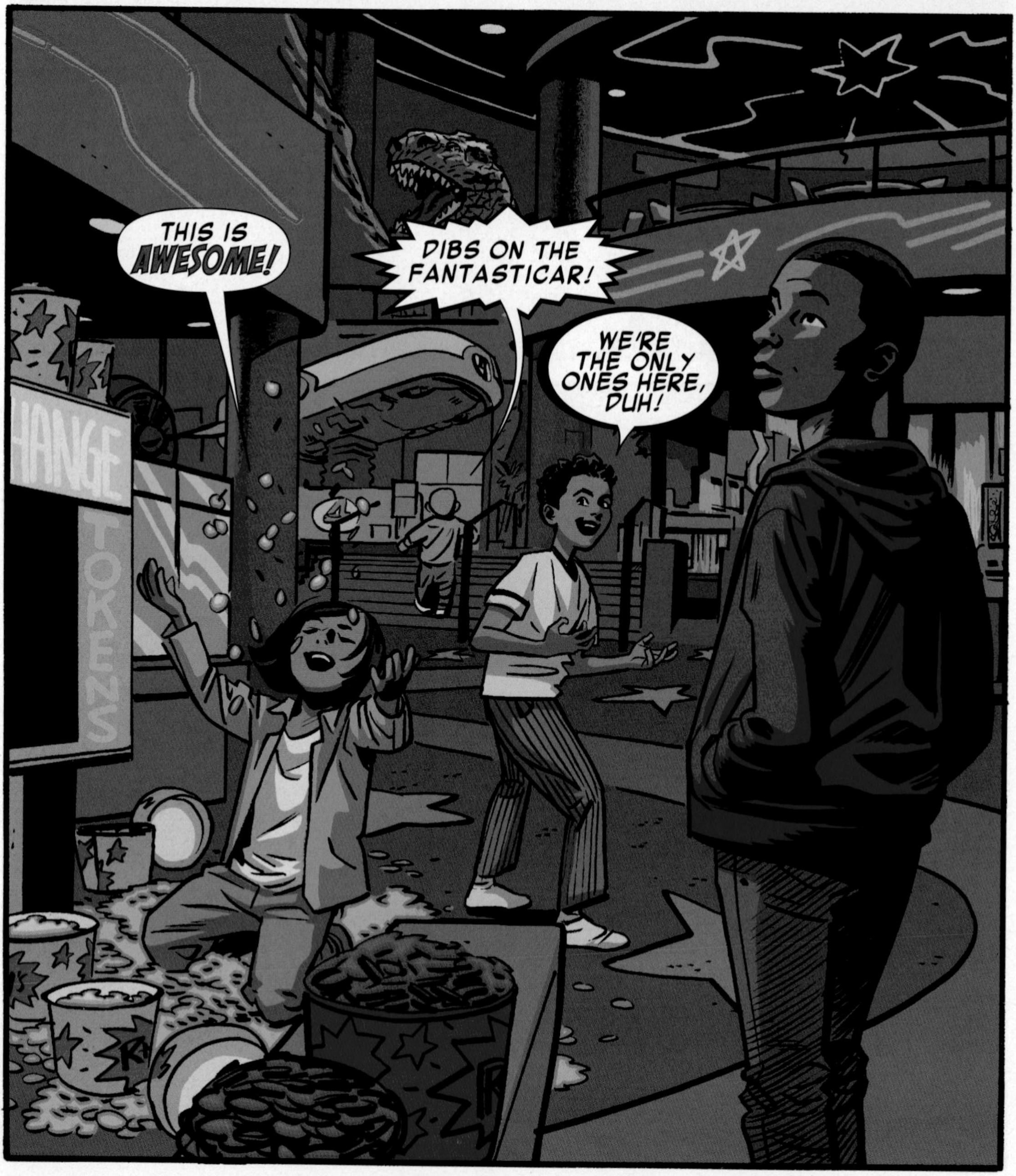
THIS IS AWESOME!
DIBS ON THE FANTASTICAR!
WE'RE THE ONLY ONES HERE, DUH!
HANGE
TOKENS

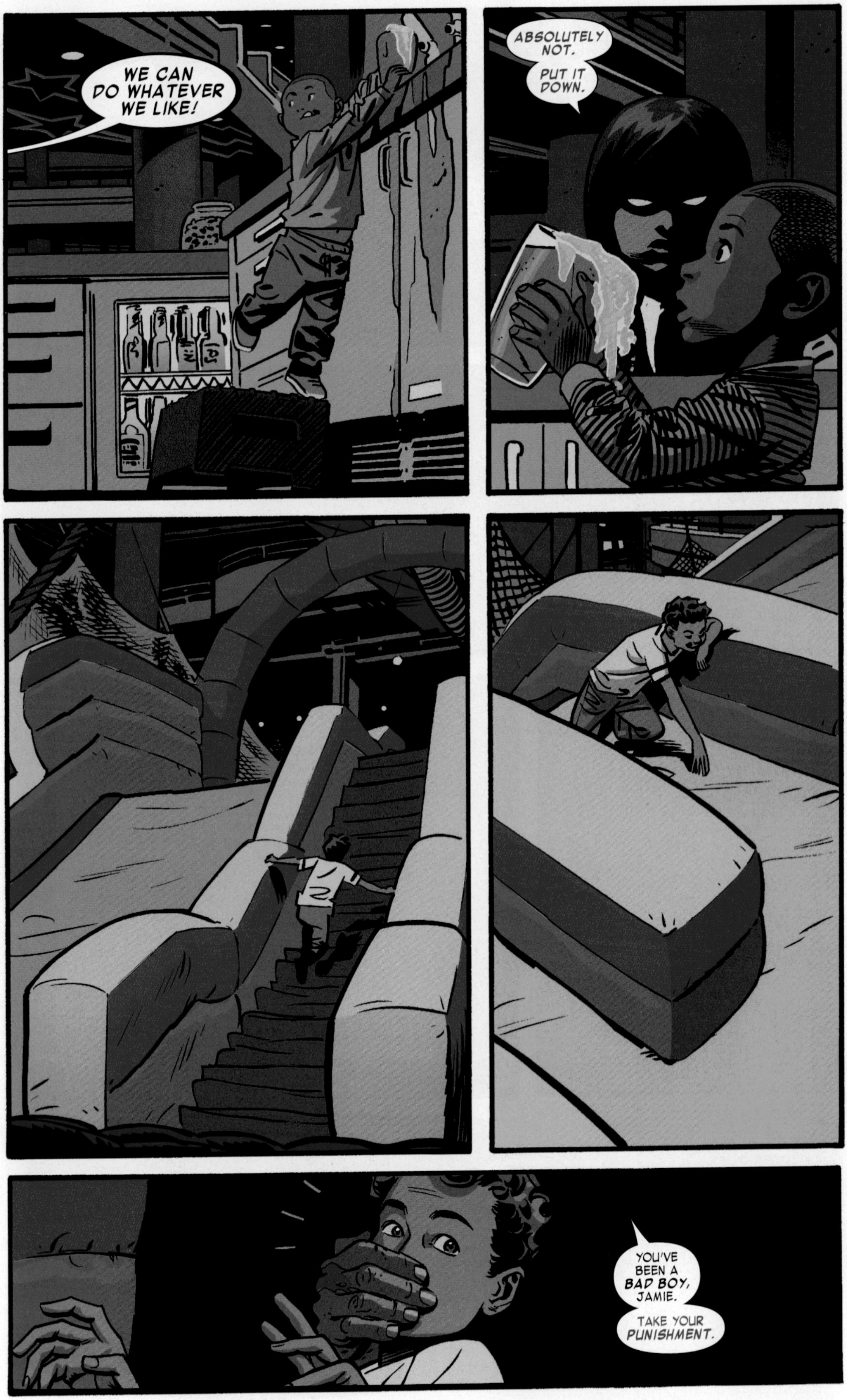
WE CAN DO WHATEVER WE LIKE!
ABSOLUTELY NOT.
PUT IT DOWN.
YOU'VE BEEN A BAD BOY, JAMIE.
TAKE YOUR PUNISHMENT.

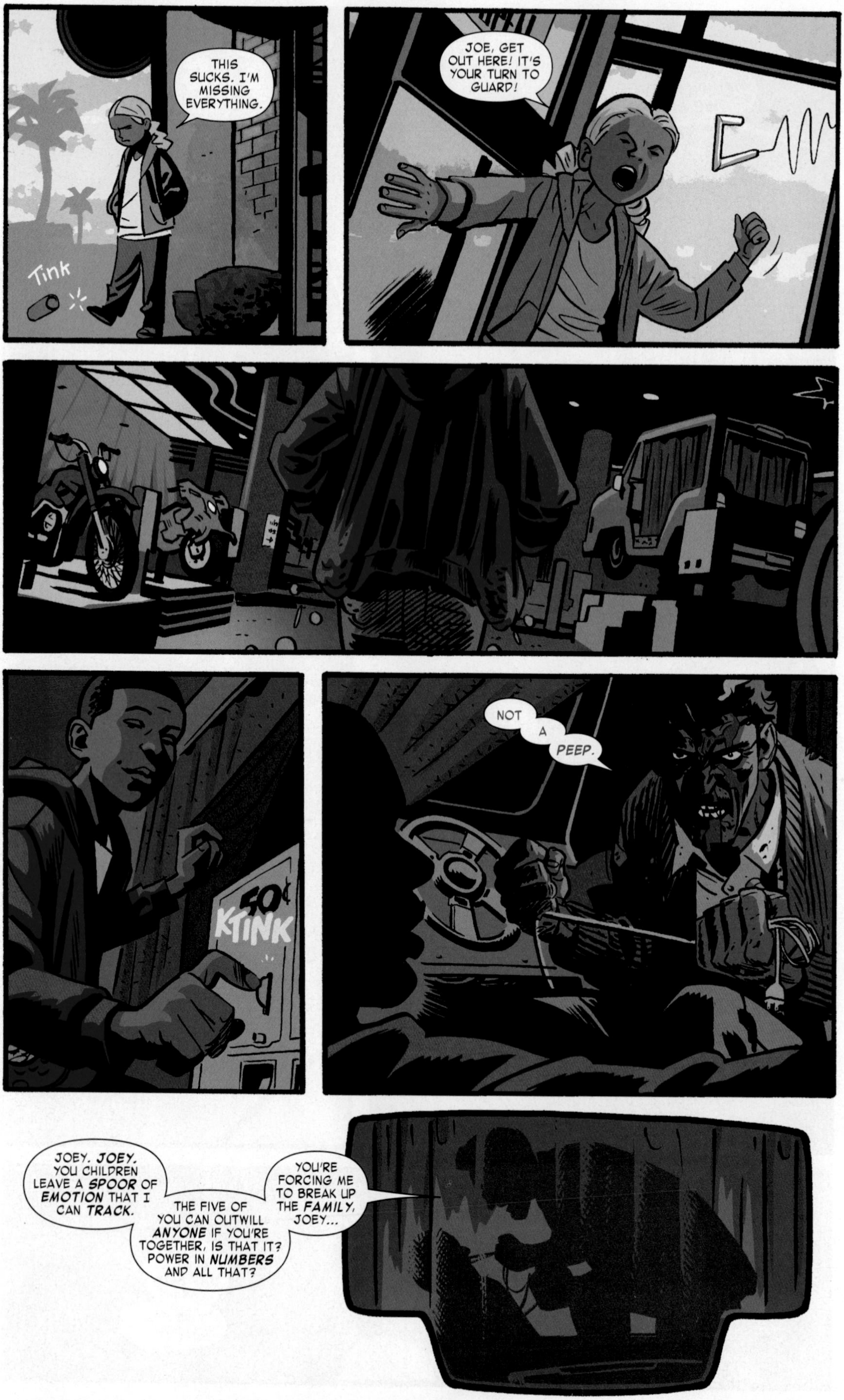
THIS SUCKS. I'M MISSING EVERYTHING.
Tink
JOE, GET OUT HERE! IT'S YOUR TURN TO GUARD!
50¢
KTINK
NOT A PEEP.
JOEY. JOEY. YOU CHILDREN LEAVE A SPOOR OF EMOTION THAT I CAN TRACK.
THE FIVE OF YOU CAN OUTWILL ANYONE IF YOU'RE TOGETHER, IS THAT IT? POWER IN NUMBERS AND ALL THAT?
YOU'RE FORCING ME TO BREAK UP THE FAMILY, JOEY...

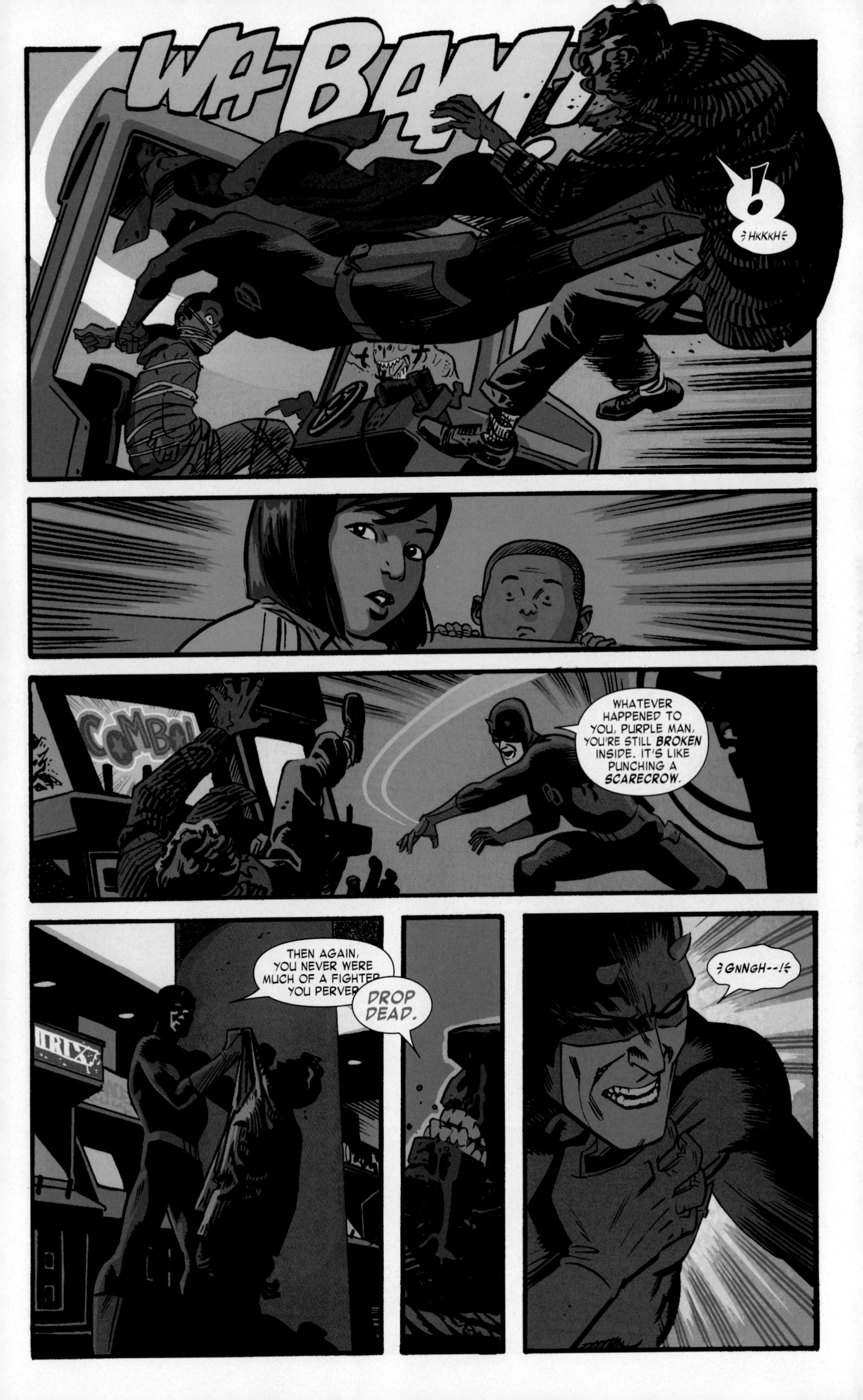
WA-BAM!
!
HKKKH
COMBA
WHATEVER HAPPENED TO YOU, PURPLE MAN, YOU'RE STILL BROKEN INSIDE. IT'S LIKE PUNCHING A SCARECROW.
THEN AGAIN, YOU NEVER WERE MUCH OF A FIGHTER YOU PERVER
DROP DEAD.
GNNGH--!

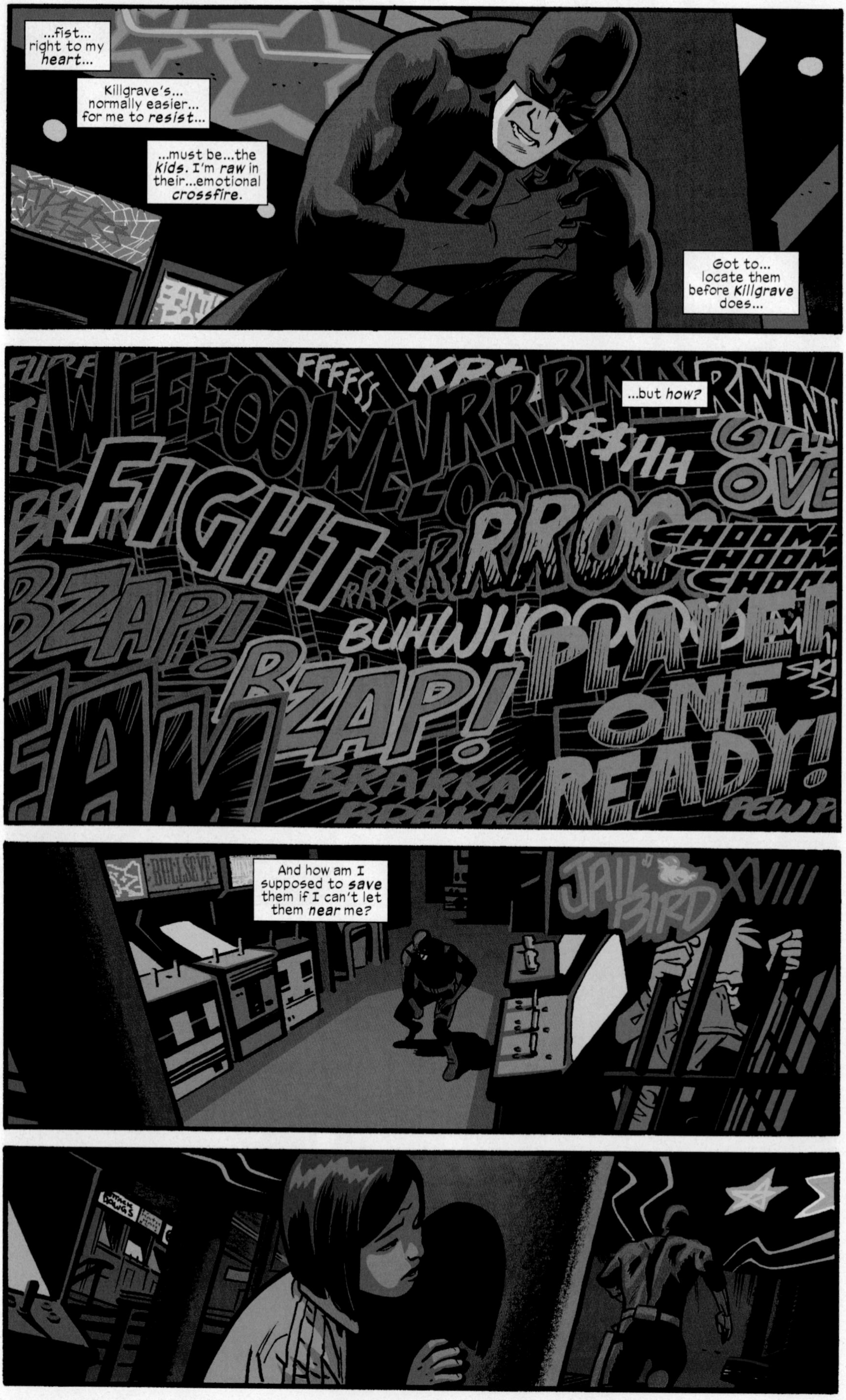

...fist... right to my heart...
Killgrave's... normally easier... for me to resist...
...must be...the kids. I'm raw in their...emotional crossfire.
Got to... locate them before Killgrave does...
WEEEOOWL
VRRRR
FFFFSS
FIGHT
RRROO
BZAP!
BUHWH
BZAP!
PLAYER ONE READY!
BRAKKA
...but how?
BULLSEYE
JAIL BIRD
XVIII
And how am I supposed to save them if I can't let them near me?

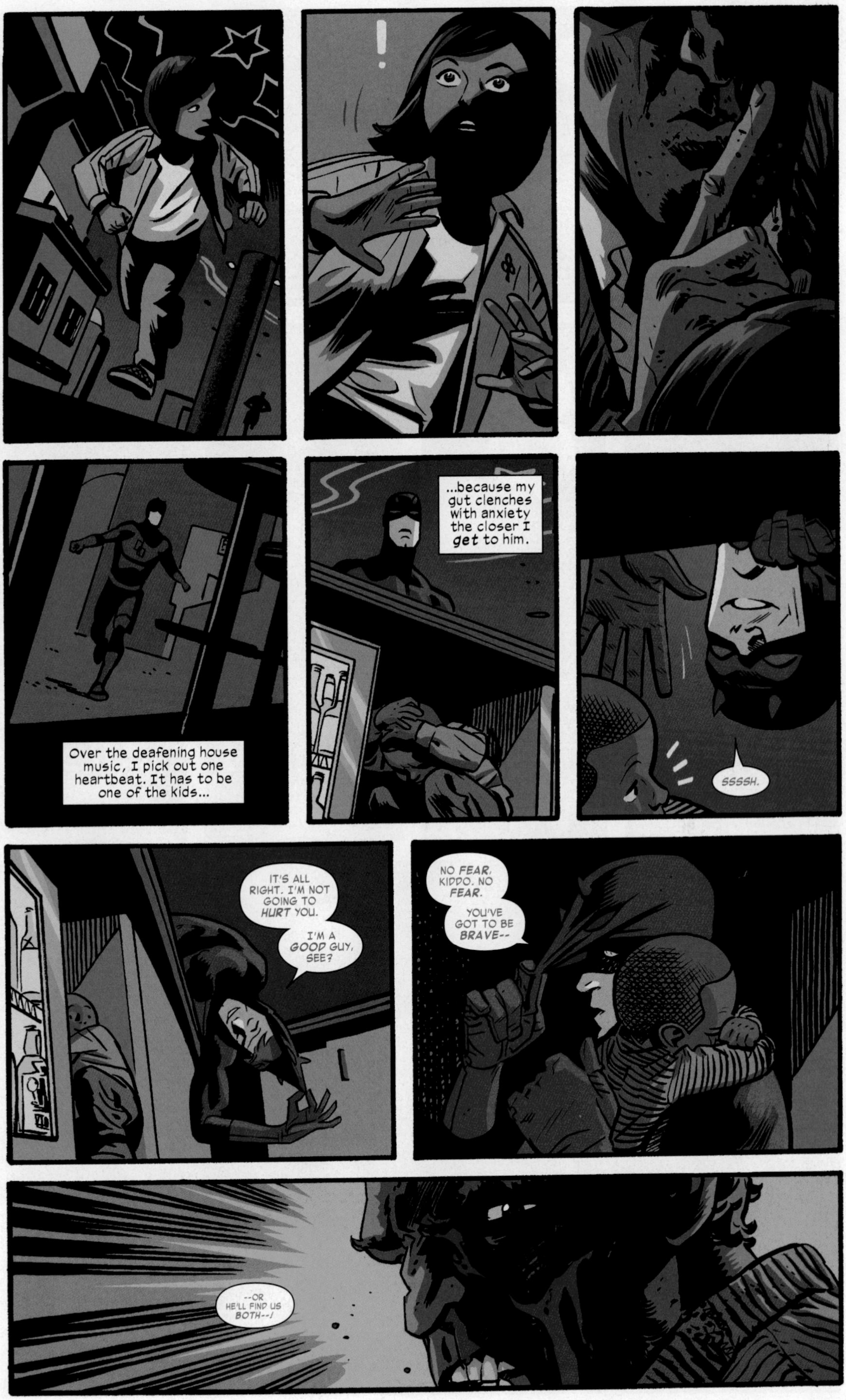
Over the deafening house music, I pick out one heartbeat. It has to be one of the kids...
...because my gut clenches with anxiety the closer I get to him.
SSSSH.
IT'S ALL RIGHT. I'M NOT GOING TO HURT YOU.
I'M A GOOD GUY, SEE?
NO FEAR, KIDDO. NO FEAR.
YOU'VE GOT TO BE BRAVE--
--OR HE'LL FIND US BOTH--!

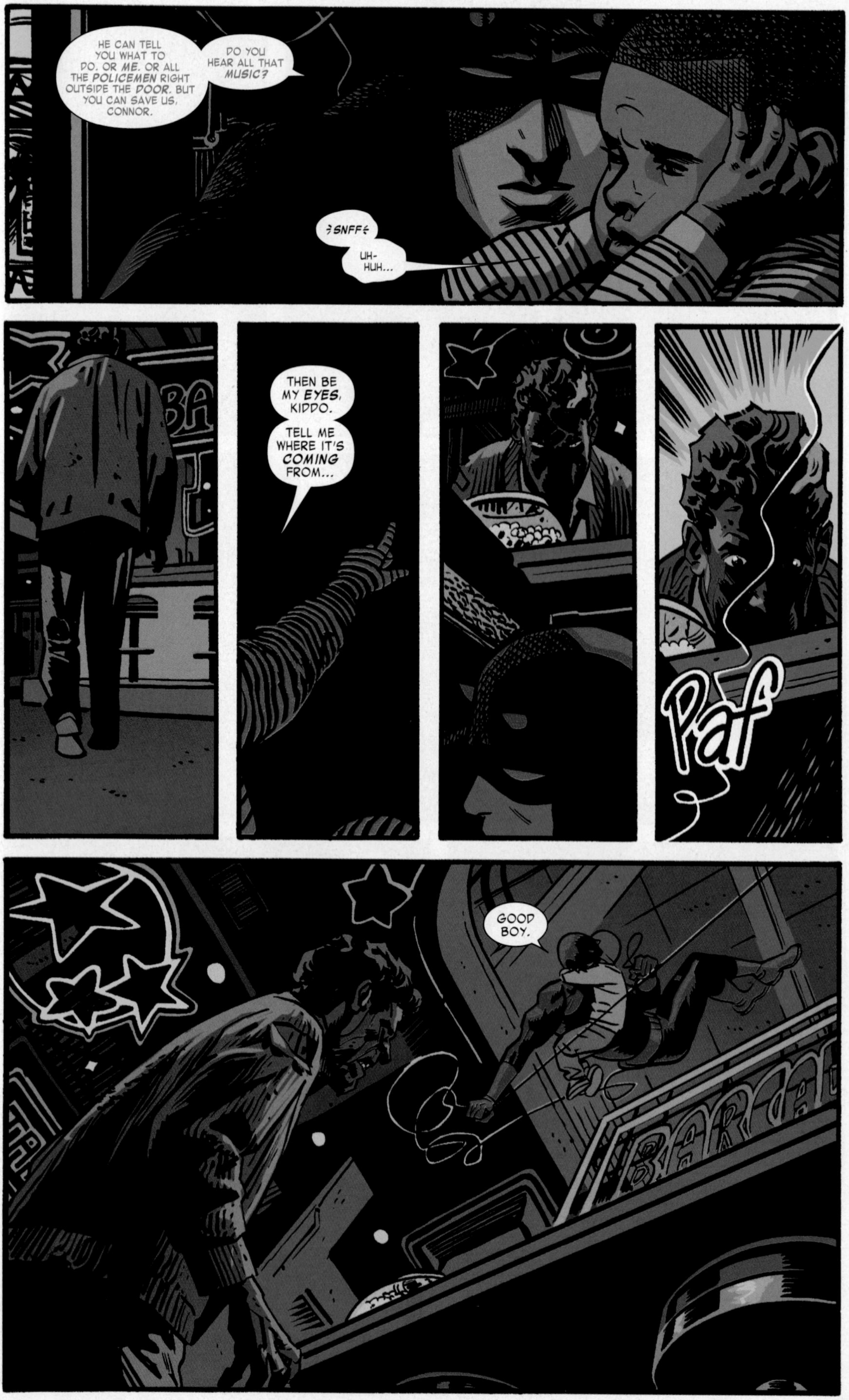
HE CAN TELL YOU WHAT TO DO. OR ME. OR ALL THE POLICEMEN RIGHT OUTSIDE THE DOOR. BUT YOU CAN SAVE US, CONNOR.
DO YOU HEAR ALL THAT MUSIC?
SNFF
UH-HUH...
THEN BE MY EYES, KIDDO.
TELL ME WHERE IT'S COMING FROM...
Paf
GOOD BOY.

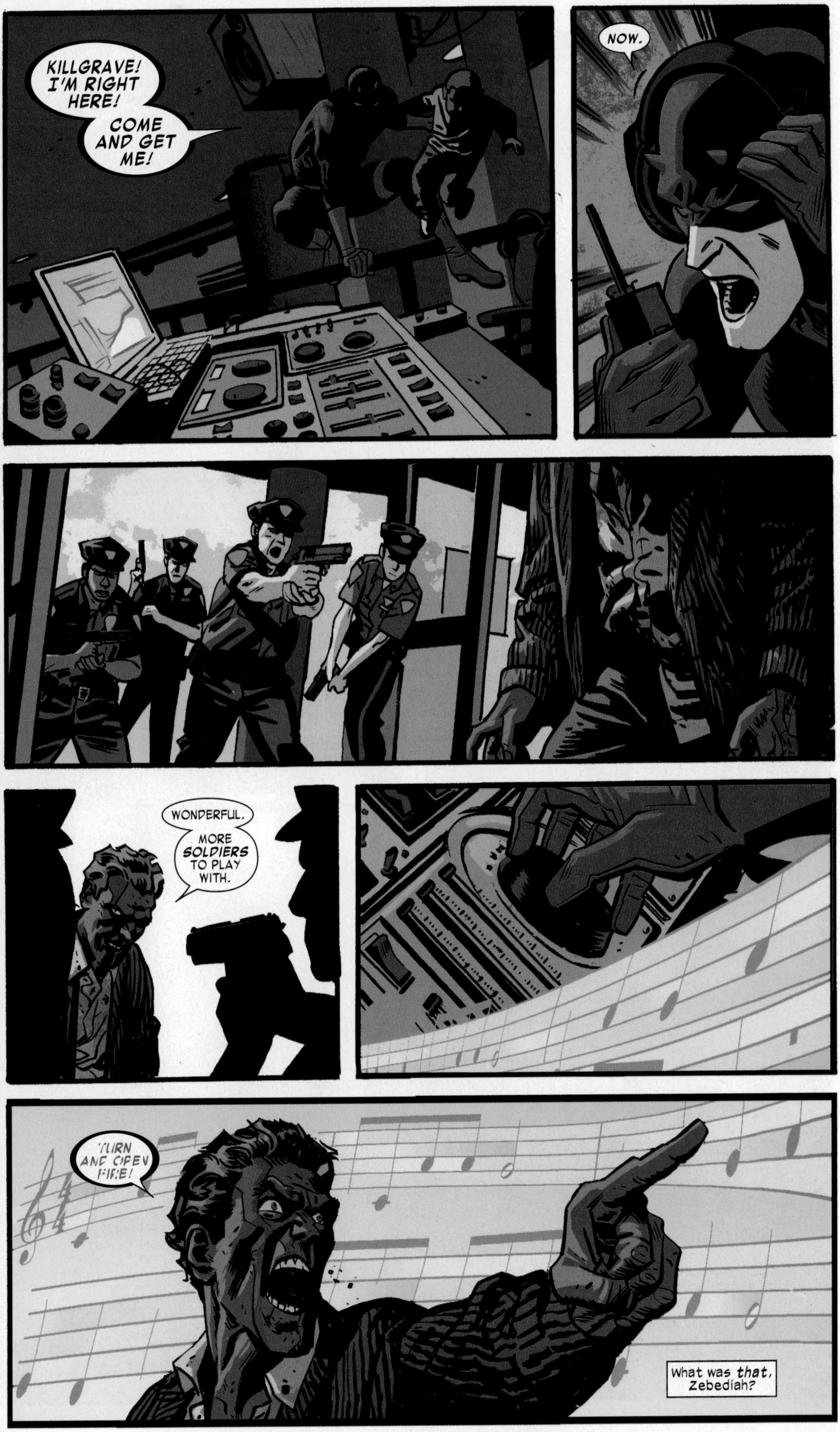
KILLGRAVE! I'M RIGHT HERE!
COME AND GET ME!
NOW.
WONDERFUL.
MORE SOLDIERS TO PLAY WITH.
TURN AND OPEN FIRE!
What was that, Zebediah?

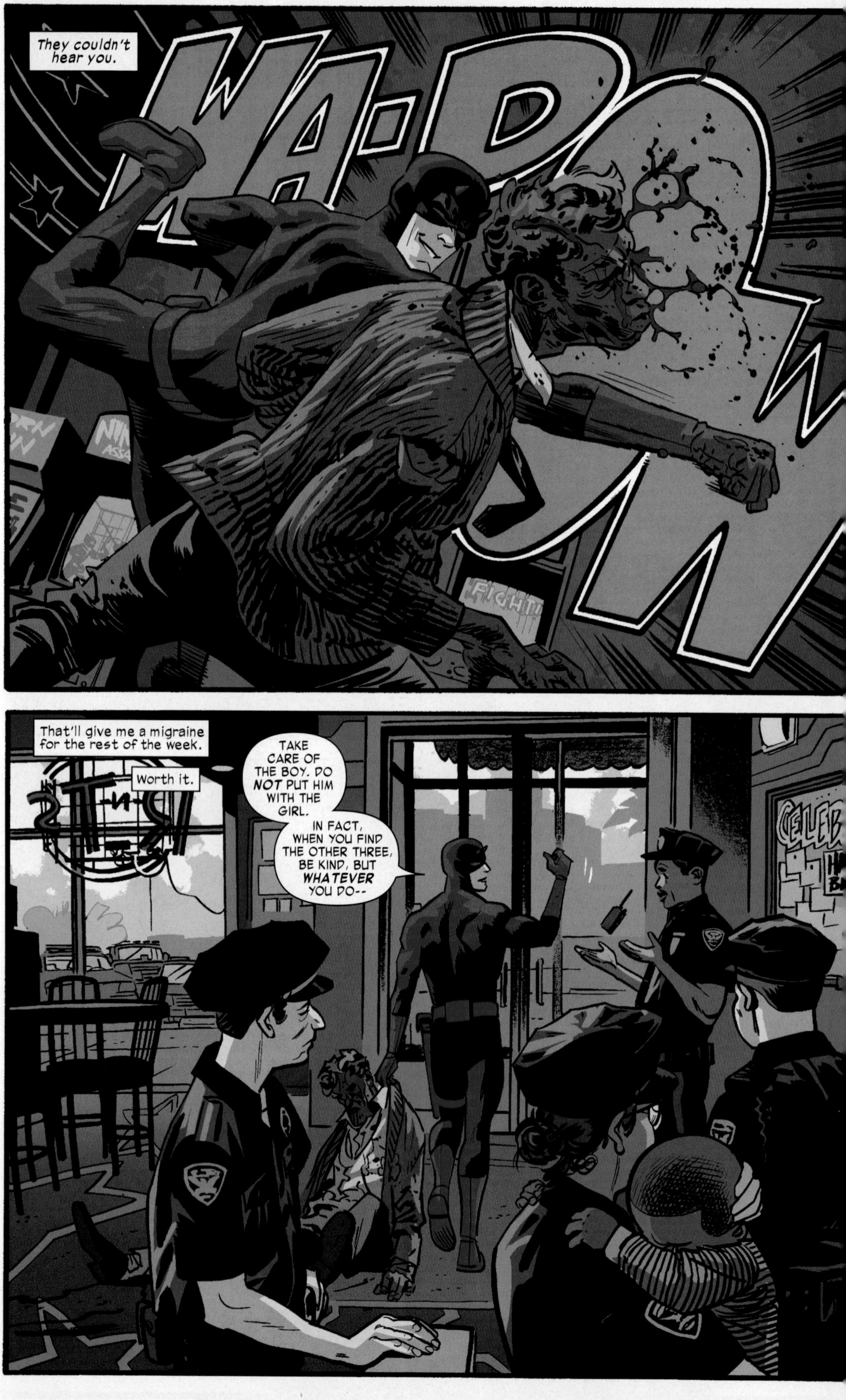
They couldn't hear you.
WA-POW
That'll give me a migraine for the rest of the week.
Worth it.
TAKE CARE OF THE BOY. DO NOT PUT HIM WITH THE GIRL.
IN FACT, WHEN YOU FIND THE OTHER THREE, BE KIND, BUT WHATEVER YOU DO--

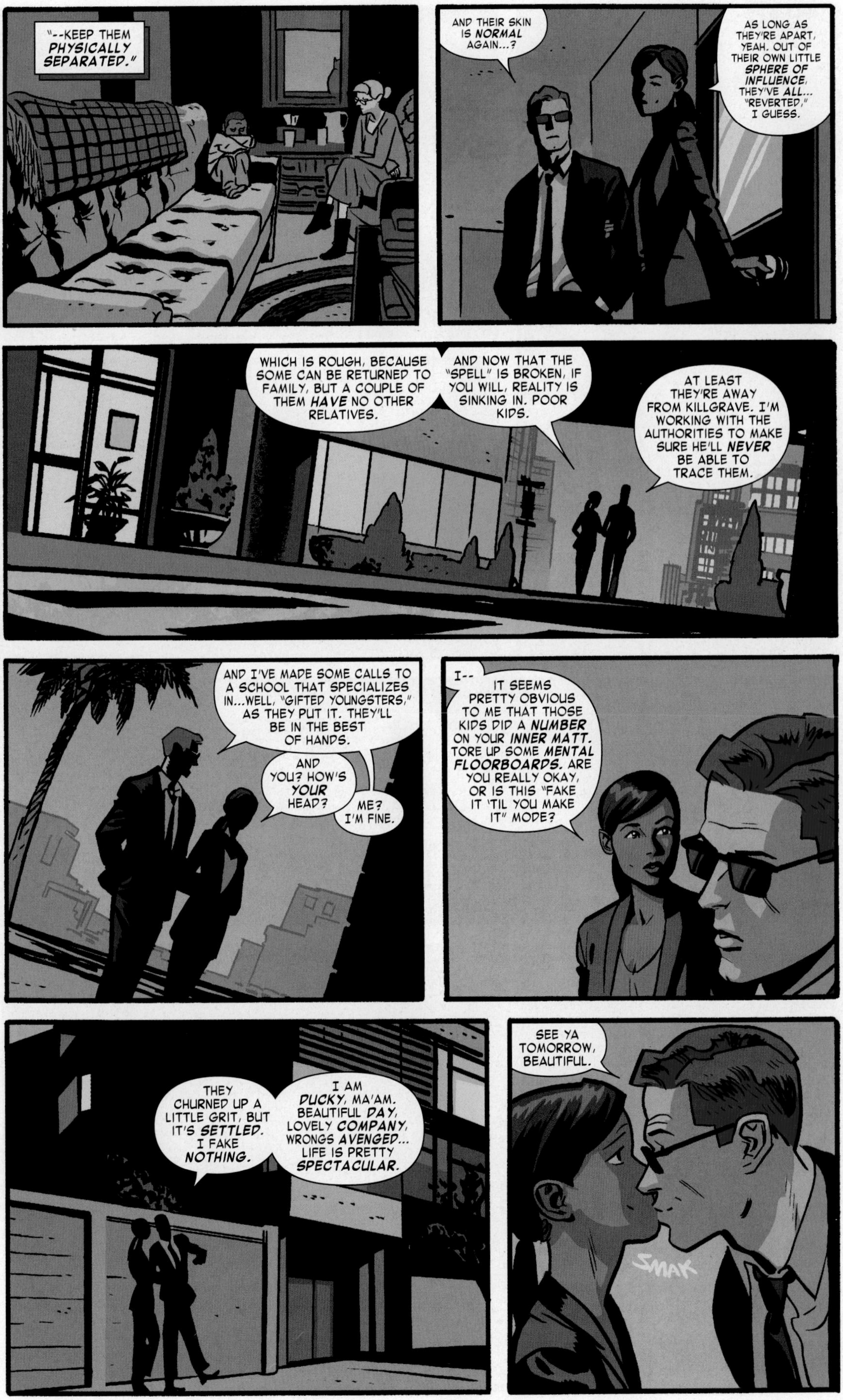
"--KEEP THEM PHYSICALLY SEPARATED."
AND THEIR SKIN IS NORMAL AGAIN...?
AS LONG AS THEY'RE APART, YEAH. OUT OF THEIR OWN LITTLE SPHERE OF INFLUENCE, THEY'VE ALL... "REVERTED," I GUESS.
WHICH IS ROUGH, BECAUSE SOME CAN BE RETURNED TO FAMILY, BUT A COUPLE OF THEM HAVE NO OTHER RELATIVES.
AND NOW THAT THE "SPELL" IS BROKEN, IF YOU WILL, REALITY IS SINKING IN. POOR KIDS.
AT LEAST THEY'RE AWAY FROM KILLGRAVE. I'M WORKING WITH THE AUTHORITIES TO MAKE SURE HE'LL NEVER BE ABLE TO TRACE THEM.
AND I'VE MADE SOME CALLS TO A SCHOOL THAT SPECIALIZES IN...WELL, "GIFTED YOUNGSTERS," AS THEY PUT IT. THEY'LL BE IN THE BEST OF HANDS.
AND YOU? HOW'S YOUR HEAD?
ME? I'M FINE.
I--
IT SEEMS PRETTY OBVIOUS TO ME THAT THOSE KIDS DID A NUMBER ON YOUR INNER MATT. TORE UP SOME MENTAL FLOORBOARDS. ARE YOU REALLY OKAY, OR IS THIS "FAKE IT 'TIL YOU MAKE IT" MODE?
THEY CHURNED UP A LITTLE GRIT, BUT IT'S SETTLED. I FAKE NOTHING.
I AM DUCKY, MA'AM. BEAUTIFUL DAY, LOVELY COMPANY, WRONGS AVENGED... LIFE IS PRETTY SPECTACULAR.
SEE YA TOMORROW, BEAUTIFUL.
SMAK

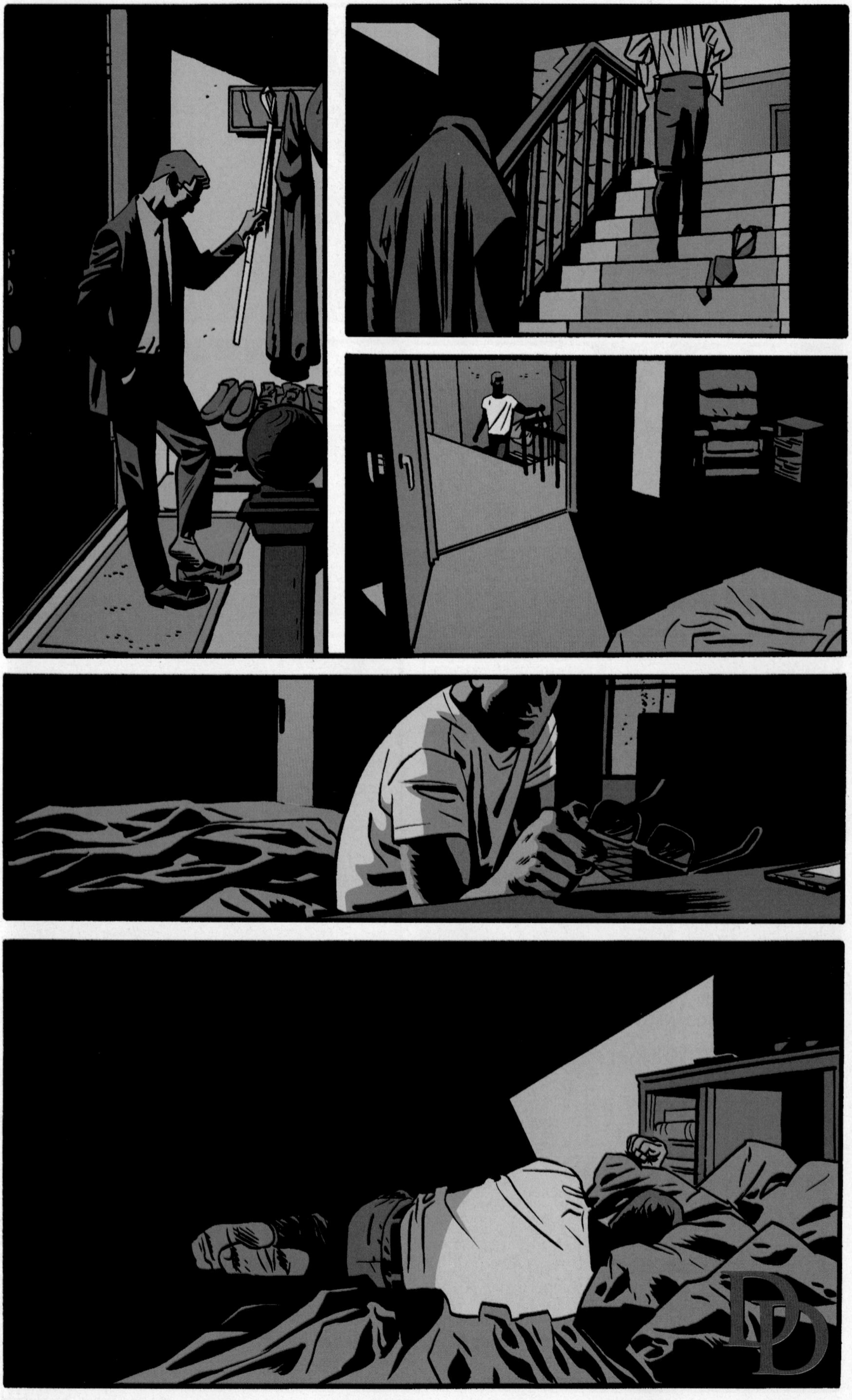

HEY--
"DUCKY"? WHO SAYS THAT? DID YOU REALLY FOOL ANYONE INTO BELIEVING YOU WERE YOUR OWN TWIN BROTHER ONCE? BECAUSE I HAVE SEEN HORSES ON MEXICAN SOAP OPERAS THAT ARE BETTER ACTORS THAN YOU!
--THERE.
I JUST...
I FEEL LIKE TALKING. YOU DON'T HAVE TO COME OVER OR ANYTHING...
OF COURSE I DON'T.
I NEVER LEFT.
CLIK
THANKS FOR LETTING ME IN.
NEXT: FOGGY, THE FRIENDLY GHOST

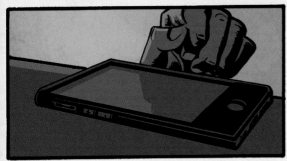

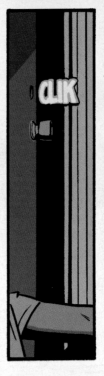

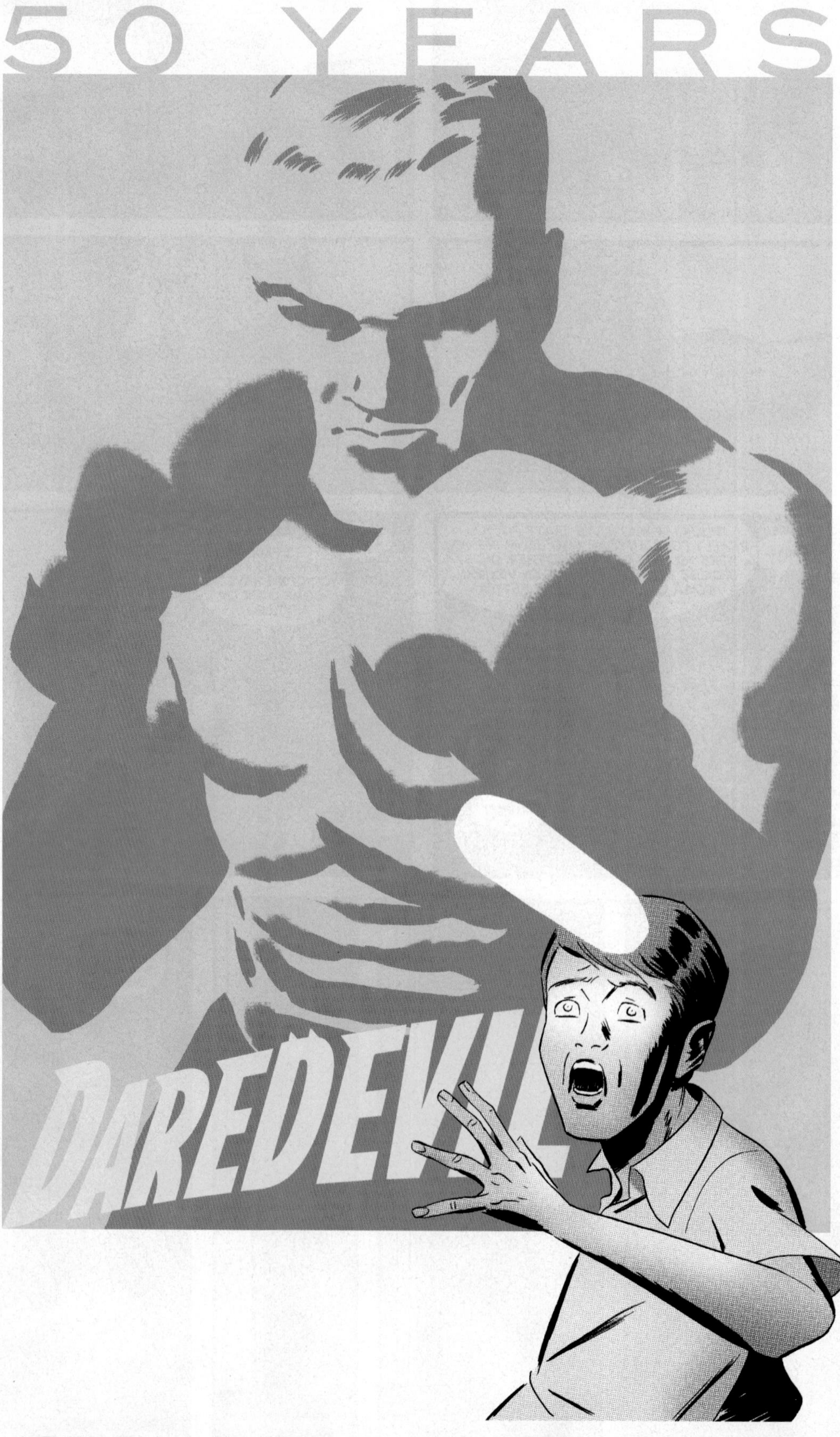
50 YEARS
DAREDEVIL

DAREDEVIL #1.50 VARIANT BY MARCOS MARTIN

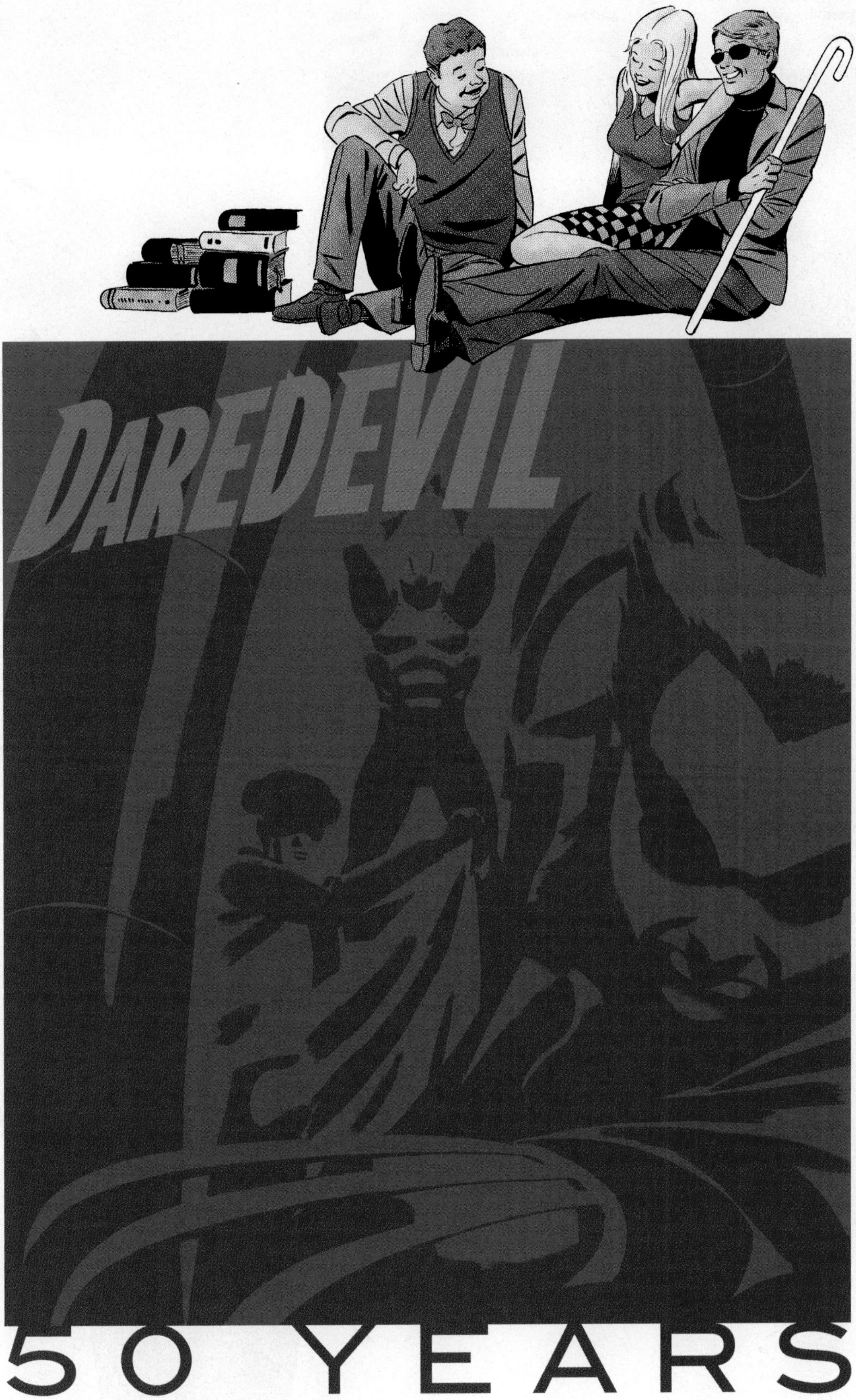
DAREDEVIL
50 YEARS

DAREDEVIL #1.50 VARIANT BY MARCOS MARTIN

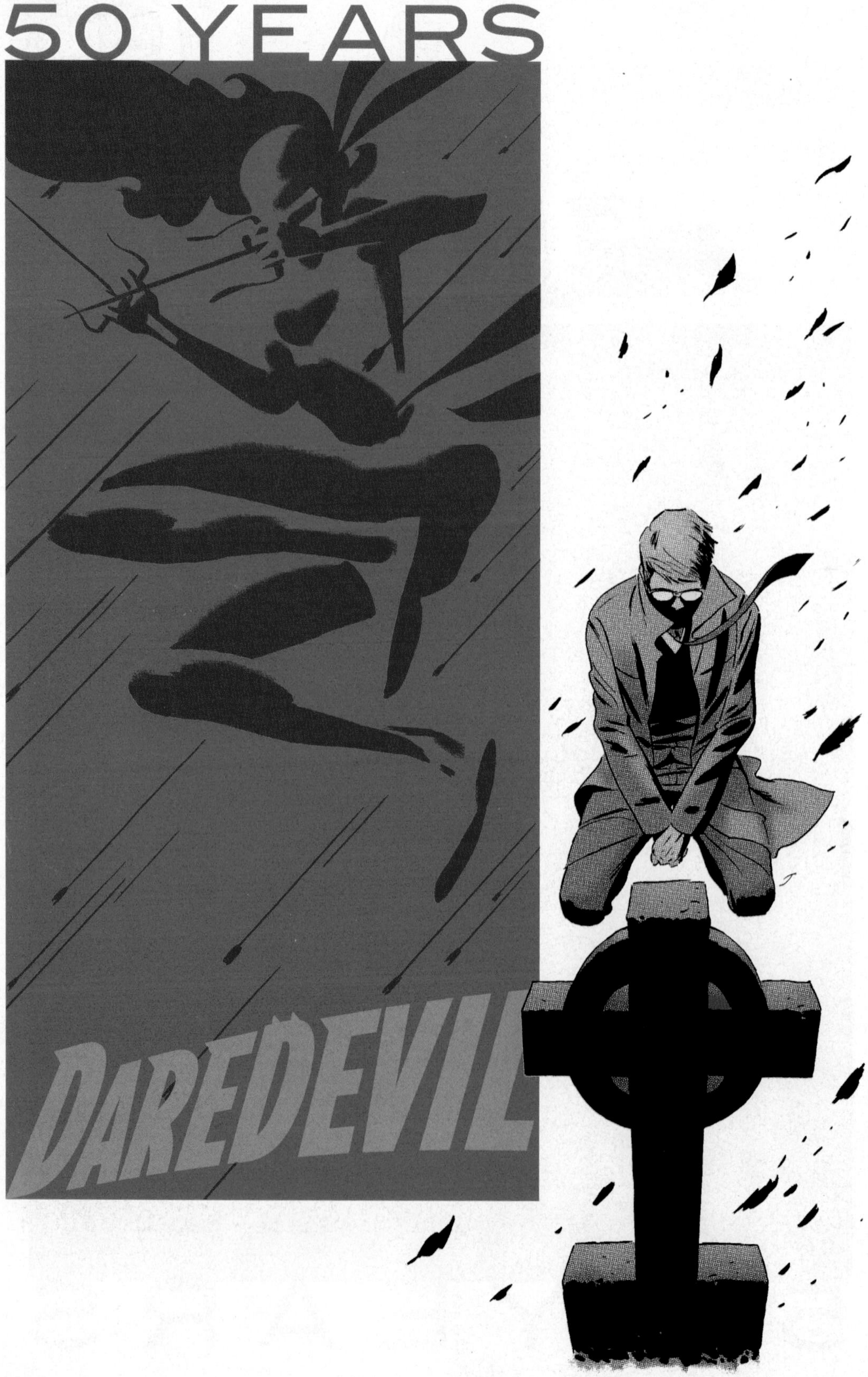
50 YEARS
DAREDEVIL

DAREDEVIL #1.50 VARIANT BY MARCOS MARTIN

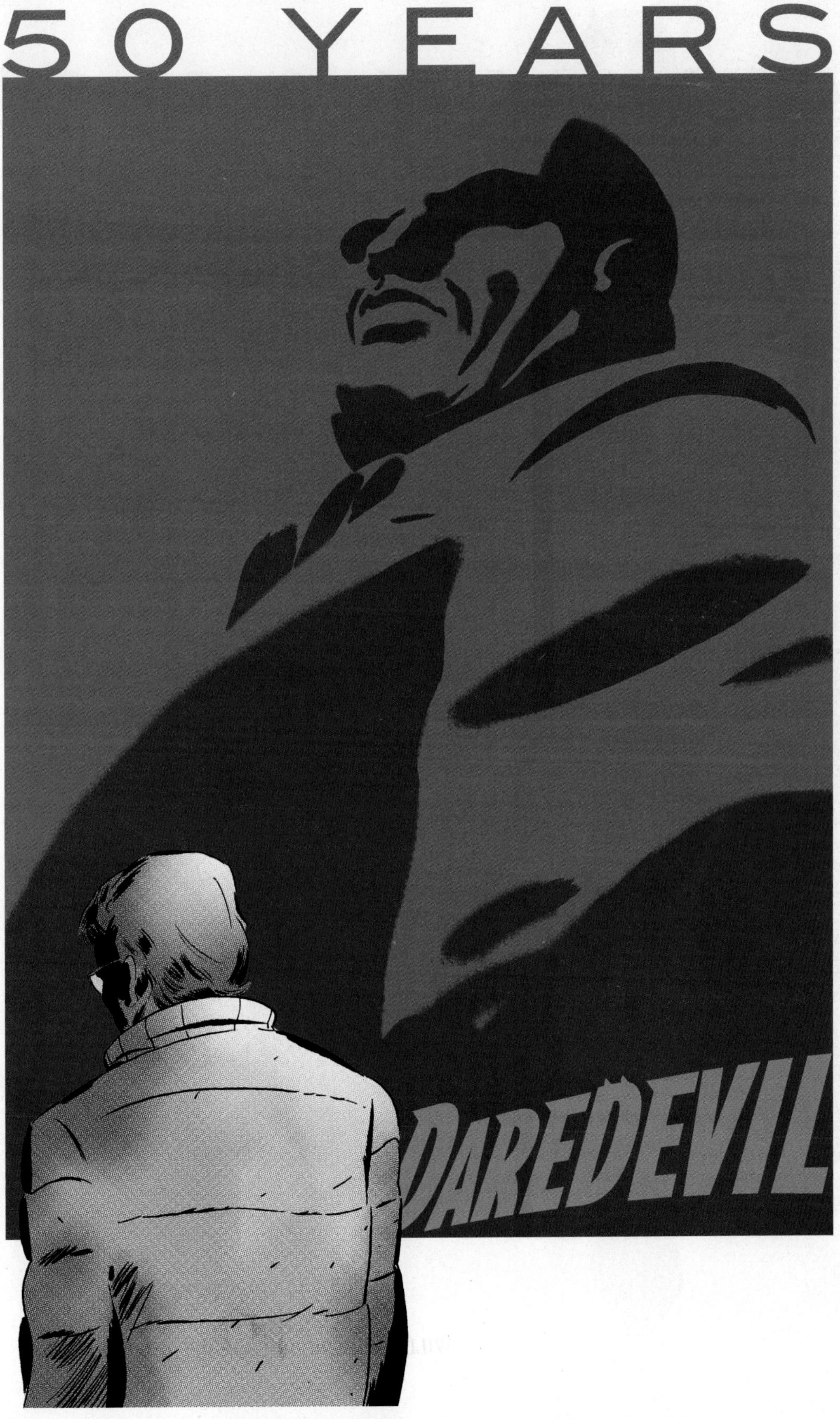

50 YEARS
DAREDEVIL

DAREDEVIL #1.50 VARIANT BY MARCOS MARTIN

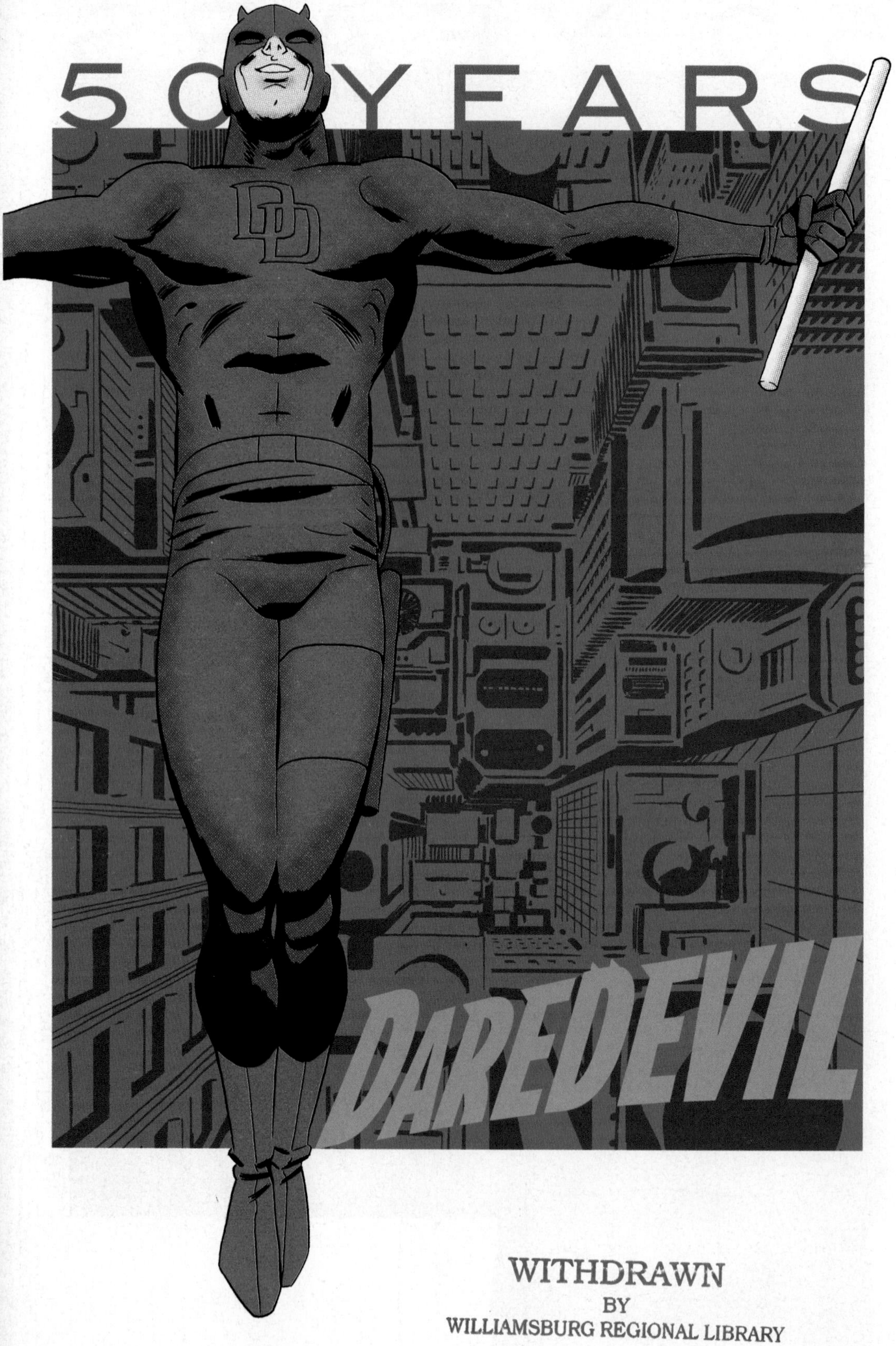
50 YEARS
DAREDEVIL

DAREDEVIL #1.50 VARIANT BY MARCOS MARTIN